W9-CLR-857

Gay Body

Also by Mark Thompson

Gay Spirit: Myth and Meaning

Leatherfolk: Radical Sex, People, Politics, and Practice

Gay Soul: Finding the Heart of Gay Spirit and Nature

Long Road to Freedom: The Advocate History of the Gay and Lesbian Movement

Gay Body

A Journey Through Shadow to Self

Mark Thompson

St. Martin's Press
New York

Design by Maureen Troy

Library of Congress Cataloging-in-Publication Data

Thompson, Mark
Gay body : a journey through shadow to self / Mark Thompson. —1st ed.
p. cm.
Includes bibliographical references.
ISBN 0-312-16853-5
1. Thompson, Mark. 2. Gay men—United States—Biography. 3. Gay men—United States—Psychology. 4. Gay men—Religious life—United States. 5. Spiritual life—United States.
I. Title.
HQ75.8.T46A3 1997
305.38'9664'092—dc21
[B] 97-20510
CIP

First Edition: November 1997

10 9 8 7 6 5 4 3 2 1

For Gail and John,
who survived,
and Kirk, who didn't

Acknowledgments

This book is not strictly autobiographical in the sense that it records every significant person and event that has intersected with my life. Rather, it is a selective memoir explicating the landmarks of my inner journey—my path of healing and spiritual discovery.

Many individuals have contributed to that process, but none more closely than my life partner of twelve years, Malcolm Boyd. The creation of this book would not have been possible without the encouragement and support of Malcolm, who is an Episcopal priest, a warrior, and a healer. We share our lives as spiritual seekers, fellow writers, and soul mates who care passionately about the same things, not the least each other. While the facts of our life together are not discussed in this particular work (that, as it's said, is a story for another time), our love unquestionably informs every line of this book. Without Malcolm, this gay body would be far less rich in the blessings of life.

In terms of the specific creation of this book, there are a number of individuals who must also be acknowledged. I want to thank Mitch Walker, who encouraged me to explore the meaning of the Gilgamesh story. Douglas Sadownick gave much advice during the making of this book. William Stewart, Cathy Toldi, Michael Denneny, and Winston Wilde offered important comments on early drafts of particular chapters. Adrian Brooks, Will Roscoe, and Wendell Jones gave astute feedback as the project neared completion. I am also appreciative of Eugene Shirley and his contribution to the discussion of the Frankenstein and Dracula myths. Gayle Rubin and Jennifer Finlay provided useful information as well.

I have been supported during the duration of this project by Ken Clements, good doctor of the soul, and Kevin Williams, expert doctor of the body. I also want to thank Chris Kilbourne, Felipe Hernandez, Roger Kaufman, Matt Silverstein, David Grubbs, Mark Simon, Jim Curtan, Felix Racelis, and Leng Lim, among other cohorts in Los Angeles who have contributed to my book and soul-making process in some way.

A special acknowledgment is due Fakir Musafar, who made my Sun Dance possible, as he has assisted so many others in realizing their journey toward light. And, as always, James Broughton remains a singular source of inspiration in my life.

Last, but not least, I want to thank my agents, Charlotte Sheedy and Neeti Madan, who always believed in this *Body,* and my editor at St. Martin's Press, Keith Kahla, who made its birth in the world possible.

Contents

⊠ ⊠ ⊠

Contents

Contents

Introduction

⊠ ⊠ ⊠

Of all the men I've loved and have seen die before their time, no parting cut as deeply as Kirk's. My brother had remained in the place of his birth on California's central coast where he matured into fine manhood and was admired for beauty of body and soul. Kirk knew all about the healing power of green, and exhibited a magical rapport with growing things that seemed downright mysterious to those not so gifted. The gardens he created were the envy and happiness of many.

Working in the earth connected Kirk with a spiritual energy that soothed a shaky past. The four children in our family were like seeds scattered in the wind to fall and sprout the best they could, he'd say, allowing that maybe we did okay. But deep down, he didn't really know the value of his own considerable worth. Not being properly seen as a boy meant that he could not fully see himself as a man. His ground of being was not as yielding as the actual soil he cultivated. Moreover, two successive life partners had passed from the plague, losses which further eroded his confidence in life. Now, it was his turn to die.

The call came late one February night; a message to come right away. I left for Monterey the next morning, driving up the coast and through the Salinas Valley: prime Steinbeck country, rimmed with low peaks dusted with a blanket of freshly laid snow. The chiaroscuro clouds above and variegated fields on either side of me shimmered in the silver winter light, a magnificent picture teetering on blowing apart—as if pixels of color and form would go flying if stared at too long. Although my hand was steady on the wheel, my mind was in dissolution. Reality, as it is thought to be, is more of an illusion than we want to know.

Kirk had suffered from various AIDS-related maladies for some time, an invading army without mercy. "It's time. I want to go," he plaintively whispered on the phone. "Help me."

His once-supple body was covered with dozens of marble-sized warts and other persistent skin diseases. One arm dangled uselessly, and muscle tissue elsewhere was rapidly atrophying. Pneumocystis carinii was just one of three infections in his lungs. He had not been able to eat solid food for days.

Despite his horrid physical deterioration, Kirk's emotional health seemed stable. He was confronting death with fortitude and clarity; the previous weeks had been spent saying good-bye to loved ones and disposing of possessions. There was nothing left to say or do.

I arrived around 10:30 on a Wednesday evening. A light rain was falling out of a strangely cloudless sky. Kirk's companion, a remarkably selfless young man who had entered his life two years before—fully knowing the score—was waiting by the door. He worked the night desk at a local hotel, a convenient escape from the scene about to transpire.

Introduction

Kirk did not want his friend present, a decision mutually understood. I turned away as they embraced and kissed for the last time. The lovers' quietly spoken words of devotion were like prayers. There was a long moment of silence, the sound of a door opening and closing, and then Kirk and I were alone.

We turned and faced one another, looked directly into each other's eyes, and then smiled. Together again, just the two of us, after so many years gone by. The patter of water droplets on glass panes intensified its drumming; a protective curtain was being drawn between us and the world outside.

"I love you, Mark," he said.

"I love you, too, Kirk," I replied. It was to be our mantra, sung back and forth throughout the night.

My brother, my lover. There was no doubt by now in either of our minds that the two-as-one had been a saving grace. We had discovered what love is in each other's arms. Two souls melded, no matter their different paths in life.

"We two boys together clinging, One the other never leaving. . . ." Surely, Walt Whitman must have written the lines of that poem for us. ". . . No law less than ourselves owning . . . Fulfilling our foray." And now there was yet one more venture into the unknown for us two boys to take.

Kirk and I spent the next couple of hours talking about our triumphs and failures, what we had learned about life—if anything. He, for one, had no regrets, but admitted that he wished we'd known each other better during the years between growing up and now. It was tough being dealt a pair of emotionally absent parents, he confessed. "But I've forgiven the past." As for what was about to come, "I just hope I'm not disappointed," he shyly chuckled. With that, Kirk painfully got up from his padded recliner and shuffled across the room.

Gay Body

I followed him to the front door, which he opened and braced himself against while contemplating the view. The rain had lulled, and the crescent-shaped silhouette of the Monterey Peninsula was clearly etched in the freshly washed midnight air. From our hillside vantage overlooking the bay, we took turns naming the distant, yet familiar lights.

"There—that one—that must be the beacon near the old bath-house in Pacific Grove where we learned to swim," he said to me. I, in turn, pointed out the row of lights sparkling like diamonds on velvet—adjacent Cannery Row. We played there as boys among the sprawling ruins of deserted sardine packing plants, by then sorry memorials to overfishing and now rebuilt as nostalgia traps for tourists. Further along the curve of the bay twinkled the lights of Monterey, birthplace of our father and us, his two sons.

No further words were necessary after this. We just stood quietly for a while, hands clasped tightly around each other's waists, until the rain began to pick up again. Kirk cleared his throat and turned to say something but faltered when his eyes met mine. I could tell what was on his mind. He took one more look at the sweep of glistening coastline before him, drinking it in as if to gather courage.

"I'm going to take a bath now," Kirk softly announced, shutting the door. It was nearing one in the morning, and if he were going to ingest the vial of deadly pills sitting within arm's reach of the recliner, he would have to do it soon. The dying process takes some hours as, one by one, the body's systems sign off.

I would have done anything within my power to save him or even change his mind that instant, but I knew what a foolish thought this was. The issue tonight was not one of life or death—Kirk's condition was too far advanced for that—but rather, how and when? Here and now, in the familiar surroundings of his home and with the support of someone dearly trusted? Or in another month or so, hooked to a hospital bed and subject to further cruel invasions in a hopeless hedge against the inevitable?

I knew the correct answer. With the sounds of splashing water coming from the next room, I began to dim lamps and light candles. There must be a right container for all passages of life, especially death, and it was my task now to transform this modest space into a sanctuary.

I had just stepped back to survey the scene when a sudden violent force entered the room. It came barreling through the front door: malevolent and greedy. Whatever it was and wanted I did not know. But it scared me. The hairs on the back of my head stood upright. I could feel my heart pounding.

"Go away, get out of here!" I shouted, making dismissive motions toward the door. The presence felt evil. I needed to chase it away.

Perhaps it was only my own inner turmoil being whipped into some kind of projective fantasy—I will never know. But the dark spirit attempting to enter the room that moment felt as real to me as anything ever experienced in my life. I happen to believe in an unseen web of such spiritual entities—both good and bad—encircling the earth, and one was manifesting itself voraciously at our front door.

I fiercely held my ground, hoping that Kirk would not see my comical motions. What would he make of his older brother talking loudly to some invisible presence, waving his arms wildly in the air? I had no desire to make the evening crazier than it already was. I glowered and cursed. The would-be invader retreated soon after.

Kirk reappeared a few minutes later, toweling his hair. He was barefoot, dressed only in jeans and a simple cotton shirt. The clock struck one. "Are you sure you want to be here?" he asked me.

I assured him there was no other place I'd rather be. There was an awkward pause in the conversation after that. All our thoughts were focused on the vial of pills and bottle of cherry-flavored brandy sitting nearby. Finally, I said I was going to step out of the room for a brief spell. My absence would allow Kirk the permission to complete what he needed to do without me having to actually witness it, which neither of us wanted.

"I love you, Mark," he said, leaning forward to hug me. We embraced and I tenderly kissed the side of his face.

"I love you, Kirk," I whispered, fighting back a sudden rush of panic and tears. With these words, I turned and went into the other room, where I sat on the bed and counted off the minutes—five of them—before returning. Kirk was resting in his chair, a sky-blue blanket pulled over his emaciated frame, the pill bottle and glass of brandy drained.

His eyes had a faraway look, as if he were trying to see into the future. I immediately got down on my knees and reached out for his one good hand. I grasped it hard. Hours would pass before I'd let it go. "I love you, Kirk. Good journey."

He was already beginning to nod off, but lifted his chin to look me in the eyes one final time. "I love you, too, Brother. Stay well."

Kirk leaned his head back into the plush folds of the recliner and deeply sighed. The light from the one flickering candle set before us was all the illumination required. The flame ebbed and surged in the drafty air. I could feel Kirk's pulse beating strong and steady. In the dim golden light, I could see one tear slide down his left cheek. I was no longer able to check my own feelings and began to silently sob, then loudly wail, holding on to my brother's hand for dear life.

The rain had resumed its rhythm and somewhere from in the building came the rumblings of a water heater turning itself on. The regularity of life was heard in humble things, its cessation foretold in the rasping sounds now emanating from my brother. He was asleep, never to awake. I was alone.

I kept talking aloud during the numbing hours ahead. My legs were painfully cramped, and I soon lost all sense of time or place. All that mattered was my grip on his hand and my repeated encouragements: "It's okay, Kirk. Just let go."

After a couple of hours, Kirk's breathing coarsened to a loose rattle and the warmth in his hand began to fade. I felt my panic rage again. It's still not too late to call someone, I blindly told myself. They could save him! But then I came to, crouched before the beatific face of horrible tragedy, and realized that all I needed to do was stay present in the moment.

"I love you, Kirk," I muttered again. "Good journey."

I held onto my brother's hand until it was as cold as ice, and pale gray streaks of dawn came pushing through the shutters. He had stopped breathing at some point during the night—when exactly I couldn't say. Maybe when the rain let up. The passing hours had been sacred, scary, and sublime. But I was at a loss to explain what had exactly happened other than the fulfillment of an awesome mystery. Kirk was dead. And with him, a part of me.

As I made my way home through the Salinas Valley the following day, I noticed that the snow on the surrounding hills had already melted. Turbulent clouds were blown elsewhere, and a good, even light blessed the abundant croplands. I felt some clearing inside, too.

My brother and I acted fearlessly, yet had also been tremblingly afraid. Still, in helping him to die some line was finally crossed within myself. Whatever it represented, I knew I would never be able to return to the other side. Keeping watch over Kirk's departure perhaps marked my final act of accommodation. I've always been ready and willing in assisting others, even when it meant doing so at my own expense. My modus operandi of survival had meant becoming an accommodationist: taking care of, being responsible for, asking nothing in return but approval and acceptance.

I knew in my heart that I had done the right thing in facilitating Kirk's passage toward death. And, for the very first time, I wanted nothing in return. Kirk sacrificed his own life that terrible night and I had learned to sacrifice my fear. It no longer matters what others think.

Being wounded is not enough. Having faced and gone through the wound of death itself means that I have died before I've died. Take back what you think, I want to tell the world, for now it means nothing.

This is the story of one crazy family and how a disembodied soul, hurtling through time and space, came crashing into its nucleus. All the rest has been about the recovery from that. This is the story, too, of others like me: How a mangled tissue of deceit and lies, stretching over generations, has impacted upon our selves. But, ultimately, this is my tale: one who survived the wreckage of splintered lives, who in tending to his wounded body—his gay body—saw what had happened to his soul.

Somewhere inside every gay man there's a wounded boy who stopped growing. Who simply gave up and shut down. He was not seen for who he really was, as pernicious an abuse as any devised. If ever he did reveal his shining inner self, it was humiliated, mocked, and scorned. And so the boy took whatever of himself he could save and hid it, burying it in that twilight zone between knowing and not knowing.

This book is an attempt to name this place, in both a personal and collective way—a phenomenon I call the Gay Shadow. "The shadow is that which has not entered adequately into consciousness," explains psychologist Robert A. Johnson. "It is the despised quarter of our being. . . . The shadow gone autonomous is a terrible monster in our psychic house."[1]

The point is, gay men like myself have much tending of our psychic houses to do. One hundred years after the invention of the term *homosexuality* in the modern west, and a quarter century past rebelling against its stupefying effects, we're either dazed from sorting out fact from too much fiction or are lost in the woods with no moral compass. Some live in denial, a kind of willful deep sleep induced by sex, drugs, or lack of reflection, while others have abdicated caring altogether, riding along on the wrong bus.

As deeply feeling men who have been robbed of feelings, we have no choice now but to know ourselves completely. Where is our joy? Our rage? Where are the stories and myths that will lead us back to where our true self lies? Asking these questions is the better act of survival.

Answers lie coiled in our bodies beneath the skin of what we *think* we know, and in that repository of all we don't: shadow. The shadow contains the inferior parts of ourself we wish to deny, the shameful and neglected aspects of personality. Every person has a shadow, for it is an integral part of one's psyche. But when left unclaimed, it becomes a dangerous thing: the repression, primitiveness, and hostility it contains invariably seeps out to contaminate others and our own being. Much of what escapes and confounds us in waking life, or disturbs us in our sleep, can be found in shadow. It is slippery, buried, frightening, and thus difficult to own.

This is a book about one gay man's quest for his lost power, his true selfhood, what I refer to here as my "queer masculinity." And how I've come to believe there is no other way to claim this elusive power than through a passionate and empathetic relationship to that hidden place called shadow.

Before there is queer masculinity, there is a lie. Named or not, we know it well. When I was a boy, people would sometimes step away and gaze nervously into my eyes, as if to retrieve me. I seemed to be no longer there, having fled the moment to a private refuge where solitude was kept, like secret wisdom, as an answer to living. My distance from others was revealed only by these incidents of accidental confession. I had learned to hide myself well. And because of this I could detect others who were hiding like me.

No matter what tactic we use to protect ourselves—covering up, acting out, or fitting in—to be gay is strange. How could it be otherwise? Our lives are portioned by the very terms of estrangement. We are strangers to those who should know us best, and thus are kept strangers from ourselves. The boy inside remains unknown to the man—the priest, the letter carrier, the lover—he becomes. And so each, in his way, continues to suffer a separate hell.

In the twenty-five years since my coming out, I've roamed and prowled, documented and assessed, nearly every stage the gay and lesbian liberation movement has demonstrated itself on. I've been peripatetic, to say the least, in my eagerness to grasp as much of the story as possible while at the same time having my own say in it. Yet I've remained distanced enough to know that the drama itself—this sprawling saga of queer uprising, resistance, and cultural entrenchment—is the most important thing. In fact, I believe there has never been any story quite like it.

We've rightly demanded that our history be told to the world, but it is acceptance from others that has mostly defined the struggle. That is why what the world thinks of us is only half the story, and perhaps the lesser half. For in whatever ways we've grown resilient against the tyranny of crude laws and moral sanctions, we remain hostage to a crueler enemy: our own self-doubt and destructive urges.[2]

Now it's time for a new way to claim gay reality, to re-envision and heal it from within. As always, we need to deconstruct and expunge the negating myth of homosexuality, a myth largely created by what the novelist Christopher Isherwood called "the heterosexual dictatorship." More important, we must invent new myths—an ontology generated from the depths of our own being rather than adapted from the values of those who oppress us.

In so doing, we must ask: Who are we? Where have we come from? What are we for? As both professional journalist and spiritual seeker, I've kept these fundamental questions in mind as my search for meaning has led me ever inward to where my own truth resides.

In this book, I weave two stories—the outer and inner—like intertwining threads. Archetypal images, historical reportage, and personal memories connect the two and show how—if one goes deep enough—the contents of one's unconscious find revelation through universal forms.

A Word About Archetypes

When asked what it's like to be on a "spiritual path," I usually don't know how to reply. In truth, the word *spiritual* is one of the most overused and least understood adjectives in modern life. What does it mean, exactly? How much have our beliefs about spirituality been colored by personal happenstance—past events and hopes about the future? To what degree have our judgments about what is spiritual or not been affected by Christianity, Buddhism, Hinduism, and all the many other entrenched-isms that exist?[3]

For some, a spiritual path means being on a kind of metaphysical thrill ride; bouncing from one peak experience to another, never settling on one consistent way. Sometimes the opposite is true: Devotees of a particular doctrine are caught in a groove, unknowingly depressed and unable to let other possibilities live. Then, what is known as spirituality becomes a palliative rather than a curative thing; an obstruction to right, lively engagement with Self. Of course, many find a middle road with its own challenges and rewards.

As for myself, I have traveled down many avenues of religion and faith—from what is generically called New Age to time-honored traditions of both East and West. The direction of modern depth psychology, however, has been an especially good way for me to explore my own complexities. Throughout this book, I employ some of the insights gleaned from the science of psychology (which is itself the science of the mind) to better illuminate what spirituality is for me.

In communicating about the world within, I rely on the language of Carl Jung. More than any other man in our modern era, this Swiss psychologist created a vocabulary about the human soul. Central to this way of thinking is the concept of psyche, the totality of nonphysical life: personal and collective, conscious and unconscious. The contents of psyche—our archetypes, complexes, persona, ego, shadow, and self—grow from an immaterial source and take shape as we do. Radiating throughout psyche and all of its parts is libido, a dynamic life force with a nature of its own. It energizes an inner world as mysterious and infinite as the one around us.

One of psyche's most evident functions is its spontaneous capacity for symbol making: creating images of self-regulation and transformation aimed at realizing our journey toward wholeness (what Jung referred to as *individuation*). These images, known as archetypes, populate our private dreams and common myths. They are inherited archaic instincts, the original model or "first-source" after which behavior is patterned and emotions are perceived. Jung showed how similar archetypal themes or mythical ideas exist among all the world's people, no matter how specific differences may appear to separate us.

Archetypes are structure-forming elements within the psyche, a treasury of crystalline seeds which give rise to the fantasies and mythological motifs informing our lives. When activated, they release a great amount of creative energy. However, archetypes are not the actual contents of the symbols or myths themselves; they are the imprinted forms or parameters in which psychological material is organized and channeled. Thus, any given archetype can find numerous expressions. The mother archetype, for example, includes not only our real mother but all mother figures ranging from positive to negative—from the Virgin Mary to Medusa.

While each individual's experience of an archetype is unique—given who we are and where we've come from—the general way in which archetypes are felt and lived out are universally determined. "The most we can do is to *dream the myth onwards*," said Jung, "and give it a modern dress."

Archetypes are not just intellectual concepts, but exist as living forces within the human soul. Psychologist Anthony Stevens describes them as a kind of unseen "author-director" standing behind the scenes of each person's life. From birth to death—through childhood, maturity, relationship—the primal occurrences of life are all subject to control by these genetically acquired, genome-bound units of instinctive information. "That there is a biological substratum for the most complex social and individual behaviour among all animals is now certain, and man is no exception," he says.[4]

Pictured in the form of gods and myths, we can see how these powerful predispositions work in shaping our emotions and needs. And, as this is a book about the lives of gay men, the archetypal images discussed are those dealing with same-sex love and masculinity. The mythic figures of Gilgamesh and Enkidu, Dionysus, Narcissus, Hermes, and Trickster are all relevant to our present-day desire for personal authenticity. But this book is not about how to become *better* men within the tradition of masculinity as prescribed by Western culture. Rather, it suggests that by going to the root of our desire—in nurturing our queerness in unforeseen ways—we become men beyond any current definition.

The Hero's Path is one archetypal image that all gay men should ponder these days. The way of the hero certainly holds unquestionable meaning for my own life—the life of a queer man coping with AIDS, laughing and crying on the edge of the wasteland. It's hard not to balk before the dark. But in risking to know the fecund, mysterious, and scary part of ourselves we call *shadow*, one can advance through the wilderness. In this way, we find our own myth. In this way, I've not only survived—but thrive.

To quest for queer masculinity is to go to the sacred source of gayness itself. And for this we must find what was taken from us: our innocence, originality, our verve. I have no better way to do this than to tell my own story—my own myth—and show what was stolen from me. There are faint clues of how this happened. Yet I know the theft occurred many years ago, perhaps even before memory begins.

When I was a boy, the centerpiece of my neighborhood was the deserted remains of a stately Victorian house. It commanded an entire city block ringed by dense hedges now grown wild. Grand ivory charm had long faded: the paint on the walls curled like slivers of dead bark and rain-stained floors glistened with a carpet of broken glass. Yet as I walked through its stripped rooms, it pleased me to believe that this house—haunted, to be sure—was mine.

Tidy suburban dwellings crowded the perimeters of this fetid pile, and stern parental warnings not to trespass onto its grounds were ignored. I played among the unkept gardens by myself or with a select posse of other boys. Using battered garbage can lids for shields and uprooted surveyor's stakes for swords, we plunged into the fantastic byways of imaginary life. We advanced and retreated in motley summer gangs, daring each other to go farther into the house, especially into those rooms where the sun did not shine.

At the end of such days I'd sometimes venture alone into the building's center. With arms outstretched like probing antennae, I edged forward in the murky light until a fearsome panic rose up to shake me. Then I'd rush out, breathless, vowing never to return again. But I always did. Until the day men came to knock the old place down.

That house was somehow *my* house, and what dwelled inside lived on to tag me. Long after those troubling grounds were smoothed, I found myself still in flight from unnameable fear. I spent years running, seething anger directed inward, all the while projecting the phony peace of a secretly despairing person.

Along the way there were so many other men found, loved, and lost just like me. They were unlike the boys I had once played with.

Gay Body

By now, we had learned to cover up the chaos, resist the bends and curves of the irrational. Always pursued, so little time for patience, we left difficult questions and deadly assumptions behind in haste.

I learned to survive, although the price I paid was never being able to confront my mystery and, without that, a man is left with no story to call his own. This was revealed to me the day I reached the loneliest moment. I could not find even the disguise of feeling, merely its absence. I knew then that the time had come to begin the search for my missing self—to find what had been haunting me.

What I discovered is told to you here. Above all else, this is an adventure story.

Los Angeles,
Winter Solstice, 1996

1

Strange Kind of Paradise

"O I say these are not the parts and poems of
the body only, but of the soul,
O I say now these are the soul!"

—WALT WHITMAN

I stand naked in front of a mirror and study my body. What I see is this: a man of middle weight, at middle life, who's from the Middle at his very core. ("Good Midwestern stock," so he's been told.) The feet stand firmly on the ground and support two legs, well-built and sturdy. The hips are too wide for a man, though, I'm loathe to say. They're more womanlike, a comparison heard all my life. The abdomen is soft, but not too flabby, tucked beneath a broad chest and rounded shoulders. The face is strong-jawed and smooth, framed by a short beard and full head of hair rapidly graying. The eyes are blue, but sometimes tend to greenish.

The assemblage of parts is not displeasing, but there is no mistaking its idiosyncrasy. My body is unique to me, a curious mixture of feminine curves and masculine juts. And the truth is, I've had a difficult time always wanting to be in it. It's been the source of my shame and others' consternation, the battlefield over which my right to selfhood has been fought. The nicks and dings of the flesh are but a pentimento of scarred feelings beneath. Still, accepting my body as it is has meant forging a larger, if not lasting peace.

My body. My *gay* body. Divided into parts, warred over, and now maybe won. It's always been not just a matter of occupancy, but rather of ownership. What of it belongs to my father? What of its realm can the mother claim? What parts are the socially constructed? What, if any, are the essential? How much of the whole is the piece called "I." And as for the unconscious rest, to what collective does it really belong? That I can ask these questions at all marks a truce of sorts. For the battle in my body, *for* my body, has been waged for as long as I can remember.

A lasting settlement is harder won. But the prize is immensely worthy: no less than the capacity to love myself. It's not that love was ever absent. In some manner or form it always circulated in the air. The problem was my inability—no, wariness—in letting it in. Love seemed so conditional during my early years. The price for love, real and complete, was too high. Perhaps, in the final analysis, this is what saved me.

As a first-born son who happened to be gay, I was susceptible more than most to the dysfunction brewing around me. Not only the dysfunction of my family, but of society. No matter how small or big the circle drawn, I was at its center, like a magnet, attracting the stray particles no one saw or wanted to see. I became a carrier of my family's toxic secrets—its legacy of violence, bitterness, and shame—and an ideal container into which the greater culture could similarly pour its disowned parts.

With bright eyes, a curious mind, and an unshakable sense of being different, I had no choice but to investigate those things others refused to acknowledge. Then, over time, an even stranger thing happened: What I observed took hold and grew inside. In this way, my fate was cast. In this manner, too, has the destiny of all gay lives been shaped.

At what point does the armor of innocence which protects the young shatter? Or does it come apart piece by piece—shine to rust, invulnerability to rot—as the years march by? While I wasn't completely impervious to the trouble around me, I somehow found a way to guard myself for a decade from the fusillades of my family's embattled truth. But then, one summer day in my ninth year, something simple yet momentous happened: I was divested of my chimerical shield by the sound of breaking glass.

I was sitting in my grandmother's spotless kitchen drinking a glass of milk when the white porcelain vase she prized above all others came crashing to the floor. It smashed into a hundred pieces, the fine petals and leaves which covered its ornate lid like an alabaster hydrangea bloom now littered the linoleum. What caused it to tumble from its enameled niche? Did someone throw it? Or had it fallen when someone slammed the door?

It seemed that doors were always being closed just a little too hard or that tension was roiling the room, no matter what the occasion. Ever-present strife and unspeakable past deeds were the polar currents which energized life around me. Yet, no matter how vehement the views expressed, some things, perhaps the most important things, just never got said. If neurosis is the refusal to suffer fully, then my family was one heated farrago of anxiety.

That day in my grandmother's kitchen arrived at the zenith of America's imperial pride; when the kind of innocence we'd diagnose today as outright denial was the rule of the land. Few people spoke honestly about what disturbed them, opting instead to stuff feelings into neat hidden compartments inside. So it came as little surprise when the round, trophy-sized jar fell and cracked into many fragments. Empty though it was, it seemed precariously full of the emotional strain fulminating in the house.

Whether the object was a family heirloom or not, I'll never know. That it had been proudly put on display was obvious. I calmly set down my glass of milk, knelt to the floor, and helped my grandmother pick up all the sharp pieces. With meticulous care, we spent the rest of the summer gluing the pot back together. We were never closer than during the countless hours of sorting shards; each minuscule scrap turned and twisted until we could figure out where it fit back in.

What are the spiritual ties between gay boys and their grandmas that make their bond so special? Grandmothers are fonts of unconditional blessing for everyone, but young queers get more than devoted hugs from theirs. Under a grandmother's aegis, we are admitted into the maternal world, clued in and trained in its ways. During the long muggy days of mending a broken pot, I got wise about a lot of things. I realized that my family was like the thing I was piecing back together, and that however much I wanted it whole, no amount of effort or wishful thinking on my part would really correct the damage done. And as I sat with my grandmother taking inventory of the ceramic puzzle piled in the bottom of an old hatbox, I learned why this was so.

Like a crone sifting through the contents of an oracular pot, she pulled out stories from the past as each chip was lifted to be studied in the crisp morning light. There were stories about family hardships; how such occasions had been overcome by some and had defeated others. Apparently, I had come from a long line of folk whose stalwartness did not necessarily spell success. Bonnie herself was born four years after the centenary in a sod house on the shorn Nebraska prairie. She was delivered in a corncrip, a cradlelike device used to dry and store the harvested crop, and had grown up resourceful enough to outlive drought, famine, flood, tornado—all manner of natural calamity. What a survivor she was!

From my grandmother, I learned the difference between a woman being hysterical and merely headstrong, and how my mother was often both. I learned what the labels on the jars in the spice rack meant, and how to pay attention to what other people were feeling. I learned about fabric and thread and how to sew a seam straight. I learned about the importance of secrets, and also about their destructive power.

Some of the lessons were new, many were simply confirming of things already known. I had been taking notes about women's mysteries, their place and purpose in the world, for as long as I could remember. The scent of makeup on my mother's face, the satin-lined box of faux jewels sitting on her bedside table, fascinated me as few things did. The powder and rouge, the brooch with phony pearls, evoked fantasies, to be sure, but also an awareness about illusion and guile. The use of these things meant more than the merely ornamental: They were exotic weaponry in the war of the sexes being waged around me.

I ducked and took cover the best I could, retreating from the rough-and-tumble tests on the boys' side of the playground to go hang out with the girls. Neither camp seemed to mind. Better yet was to seek invisibility altogether. The ideal place for disappearing was the movie house in the small town on California's central coast where I spent my grade-school years. There, in the embrace of darkness, it was easy to escape into dreaming. I attended Saturday matinees nearly every week, scurrying down cypress-shaded alleys so as not to be late. The afternoon typically climaxed with the ruin of modern Tokyo or ancient Rome, universes away from humble Pacific Grove.

Way too stimulated to go right on home, I meandered, listening to the basso tones of a foghorn announcing the imminent dusk. Then, as if on some automatic track, I retraced my steps back to the theater and the Greyhound bus station next door, where the last hour of daylight was spent riffling the pages of racy men's magazines. These racks were known to be off-limits to boys my age. But at five o'clock, while the grumpy clerk attended to the final busload of the day, I'd edge past the sign warning "No Minors" and trespass into the adult reading section.

There my mind was inflamed all over again, but only by exotic fantasies of a different kind. Row after row of lurid covers advertised the forbidden in a frenzy of color and action: ruddy hunters with big guns blazed at charging stags; tattooed soldiers-of-fortune leered at women in torn slips; other women tied to a chair or bed recoiled in wide-eyed terror from threatening shadows.

Such was my initiation into the world of men. It seemed like an impossibly foreign world, and never more so than after these nervous excursions. After a heart-thumping minute or two, I'd dash out of the dusty station and into the street. Inhaling a long draught of damp evening air, I started the walk home, trudging up a fog-shrouded hill while contemplating a weird mixture of guilt and glee.

During the summer months, my mother escorted my younger brother and sister and me to the community's crescent-shaped beach nestled in a rocky outcrop known as Lover's Point. Decades ago, when Pacific Grove was being established as a Methodist summer camp in the late 1800s, the place was called *Lovers of Jesus Point.* But by 1960, the encroachment of time and secularity had managed to dispel much of the town's religiosity. For a while we were dutifully packed off to Sunday school, but that's about as far as our instruction in matters of God went.

Our mother was an indefatigable humanist, and taught us to embrace life with an open mind rather than by rote. She stimulated our intellect, whetted our curiosity in all kinds of ways. With modest means, she was somehow able to provide good books and music lessons, planned trips to museums and the great outdoors. Many a day was spent down by the shore, pant legs rolled up, and the cool, salty brine of the tidepools splashing over our toes, as she helped us examine the squiggly sea urchins and other odd creatures living there.

After a picnic lunch, my sister, Gail, would wander off to collect the pink and silver shells that dotted the beach, while my brother and I clambered up succulent-covered cliffs to adjacent railroad tracks. Scraped and dirt-streaked, we plundered our pockets for pennies, which we balanced on the rails. Then we'd lie low and wait for the train loaded with sand, mined a few miles down the line at Spanish Bay, to lumber past. Flattened copper coins and bits of shells jingling together in the bottom of a plastic pail were the souvenirs of countless perfect days. However, we were oblivious to storm clouds on the horizon of our happiness, the tumult brewing in our mother's gifted but troubled mind.

Much of the summer was spent in the town's saltwater pool, where we were given swimming lessons. But I was less interested in splashing about with the other children than in exploring the grottolike recesses of the grown-up locker room. A dank bunker constructed of local stone and concrete, it was usually filled with naked men whose ease with their bodies only underscored the shyness I had about mine.

It's where I first saw my dad naked. We were there together after one Sunday at the beach: He slowly peeling off his wet suit, me standing in rapt attention. The sight of his firm, pale butt and meaty penis transfixed me on the spot. I could not avert my eyes. But he caught my admiring gaze and countered it with a contemptuous look. This lightning flash of truth between us was too much to comprehend at that moment; my only response was to blush from head to toe.

Still, I couldn't resist returning to those murky corridors, taking pleasure from the banging sounds of locker doors and the sight of bare flesh. As with all gay boys, my sexuality was informed by furtive looks and an ever-present dread of discovery. I have no doubt that my lifelong tendency for keeping veiled what others casually reveal was incubated in this seaside cave of male mystery.

The safest place to hide was the town's library. I could lose myself for hours on one of the window seats lining its spacious front room. There I read and reread all fourteen of L. Frank Baum's Oz books; his phantasmagorical land was the farthest point from Pacific Grove of any yet found.[1] The annual broadcast of *The Wizard of Oz* during the fifties and early sixties was always an eagerly awaited event in our house. Yet I'd unfailingly break down near the end of the movie when Dorothy must say good-bye to her newfound friends, click her ruby heels together three times, and return to Kansas.

"Mom, Dad! Mark's crying again!" my brother and sister would jeer upon seeing my tears. Their loud taunts, however, did little to stem the embarrassing flow down my cheeks. I couldn't help it. More than gross sentimentality, I was being moved by the sheer frustration of the moment: Who would want to leave such a fantastic place?[2]

Dorothy's departure from Oz resonated with my longing to escape a harsh and unwelcoming world. But it was not her character on which I projected that wish. Dorothy, at least as portrayed in Baum's books, struck me as being more selfish than virtuous, thickheaded than smart. She's the least interesting of all the Oz figures, and thus the hardest to relate to. It was Ozma of Oz, ruler of the realm, who captivated me.

A powerful queen, Ozma is riding a magnificent golden chariot drawn by a great lion and an immense tiger, when she is first seen by Dorothy. Clothed in dazzling silver robes and wearing a bejeweled crown, Ozma holds an ivory wand with two prongs tipped by the diamond-encrusted letters *O* and *Z*. As a baby, Ozma had been transformed into a boy by a wicked witch, and many years passed before she knew she was a girl. When restored to her natural form, Ozma also discovered she was the only child of the former ruler of Oz and entitled to govern in his place. Strong and brave, Ozma took control of her destiny. She was never a hapless victim, surrendering her fate to circumstance alone.

I identified myself with her character, a person with ability and might, rather than the ill-fortuned Dorothy. Ozma spoke not only boldly, but truthfully as well. Empowered as she was by her contrasexuality and royal stewardship of the land, Ozma's image registered deep in my psyche. By age ten, this numinous figure had leaped off a printed page to come home and live inside me as companionable kin—a sister. She appears in my dreams to this day as a silent witness of deeds, other times as a fateful instigator of them.

The habitation of secret realms and a hoarding of shame was my introduction to that place inside known only as shadow. In fact, it felt more comfortable to be a citizen there than of the real world and, as time has gone by, I've come to see what company I keep. Every gay men should have a map of this inner domain and learn to navigate its landscape. We may fear to descend and venture there, but there are energies below, like magma, which can arise and erupt with awesome consequence.

Few people are cognizant of the fact that we inhabit two worlds simultaneously and that each is but a mirror of the other. I am reminded of this when relationships sour when least expected, or things that should come out right take a wrong turn. Then I realize that how we relate to others and, in turn, are seen by them, is a reflection of the unconscious world. It has a geography of its own, and outer life is shaped as we move down its pathways of instinct and feeling.

We live in two worlds, and thus have two stories to tell. Understanding this basic truth has helped me to see how a rosy-cheeked grandma with lustrous white hair was, on another level, Great Mother with her boons. And how the instant I saw my father with a tumid cock, he was transformed into an embodiment of queer Eros itself. What's the point of talking about mothers and fathers otherwise? It's not a question of sentiment, at least not here. The real issue is how certain people are carriers of the archetypal energies we are all naturally inclined to project upon each other.

It's important to see the world symbolically. Yet the ability to do so has atrophied within the minds of most people today, resulting in the neurosis of the modern psyche. We are healed by knowing the language of the unconcious as revealed in our dreams, myths, and key figures around us. By integrating the symbolic meaning this information holds, our individuation is furthered. Like many gay men, I'm as adept at "seeing" things in my mind's eye as I am thinking about them; so uncovering the significance of archetypal imagery is as natural as it is transformative.

And so, too, has the image of a queen spied long ago in the pages of a book held true as I tool down the freeways of my own inner Oz.

The Big Tumble

My grandmother's tales about life on the Nebraska plains were no less fantastic than Dorothy's: hailstones the size of golf balls, swirling funnel clouds and snowdrifts as high as houses, endless seas of amber grain, armies of locusts advancing in the summer heat, the odd propriety and dampened passion of small-town lives. For a precocious queer boy growing up on the fair Pacific coast, such stories couldn't be more remote from my own experience than if I'd been carried off to Oz myself.

Whether sitting in rapt attention by her side or hidden away with my nose stuck in a book, I was instructed by a fabulous mythology perfectly calibrated to my mind. I learned how women survive; indeed, how they get what they need. And more than anything else—more than wearing my mother's things or even the ruby slippers—what I wanted was my father's undivided affection.

Howard was a handsome man, tall and broad-shouldered, with the musculature that comes naturally from hard work and outdoor living. Mainly of Scottish descent, he was proud of his Oglala Sioux bloodline inherited from a maternal great grandmother. Butch (as he was affectionately called) loved to fish and hunt. Stuffed deer heads lined the garage walls, souvenirs of his expeditions into the mountains just south of where we lived.

During the Depression, he'd go out into the woods and bring back game for the family table. He was deemed a champion in other ways, too. At ease in his body and with a knack for making others laugh, Butch scored with the girls and won with the boys. He was a star quarterback in high school and, after a valorous stint of duty in the Second World War, proudly worked as a forest ranger. My dad unquestionably possessed the clean-cut, sexy swagger so much in favor among gay men today.

Whether he had any homosexual experiences himself, I'll never know. But the probable odds, as laid out by Alfred Kinsey and company in their groundbreaking 1948 study of the nation's sexual habits, suggests that he did. A blow job at sea or a furtive locker-room grope is of little concern to me, however.

What seems evident now, after so many years of knowing so few things of real importance about him, was that my father had become a masculine icon to me almost from the very beginning. My attraction went beyond the acceptable bonds of parent and child: He became the exemplar of my need. All of the feminine skills I acquired—indeed, the very language of romance—were for him.

What risky business this was. For one so young, there was no conscious knowledge that this is where my passion was being sown. He, of course, already sinking in the mire of a sorrowful marriage, hadn't a clue that his oldest son was projecting the sum of his self-worth and fulfillment as a queer male onto him.

Straight men have a hard enough time figuring out what is happening inside them, let alone pondering what their gay sons might be feeling. There is no education, for either party, about such things. Invisible emotional currents are doubtlessly broadcast and received, but without the information that this programming between a father and son is as correct as any other, the transmission is more garbled than clear. With no way to comprehend, and perhaps distressed by what little he did perceive, my father simply tuned out.

I am not without some satisfying recollections of my father. Our best moments were those rare times alone. I remember him coming into my room at dawn, gently shaking me awake, telling me to dress while he finished loading the truck. With a thermos of strong coffee warming the cracked vinyl seat between us, we'd set off down Highway One, over the ridge that divides the Monterey Peninsula like an arched spine, past the stuccoed dome of an ancient mission church, through artichoke fields tilled near a windswept bay, and then, free of civilization, into the wild headlands of the Big Sur coast. There was a stillness that time of day which made conversation unnecessary. Only the creaks of the old Chevy and the surf's cyclic roar interrupted our calm.

We'd drive for an hour, the lifting fog making each turn along the ribbonlike highway a discovery. Few roads in the world are as improbable as the one carved out of the sheer cliffs of Big Sur. It could only be completed in the 1930s, when the New Deal commissioned a series of bridges over the narrow canyons splitting the coast. Men died making the concrete trestle resting high above Bixby Creek, my dad said, each time we crossed it. They had fallen into the foundations just as the cement was poured, he'd add with a wink, buried alive and entombed there still. I always thought about their ghosts prowling the majestic span.

We reached our destination soon after, an outcropping of rock where abalone was harvested at low tide. It took good balance on the wet stones and a crowbar to pry the large oval-shaped shells from their roost but, within a couple of hours, our burlap sacks were filled. Brine encrusted, we'd then head home, the sun now high in a blue sky.[3]

Despite such expeditions, my father knew I was not like the other boys and so, for a short while longer, he sought tougher remedy. We'd go pigeon hunting in the woods: Dad shooting, me scrabbling through the underbrush to retrieve the bloody, twitching birds. I would hurriedly stuff their corpses into a grimy canvas bag, horrified, but not wanting to disappoint. I was desperate to keep up my end of the bargain.

Years later, I wondered about the initiation rites of certain aboriginal tribes. Young boys, the same as Mark-the-bird-gatherer, were tested through fierce ritual, their coming-to-power inscribed on flesh. I had often imagined myself alone and naked in the forest, sharpened stick in hand, pursuing the shadow of a bigger man: the man I hoped I would grow up to be. Instead, I had been left with a sack of smelly pigeons.

As hard as my father tried, there was neither a rite of passage nor reciprocated romance. Soon after, I was abandoned to my own devices and never really saw him again—as he did not see me—until some decades later. We were strangers in the same house, passing by but never looking.

I retreated into an isolated world, my psyche fed more by fantastic words and pictures and less by physical doing. While nongay boys might translate such fuel for an active imagination into actual deed (Superman not only saves the girl but gets to have her all the way), I stayed safely within the confines of my imaginal cocoon. Rebelling against and sending up the traditions of family and state, or flying to Mars and back, if even in one's head, might in some way aid in the resolution of the Oedipal dilemma; with that important separation from the ties of the womb done, boys are presumably free for manhood and its procreative responsibilites.

I dared not stray into a world fraught with the complexities of real relationships—either with girls or boys—but opted instead for the simplicity of what I could control in my own head. I chose to inhabit a denatured, pacified world; a place populated with Disney characters and soft television fictions, where any problem could be fixed by special effects and Mr. Spock was superior in his lack of emotion.

Precocious yet introverted, I could not risk letting the outer world in. Instead, I projected what was inside me on it. I'd take walks down by the ocean to a private place where I sat and watched the waves. There, against the tapestry of dark water and kelp, images would often form. Out of the sea arose visions of amphibious men, godlike and tacitly appraising. Somewhere, from down deep in the oceans of my soul, I was seeing a split-off part of myself.

As the sole occupant of my nowhere no-man's land, what else was I to do but have these conversations with myself? Like all queer children of the world, I was orphaned: Adept with the mysteries and materialness of the maternal world, but not really of it, and divorced, too, from the place of the father. I was straddling a thin line perched on my lonely rock, facing neither past nor future, just vast present emptiness. Little did I know it would prove the most important lesson of all.

My urge to go beneath the surface of things was hastened the day I finally saw that my homosexuality possessed its own immutable truth, an inner reality existing beyond any outside reason. It was as if a great hole had opened beneath my feet, and down I went screaming. After all, declaring one's otherness requires a death, a real submission to the fact that nothing in your life will ever be the same. Believing otherwise is a lie.

Perhaps what those apparitions I'd spied in the waves were really saying was good-bye: Farewell to falsity and fake illusions; now it's time to go find real values to fill the void. But, as I soon enough discovered, no amount of earnest ideals or crafted theory will satisfy the appetite for knowing if what we claim as truth is simply not so. Grafting made-up meaning to our homosexuality is not necessary; love, after all, needs no justification.

Yet I persist in my belief that queer eros holds multiple purpose in our lives—pedagogic, religious, creative, even altruistic—beyond the near-meaningless context it's been assigned. No matter how it's dealt with, being gay must certainly encompass more than whom we choose to have sex with. We're not different because of what we do in bed. The difference comes from what's happening under our skins, not the sheets.

A psyche-based paradigm of gay nature puts homosexuality in a new light. To be gay, as currently defined, gives us a limited place to stand in the world and a lever with which to somewhat move it. But an understanding of our lives stemming from psychological mindfulness permits a much better view of society's queer men as potential healers, soul guides, and culture makers for all people.

There is a wealth of archetypal forces residing within us; as many, one might say, as there are gods in the heavens. Some archetypes can be literally imagined, such as the Questing Hero or the Wise Old Man. (In Western culture, major archetypes are seen in the personae of ancient deities, on tarot cards, or in the image of certain pop icons.) But others are representational of more abstract images and ideas, like Self or Individuation, which are known as archetypes of transformation.

Some archetypes are widely experienced in Western culture (the Senex, or Judging Father, is one). But other archetypes are more acutely felt, for reasons of biological or social inheritance, within individual minds. Archetypes of the Same or Double, the Wounded Healer, Divine Child, Lunar Phallos, and Trickster are especially ascendant and at work in the psyches of gay men today. I believe the fundamental basis of being queer is an archetypal matrix, or inner constellation, characteristic of those who have been so labeled. This biologically determined psychic structure is further organized according to the vicissitudes of one's personal and collective upbringing.[4]

Because these archetypes contain energetic forces vital to challenge and change—necessary to the discovery of new ideas and modes of being, but revolutionary in that they upset the established order—individuals acting out the contents of these archetypes are shunned and suppressed. Recognizing this helps us to see how certain capacities of the soul could be assigned as "gay" throughout time; their value, adaptation, and even survival contingent on the specific cultural milieu in which they're perceived.

Seen from this vantage, being gay is more about what we do—our social role and function—than about what and how we've been sexually labeled. It is a subjective, multidimensional view of same-sex love, not a further justification. After all the damage that's been done, what recourse do we have but sublimity?

In ways both covert and blatant, a large percentage of us are soul-wounded early in life. We know this hurt better than any lover. And so we wonder: Are we damaged due to too much love from one parent and not enough from the other? Despite the rhetoric of gay pride, maybe there really is something "abnormal" about being homosexual. Then again, perhaps there's nothing wrong at all except for society's prejudice. Whatever the reason for rejection, is our wounding a curse or a spiritual occasion? Maybe it's an opportunity to take the road less traveled.

Because a false self and its sensibility of shame has been implanted in our souls, not many have been able to see clear enough to answer these questions. Our culture's legacy to its queer folk is decidedly poisonous. That is why striving to create an autonomous awareness is not only called for, but crucial. What choice do we have but to become literate of ourselves?

As someone who assiduously tended to the wounds of his own soul, some of Jung's insights about same-sex love hold value for us today.[5] For it was he who finally grasped, better than any of his peers, the one truth essential to any gay person: Our homosexuality has a meaning peculiar to us, and us alone. Taking the downward tumble into our own depths demands that we become conscious of that meaning.

On the Razor's Edge

Psyche is an ever-changing cosmos, but somewhere at the center of that inner world is Self. Described by Jung as the totality of the personality, the conscious and unconscious, "the self is our life's goal, for it is the completest expression of that fateful combination we call individuality."[6] Symbolized by mandalas of the magic circle or square, Self is the archetype of wholeness and includes, in early developmental stages, a great deal we don't yet know: shadow.

When we hide our feelings or compromise who we really are, as gay people must do nearly every day of our lives, a false or defended self is created. Like most people, gay men go through life without any realization of their true Self. So bound are we to our idealized, conforming false selves, that what has been buried in shadow is seldom found.

By my fourteenth year, I had become a censor of my own life, cautious and ever guarded against the thing haunting me. I never saw it, but nonetheless felt its stalking. Surely, any day soon, I would be cruelly exposed and humiliated for being who I really was. The fear fed doubt, which had grown into a disbelief about the adequacy of my very person. The creation of my false self was complete.

By now, the sense of not living in my body—of having separated from it to some distant, ethereal zone—was total. While I appeared stolid enough to avoid detection by others (how could anyone so glum be gay?), I could not fool myself. It was all a con game on my part, a desperate ruse in the service of self-protection. But the price for this defense was high; I may have been safe but was emotionally locked up. Never has a better prison been constructed.

My exile from Self was not without some advantage, though, as it sharpened my voracious watch of other people's lives. None fell under my inquisitive eye more than my parents: Why were they so unhappy, I wondered. And what relationship did I have, not only to them but to all that grief? Like most children of angry, dysfunctional families, I internalized the rage and hurt rather than seeing it as mere misfortune. Victims of brutal assault often believe they are the ones to blame, until otherwise taught.

Life was not all Sturm und Drang and retreat into dark corners, of course. My greatest source of comfort came from the abundant raw nature around me. Strange though it seemed, I was living in some kind of paradise: the Monterey Peninsula. A rugged point of land one hundred miles south of San Francisco, these twenty-five square miles of rolling dunes, low hills, and twisted trees have been celebrated by many—from early Catholic missionaries to authors such as Robert Louis Stevenson and John Steinbeck.[7]

My father came of age in this idyllic setting while living in a small, Monterey colonial-style house built by his father. He worshiped his dad, a hard-working, conscientious man who had suffered shell shock during the First World War. Life in Monterey during the two decades following the war remained "lovely and soft," in the words of his sister. Only the frantic pace of the sprawling sardine canneries along the bay intruded upon this sleepy pace.

My mother was born in Geneva, Nebraska, the modest seat of Fillmore County, a district of low-rolling croplands in the southeast corner of the state. By all accounts, Patricia grew up to be the brightest girl in the village. During the hardscrabble years of the Great Depression, her natural intelligence and thirst for learning led her to the town's Andrew Carnegie–built library, where she read nearly every book. Inspired by literature and the determined women she saw portrayed in the movies, my mother strove for independence from the prairie's confines.

Soon life everywhere was to change with the intrusion of another war.[8] Like many places, Monterey was wrenched from an isolated past. Local upheaval followed the nation's with the opening of Fort Ord, a nearby military training camp. Day by day, Howard saw his father change. The man hated the idea of his only son going to war; the worry stirred painful memories and he turned to alcohol for relief. But drinking only hardened his mood. Howard tried to soothe his father's violent fits, but often he'd come home from school to find his mother knocked unconscious on the kitchen floor.

One day in 1942, Howard arrived to discover his father dressed only in underwear and holding a loaded shotgun at his mother and sister. The episode ended when he slumped to the floor, a victim of a stroke. The family nursed the sick man for a year, but after a brief recovery he collapsed again and died. My father was devastated by the mental decline and death of the man he had once idolized, and so, with the war in the Pacific still raging, he enlisted in the Navy at age seventeen and sailed away.

There was not much direction in Howard's life after his safe return from the war. He was embittered over the loss of his dad, feeling that his mother was somehow responsible. Howard hit the road for a while, but eventually resettled in Monterey. In 1948, he met Patricia, who was working in a bank in nearby Pacific Grove, and soon after they were married.

She had recently arrived on the Peninsula, having come with her family for a fresh start in the Golden State. Though poor and ever struggling, Waldo, Bonnie, and their three daughters were one of

Geneva's most respected families, having descended from the simple German farmers who settled the region in the 1870s. Waldo, a neatly dressed man of slight build, had departed from the work of his folk by becoming a newspaperman. He wrote articles, sold ads, even set type for *The Signal,* Geneva's weekly journal of record. His cramped brick office was filled with those who stopped by to gossip, seek advice, or mull life's problems with a kind and thoughtful listener, well-liked by everyone.

But in California, Waldo could do little to keep his own life from souring as he increasingly succumbed to bouts of sleepless depression. Hardy though they appeared, his forebears had suffered a long history of mental illness. While Waldo was living in Geneva, it's possible that his best friend, the town pharmacist, eased his symptoms by supplying cocaine. Now that he was fifteen hundred miles from this alleviating source, Waldo worsened, his despair aggravated by the burden of providing for an uprooted family.

Apocryphal or not, such conjecture is of little importance. One mild afternoon, while Bonnie fried eggs in an adjoining room, my grandfather took a double-barreled shotgun to his head and pulled the trigger. He joined a sizable list of relatives who had taken their lives in identical fashion.

News of the suicide was quickly hushed up, and my grandmother, with no clear idea of what to do, shuttled between Geneva and Pacific Grove before deciding to stay on the coast. She found employment caring for other people's children, mainly those who lived in neighboring Pebble Beach, a gated enclave of the rich and privileged.

My mother, just a few years out of high school, must have deeply internalized the grief and shame she felt over her father's death and mother's hardship, for I never remember her discussing it. In fact, she seemed to have an iron-clad contract with her emotions, determined to keep them under control whatever the case, unless it suited her purposes to unleash them.

She could focus her considerable will laserlike, as she could her scorn, when she wanted to. They were often applied in tandem, as my father soon enough discovered. Although impressed by her drive and tended good looks, he voiced second thoughts about marriage and tried to renege on his vow. It did not take long for my mother to correct this momentary lapse. Soon they began to raise a family, lifting their cues, like so many others, from the promissory script of the post-war era. It was not the time to air disturbing questions; truth was easily deferred and thus subverted.[9]

Years passed before they began to openly wonder about the shy, sensitive boy they called their oldest son, who by now had learned to read his mother's sadness. But, by then, neither parent had time to investigate curious hunches about my life; their own lives were failing. The era of suburban striving had taken its toll and was now replaced by one long season of relentless hostility. There had been too much suppressed emotion, too many conforming pressures, to find mutual understanding. Their world was an imperfect mirror.

The fractured image my parents painfully saw in each other was symptomatic of an entire generation's denial. Few survived unscathed. My mother eventually retreated into a hellish world of debilitating fury, her dreams lost forever. Today, the tragedy of something fervently desired—but never found—is permanently etched on her face. Sometimes, I see this awful grief cloud my face, too.[10]

My mother's distress, though more exaggerated than most, is part of a larger picture. I believe our relationship is typically reflected by other gay men and their mothers. We are ideal containers into which their own aspirations and anxiety over not realizing them can be poured. As we'll see, gay male psyche and the feminine shadow are inextricably woven together in many ways. Reasons for this can be found throughout patriarchal Western culture, where the fate of women and homosexual men have long been shackled together. The destiny of each are swayed by rude forces which serve only to confound their souls' intent.[11]

I'll never know why my father finally consented to marry my mother, but I do understand some of the underlying dynamics at work in his decision. Psyche's impulse is always toward completing the opus of a human life, and the way it does this is through the forging of opposites: a *coniunctio* or union of masculine/feminine, yin/yang, light/shadow. A nongay man's individuation process compels the integration of his masculinity with his inner feminine, an archetype Jung called the *anima.* (The archetype of the inner masculine in a woman is correspondingly known as the *animus.*)

When a different-sex couple falls in love, the man is enabled in the assimilation of his softer, more emotional and spiritual side through his romantic projection onto the woman. But this inner marriage can successfully occur only when the man is able to free himself from the sphere of the personal mother and her claims on him. His anima projection must be cast elsewhere, onto a more suitable feminine form. A new relationship with the mother, one neither too distant nor too close, must be established.

The archetypal Mother, in all her many guises, from creator to destroyer, possesses soul mysteries for every man. But gay men seem to have an alliance with the inner feminine distinctly our own. She dances with us and nurtures our deeds, but hers is not the primary romance we seek. That which paves the way to our selfhood wears a masculine mask. Masculinity itself contains opposites—solar and lunar dualities—to be joined as one.

Jung's thinking about the cause and nature of same-sex love evolved over the years. Homosexuality in men, he basically concluded, was the result of excessive identification with the feminine. But there is a further view now perceptively stated by Jungian theorist Robert H. Hopcke, among others. "Is it impossible to imagine that male homosexuality might be the result of an identification with masculinity and not simply the result of an identification with femininity?" posits Hopcke. "Can we ignore masculinity and all its archetypal roots?"[12]

While gay men today have obviously learned to adopt the outward postures of virile masculinity, the struggle to forge a more substantive link to the inner masculine—to realize our own *coniunctio* born of sacred love—is equally clear. It is a conflict that begins with our first and most important masculine source: our fathers.

Like all children, we project a libidinal instinct for soul-bonding within the first years of life. But it is not with mothers, but rather our father (or his surrogate image) that we identify this longing. It is on him that we project our erotic feelings. In a queer psyche, the libido itself is homosexually oriented.

In his unconscious romancing of the father, the young boy mirrors traits and behavior modeled by the mother, competing with her for the father's attention. This is one way in which gay men become conversant with the feminine and its vernacular. By the time most gay boys reach five or six years old they are rejected by the father, who begins to identify his son—in ways subtle or dramatic—as a sissy. The father's own homoerotic feelings have been uncomfortably stirred, and his son's initiation into the masculine world is left painfully incomplete. The boy is left bereft with a rupture of feeling. A wound is formed. A scenario of emotional distancing, from himself and others, is written.

Richard A. Isay, a psychiatrist who has worked extensively with gay men, explains it this way: "The child's perception of and response to these erotic feelings by themselves may account for such 'atypical' behavior as greater secretiveness than other boys, self-isolation, and excessive emotionality. Other traits that they soon label as being 'feminine' may also be caused by identification with the mother or mother surrogate. Such characteristics usually develop as a way of attracting the father's love and attention, in a manner similar to the way the heterosexual boy may pattern himself after his father to gain his mother's attention. . . . Such behavior in turn frequently affects the response of peers and may result in further isolation and unhappiness."[13]

Many gay men recognize this reality as an underlying truth in their lives: As it is below, so it is above. The aborted connection with primal maleness in early life afflicts our sense of Self as we grow into adolesence and adulthood. Once rejected, the inner masculine can be crippled forever, or masculinity itself becomes overly compensated for—even caricatured—in the life of an individual. Both extremes are apparent in gay men today.

Surely, my mother must have sensed some of the dynamics just described, whether intuitively or in the coolly reasoned way she deduced most things in life. By my freshman year in high school, there was little denying the fact that my dad and I had run out of words to say. As for her own culpability in the shaky course of my life, she remained clueless. Her own precarious psyche demanded that what was given one moment be taken away the next. I was either being exalted for my smart deeds and artistic promise or excoriated for my lack of the right stuff.

If we don't work to bring to consciousness the inner contradictions that confound us, then we are fated to project this unfinished business on the outer world—usually on those who are closest, our family and friends. It amazes me when people fail to grasp this basic psychological truth, but then we are blind to ourselves as to none other. Though unforgiving of the shortcomings of those around her, my mother was impervious to her own failings.

I was well-schooled in her twists and turns, but Patricia quite surprised me one afternoon by pulling up a chair in front of the television set and asking me to sit down. Usually during this time of day she was commanding me to go outside and be "like the other boys," rather than hiding out in my room with a book. While my father was long resigned to my lack of athletic prowess, my mother remained disgusted by it. Still, here she was, inviting me to watch a movie in broad daylight. Odd though it seemed, I could tell this was to be an important moment between us.

The movie was *The Razor's Edge*, the 20th Century Fox adaptation of W. Somerset Maugham's best-selling novel. Made in 1946, the film stars Tyrone Power as the soul-searching Larry, Gene Tierney as his shunned fiancée Isabel, Clifton Webb as her effete uncle Elliott, and Herbert Marshall as the Maugham-like narrator of the piece. I can only imagine the effect this cosmopolitan drama about lost love and spiritual seeking must have had on a young girl sitting in Geneva's one movie theater. Obviously, the picture had made a big impact. I dutifully did as my mother asked, and with a slight, almost conspiratorial smile, she left the room.

The Razor's Edge was tedious in spots, and I remember little of it from that viewing other than its touching some secret inner place in an inexplicable way. Certainly, I recognized myself in the asexual Larry: a young, idealistic seeker, a loner if there ever was one. But then there was Elliott to consider; waspish and uptight, more concerned with the outward appearances of things than with what was going on inside. Here, in one old movie suspiciously watched, were the polarities of my own character revealed. Could my mother have possibly known what she was doing?

What was it about this film that had touched her so? Perhaps there was something about the noble protagonist who wanders the world looking for life's meaning; he ignores society's conventions and holds onto his high principles no matter how his quest disrupts the lives of those around him. Maybe my mother saw her own need for healing reflected in the hero's search for self. Whatever the case, it was obvious to me that day that the handsome Larry was a gay man much like myself, in pursuit of one ineffable thing as surely as he was being pursued by something else. Maybe they were the same.

Sometimes, when gay men internalize the rejecting father they look elsewhere for male authority and may become addicted to the search. If this happens, sexuality becomes detached from emotional groundedness; an experience outside sustained intimacy. Never being satisfied with the relationships he does manage to forge, a father-wounded gay man moves on in narcissistic pursuit of a lost love that can never be restored—his father, himself.

While not explicity stated, perhaps Larry's constant seeking was motivated in part by his own father wounding. Whatever the reason, his propensity for flight was recognizable enough. Like all enduring works of art, Larry was made out of whole bits of the truth. Years later, my hunch about Larry was confirmed by Maugham's admission that the character was an aspect of his own younger and yearning self.[14] The author had in effect split himself in two parts; the other being the suave narrator of the story who speaks directly to the reader. A youth lost in the world and an elder other who survives by superiorly sailing above it: both figures mirrored like aspects of my own confused and inscrutable self.

None of the characters in *The Razor's Edge* are admittedly gay (Maugham did not publicly confess his own homosexuality until near the end of his life in 1962), but a queer sensibility clearly permeates both book and film. Maugham asked an openly gay colleague, the writer Chrisopher Isherwood, for help in understanding the subtleties of Vendantism, the Hindu philosophy his alter ego expounds, and based the flamboyant Elliott on the lives of several prominent gay men of the time. Of course, none of this was known to me that afternoon, but I have no reason to doubt that my intuitive gay radar picked up the queer signals and subtexts emanating from the screen.[15]

In return, I facilely projected my own spiritual longings on the movie's beautiful leading man; for all of Larry's poise and clarity of purpose, he seemed deeply hurt inside. I could relate to that. But as the movie progressed throughout the afternoon, I could feel a mounting horror as Elliott's character took shape and unfolded. True to Maugham's text, Webb played the part of a supercilious old queen with élan. Apparently, it was a portrayal not far from the facts of his actual life. (Webb, a bachelor in real life, was famed for his unerring good taste and arch wit. He devotedly lived with his mother until her death, a passing so mourned that one wag was prompted to call the inconsolable actor "the world's oldest living orphan.")

Elliott, as personified by Webb, was a fascinating creature to behold. "It may have escaped your notice, but I am not an ordinary man," he haughtily informs a friend. Yet despite his bravado and polished charm, Elliott contained a fulsomeness that made me cringe. It was the dark side of being gay: emotionally crippled, socially lethal, and undeniably sad.

When the movie's end credits finally rolled, I knew my mother had done me a great service, although not the one she had probably intended. In her mind, I was Larry: a sexual enigma; a self-sacrificing caretaker of woeful others; a soft man easily manipulated. But as night fell, I realized that it was Elliott who lived most heatedly inside: sexually frustrated, protective and selfish of his own neurotic concerns, brittle, even false; if always resilient and nobody's fool.

Somehow, I had to sort through the good and bad qualities of both characters and integrate what was worth saving back into my being. Larry and Elliott were but opposite faces of the same inner figure: the archetype of my gay manhood, with all of its complexity, pain, and shining promise. I had to forge my own *coniunctio* of opposities. It would no longer suffice to stay lumpish and unaware of my own devout quest.

I had much to commit to, this much I knew. But as to where and how to begin, I hadn't a clue. Maugham himself offered little hope or direction. After all, he said, his book was mainly a comedy. But with sage and jaded eyes, he was able to isolate one helpful truth, a quotation from the Katha-Upanishad with which he starts his book: "The sharp edge of a razor is difficult to pass over; thus the wise say the path to Salvation is hard."

Difficult or not, from that day on I had no choice: It was time to come down from the razor's edge.

2

⊠

We, Two Brothers Clinging

Gay men do not bring real children into the world as much as they give birth to one another through passion's fire. The child made of gay spirit was born inside me the night my brother Kirk climbed through an open window and entered my bed. There we embraced and made love until the sun came up, the first of many trysts where few words were spoken, the most important things said by touch. We had no choice but to love one another or die.

All around us, life was in shambles. Our parents were ill-matched people who had long ago encamped as mortal enemies do; trenches dug deep, volleys and shots fired in pointed exchange. The weapon of preference was words—vicious, lacerating words. They knew each other's vulnerable places well, took aim and discharged with accuracy. The night Kirk appeared like some savior angel marked the end of one more shattering round in which screams cut like knives do and the cops were called yet again to the Thompson domain by troubled neighbors.

I seldom remember a time when it felt safe to have friends over, or when a holiday dinner didn't end with bitter tears, or my brother and sister and I stopped looking for new places to hide. The trappings of our middle-class life offered little insulation. To us, the piano, good books, and nice toys were like detritus strewn across a field of battle; more evidence of casualty than comfort to three sad and lonely kids. Survivors that we were, my brother and I sought solace in each other's arms. Walt Whitman's romantic image, "We two boys together clinging, One the other never leaving . . ." was as apt a description of our condition as any imagined.[1]

Kirk was my first lover, and all other men with whom I've been intimate in the years since are unaccountably compared to him. He was beautiful, an archetypal California golden boy blessed by the elements of wind, water, and light. Lean and agile, he was usually tanned from long days spent roaming the nearby beaches and hills. Tousled hair was streaked blond by the sun, and from his skin emanated the sweetly acrid scent of toasted almonds. Kirk fit as gracefully in his body as I was clumsy in mine, but that difference and the three and a half years separating us in age was leveled during the midnight hours when we'd sneak into one or the other's room to press our naked flesh together.

The floor would be littered with pajama tops and bottoms in a matter of seconds. Then we'd dive under the warm covers and rub hard dicks against soft bellies. We eagerly explored the curves and crevices of a brother's body as if we were travelers in some exotic new land. The hot, coursing vein on a throat, the graceful arch of a butt, each glistening pearl of semen was beheld as the wonder it is.

Once in a while our sighs and whispers would abruptly come to a halt when a noise was detected elsewhere in the house. Was someone coming? Would the locked door be pounded on and stern inquisitions issued?

"Quiet!" I'd anxiously whisper, gripping Kirk tight. "We have to be *quiet.*" I could hear my heart beating loudly in my chest, and thought for sure its pounding would give us away.

"Hush up yourself," he'd giggle, sinking down under the blankets. He was the rebellious one, and it didn't seem to matter to him whether we got caught or not.

But it was always the creak of drying timber, or a pet rustling in its pen, or some other distant murmur that was overheard. After another nervous minute or two, we'd exhale pent-up breaths and resume our lovemaking.

Sometimes we'd just lie naked under the sheets and talk. "Why do they hate each other so much?" Kirk asked me about our parents after one especially stormy row. Earlier in the evening our father had actually pulled his hunting rifle out of the hall closet and aimed it menacingly at our mother. It was an act of desperation on his part, I suspected, born of frustration as much as rage. The month before they had tried to run one another over with cars. As usual, it was my role to step between them, to argue for peace. It was a no-win situation, debilitating for all concerned.

But I really didn't know what to say to Kirk. Older brothers were supposed to have answers, particularly one who had just finished his second year of high school, but in this case I remained mum.

"Why'd they have to go and get married in the first place?' Kirk persisted, ignoring my silence.

"Well, if they hadn't gotten married, then we wouldn't be here," I said, trying to sound wise. It was a late April night, and a humid breeze carried the ocean's clean scent through the open window. Kirk was a precocious youngster, an "early bloomer" as some might say, but his lithe, brown body, usually taut with wiry energy, seemed deflated that night. I traced the delicate curves of his chest with the back of my hand, wanting nothing more than to assuage his doubt, brush away the pain we both felt. The tension in the house had grown steadily worse over the years. Any tenderness now in our lives came from stolen moments such as this.

I pushed a flaxen strand of hair away from his hurt, blue eyes and tried to look into them. But Kirk turned away and buried his head in the pillow. "I . . . I don't know why it has to be this way," I falteringly said, "but somehow I know we'll get through it okay. At least we've got each other." But I knew my words were of little comfort, for I could feel his curled-up body shaking.

During the hot days of summer, we'd hop on the back of a cantankerous motor scooter our father had given us and go riding off through fields of artichokes cultivated between our house and an isolated spot along a river not far away. There wasn't much water flowing in the dry season, but enough for us to strip off our clothes and splash in the pools and trickles that remained. Then we'd roll in the coarse sand lining the banks and engage in wild games of chase through the nearby stands of poplar and birch.

Despite the trouble at home, I was never happier than during those blissful afternoons, when heaviness dropped as easily as a pair of drawers, and victor and loser alike were rewarded with a kiss. When the sun fell low, we climbed back on our battered bike and headed home over rutted dirt lanes, Kirk's arms clasped tightly around my waist. The sharply rising hills around us were painted in amber hues, accented with swathes of blue lupine and orange poppies, petals quickly folding in the chill dusk air. It was always the hardest part of the day.

We had left Pacific Grove several years earlier when my mother announced that my sister required a horse. My father countered that boys need a dog, and off we'd gone to a five-acre plot of country land many miles away. But the rigors of rural living proved more difficult than they'd thought, so after a while we moved back to the ocean, on the other side of the peninsula from where my childhood was spent. My parents had found a ranch-style house in serious need of repair near the mouth of Carmel Valley, and, with little ceremony, reestablished their family of three adolescents and one new, if somewhat unexpected, baby.

Now I was within walking distance of Carmel, the fabled artist's colony with a storybook veneer. I wasted no time in adapting to this new environment, for it would be hard to imagine any place more charmed. The town itself lies tucked in a manicured forest of pine, an evergreen carpet on a hillside overlooking a pristine bay. The buildings are vine covered and picturesque; a photo opportunity awaits at every turn.

The downtown district comprises a couple of dozen blocks divided by Ocean Avenue, a main thoroughfare that runs about a mile from the top of the hill to the beach below. The curved shoreline is plushly lined with powdery white sand, and turbulent eddies clash against sculpted rocks to spectacular effect. A good part of the town's commerce stems from the peddling of expensive artworks depicting these waves, grandiose images as manufactured and trite as portraits of bug-eyed children or sad clowns. In fact, aside from nature's beauty there is little about Carmel that isn't disingenuous.

What had constellated by the twenties as a place for serious artists and writers to pursue their muse had, by the sixties, devolved into an artsy enclave for the rich and famous and those envious of them. Recalcitrant locals held on to memories of the days when Lincoln Steffens, Mary Austin, Edward Weston, Robinson Jeffers, and others had made Carmel's reputation as a creative colony. The town still retained the scent of their celebrity, but poets' cottages had long been remade as pricey shops. This mecca in the woods was little more than a theme park for well-heeled tourists.

Precious to a fault, Carmel exudes about as much reality as a Hollywood backlot. But at fifteen, and still enamored with any world but the one I was in, I could scarcely note the difference. I lost no time in proclaiming Carmel-by-the-Sea as home. Little did I realize how like a hometown boy I really was.

Cultural pretensions were preserved by the gay men in the village, a kind of queen's guard who stood watch over the expensive boutiques. I was able to single them out from the other townspeople almost at once; a kind of ineffable gay radar was at work. The more I saw, the more I became aware of this stylish clique among the pines. Cashmere sweaters and crafted good looks seemed the uniform of choice. Conversations were invariably sprinkled with sardonic quips, usually a line from a Broadway show or old movie that escaped my reference. I had heard about homosexuals, and knew that I was one, too, yet I was made profoundly uncomfortable with the thought that someday I might be like these gentlemen of Carmel.

Certainly, they were gentlemen. Aside from an occasional knowing smile, they never overstepped their bounds with me. Polite to a fault, Carmel's gay men graciously tended to its image and seemed to ask nothing in return except to be left alone. But I heard the stories. Like the night the director of the town's small dinner theater was seen sobbing alone on the beach. Or the times a well-known married art teacher would disappear for days, saying on his return that he had only gone "painting." Or the hushed-up rumors of suicides and bitchy alcoholic spats in public.

These currents of innuendo and gossip, which circulated around the town like a malicious ether, became known to me. They penetrated my frightened consciousness. I was afraid—and achingly so—that some day such things might be true about me. So I kept the fact that I knew these stories closely guarded. It was one way, I must have thought, to buy protection against exposure of myself, as if knowledge, in this case, was power. Still, the hoarding of such secrets meant that I was living a life as lonely and prepossessed as the older gentlemen around me.

Now I saw Carmel's gay men with different eyes. Being a wounded child myself, I could see past polished personas and into the private inner place where their own frightened kid still lived. It must have been some kind of hell behind those formidable walls of defense. Now I knew the superior airs and posturing were but little more than a lame cover-up of deeply compromised lives.

Most of these men, sophisticated though they were, somehow still lived in their mother's houses. This was literally true for some, as they went obsequiously about tending after an aging parent or one of the many other widowed old ladies in town. For others, it was easy to see how they were figuratively preoccupied by the feminine. Indeed, inculcated with its affects.

It was all communicated in code, of course: faggot patois bleached to a kind of camp minimalism. Still, it was possible to hear one addressed as "dear" or "darling," exclaimed with hand on hip or eyes rolling with insinuation. Manners of all kinds were used as a coy means to manipulate others rather than as a way to plainly ask for what was wanted. My observations here are no harsher than the ones they traded about one another. Subtlety notwithstanding, these men were hurting inside—and it showed.

Where feeling that ought to move freely in our lives is repressed, a psychological complex is formed. Composed of elements related to the personal unconscious as well as to the collective unconscious, "complexes are psychic fragments which have split off owing to traumatic influences or certain incompatible tendencies," states Jung.[2] "The characteristics of conflict—shock, upheaval, mental agony, inner strife—are peculiar to the complexes. They are the 'sore spots,' the *bêtes noires*, the 'skeletons in the cupboard' which we do not like to remember and still less to be reminded of by others, but which frequently come to mind unbidden and in the most unwelcome fashion."[3]

Complexes contain memories, wishes, fears, needs, or insights which somehow we can never really deal with, and for this reason they "interfere with the intentions of the will . . . influence speech and action in an unconscious way." Because these black holes of inert emotion have a burdensome gravity, complexes must be identified and dealt with before an individual can liberate himself from their secret domination and proceed on a more self-determined path.

Not surprisingly, a great number of gay men are confounded throughout their lives due to the effects of a mother complex. They're stuck on the razor's edge: between a father who did not properly love and a mother who provided love with an agenda. Symbiotically enmeshed, they are unable to differentiate their needs from her desires, which more often than not lacked fulfillment in other ways.

The consequences of such a complex are not only traumatic but ongoing. Even the act of coming out is hindered when many a gay man's inner mother—a secret lover now left behind—seeks revenge. The figure of the negative mother appears in many forms: whether manifested as impotent bitch, devouring matriarch, or mad queen, the dark and possessive feminine is axiomatic in gay male culture.

A mother complex is a two-sided thing, however, as is any psychic organism. Not all is bad under the mother's roof, and it was Jung who was able to most tellingly elucidate the dual qualities of living there. To begin, he was able to advance the notion of a mother complex as a "feeling-toned group of representations," that is, images and emotional associations which coexist in psyche along with the mother archetype. The complex performs as a kind of filter through which aspects of the archetype are distorted or enhanced. While the negative tendencies of such a complex were clear to Jung (and seem self-evident to aware gay men), he was among the first to articulate its positive benefit:

> Since a "mother complex" is a concept borrowed from psychology, it is always associated with the idea of injury and illness. But if we take the concept out of its narrow psychopathological setting and give it a wider connotation, we can see that it has many positive effects as well. Thus a man with a mother-complex may have a finely differentiated Eros instead of, or in addition to, homosexuality. . . . This gives him a great capacity for friendship, which often creates ties of astonishing tenderness between men and may even rescue friendship between the sexes from the limbo of the impossible. He may have good taste and aesthetic sense. . . . He may be supremely gifted as a teacher because of his almost feminine insight and tact. He is likely to have a feeling for history, and to be conservative in the best sense and cherish the values of the past. Often he is endowed with a wealth of religious feelings, which help to bring the *ecclesia spiritualis* into reality; and a spiritual receptivity which makes him responsive to revelation.[4]

Jung's insight suggests a spiritual richness most gay men would gladly own if not for the impoverishment of their false, defended selves. To be sure, I saw the good and healthy traits that Jung describes modeled well enough by the gay men of my village. Despite the arch moves and queeny banter, their appreciation of life's finer things and caretaking of others—indeed, their abiding concern for the town itself—were fully evident. It was an introduction, of sorts, to all the pluses and minuses that a queer life could offer. That is, if one wanted to live life in a ghetto, no matter how pleasant it might be.

It did not take long for me to become disaffected with Carmel's glamour. Now I could understand why some of my high school classmates criticized their hometown as a "gilded cage," an island of privileged white folk shut off from the social upheaval fermenting around us. Although I could not say so to them, I mainly saw the place as a cage for men like me. Men, who for all of their gifts, were crippled by a terrible rage turned inward. For the gentlemen of Carmel, gilding the outer self must have been a way of keeping souls heavy with grief from bursting.

I began to scrupulously avoid going downtown except for necessary errands. Besides, except for tourism's ebb and flow, Carmel seemed changeless. It was the late sixties, and, everywhere else, the world was in rapid flux. I heard about Dr. Martin Luther King, Jr., and civil disobedience the day Joan Baez came to sing to my sophomore class on Carmel High's spacious front lawn. Fritz Perls and Michael Murphy were expounding the values of "human potential" at the newly formed Esalen Institute just a few miles down the coast in Big Sur. I tried marijuana for the first time while staying up all night working on the controversial student newspaper. And hirsute young men hitchhiking on Highway One, which bordered the campus, came forward and talked about the horrors of an immoral war in Southeast Asia.

Much of my time was spent at school, partly to dodge the turmoil at home, but primarily to partake in the progressive climate established by its principal, a forward-thinking educator imported from

Great Britain. He'd set forth an imaginative curriculum, filled with electives in everything from the Zen of pottery to experimental film-making. I wasted no time in picking up a camera and trying my hand at movies. My first assignment was to make a simple animated film using cut-out scraps of paper and lines from a favorite poem. I selected some words by Langston Hughes from a work titled "Harlem."[5]

I knew nothing of Hughes except the fact that he had once lived in Carmel and that his books were well-stocked in the library. Of course, Harlem was just a name to me. The poem had a visual emphasis that was easy to picture, yet there was something else about it that resonated closely with my own situation, as far away as it must have been from the author's. Years later, when I learned that Hughes was, in all probability, a deeply closeted gay man, I understood my empathy on a new level that transcended the bonds of class and race.[6]

"What happens to a dream deferred?/Does it dry up/like a raisin in the sun? Or fester like a sore . . ." begins Hughes's poem. Even though he was writing about the plight of black people in a slum on the other end of the country, I could relate to the image. On the outside, I was a young white man living in luxurious surroundings, promise at my fingertips. But I felt none of this at all. I lived in two realities, and it was the one inside that counted most: a place of scorched earth, where dreams don't stand a chance against the nightmares of crazy parents.

What happens to a dream deferred? Hughes concludes by wondering: "Maybe it just sags/like a heavy load./ *Or does it explode?*" Oddly enough, it was this final thought that gave me the most hope as the ranting and raving at home escalated to an unbearable pitch.

It was clear by now that just as I lived in two worlds, I had two mothers: good and bad. Her anxiety attacks and increasing shrillness had undermined the confidence of the entire family. In fact, I began to suspect that my lack of self-esteem had more to do with her chronic instability than with my incipient homosexuality. From the day of my birth, she had not been able to properly see me for who I really was. I was a pliant object which she could manipulate to fulfill narcissistic needs unmet by her own mother. Crimes of omission in Geneva, Nebraska, had soon enough become crimes of commission in Carmel, California.

I unconsciously learned to anticipate and mirror her expectations and moods, thereby gaining approval at the expense of my own emotional autonomy. Spontaneity of spirit was sacrificed to a very conditional type of mother love. Well-known author and psychoanalyst Alice Miller points out that a mother who was not healthfully mirrored in her childhood "tries to assuage her own narcissistic needs through her child, that is, she cathects him narcissistically."

Despite her good intentions, the narcissistically wounded mother "loves her child as her self object, passionately, but not in the way he needs to be loved. . . . What these mothers had once failed to find in their own mothers they [are] able to find in their children: someone at their disposal who can be used as an echo, who can be controlled, is completely centered on them, will never desert them, and offer full attention and admiration."[7]

Another way my mother maintained the fealty of her children was to undermine the worth of her husband. No matter what our father did, it was never good enough. Money was the main point of contention, as it is in many families, but she went even further by holding his masculinity up to scorn. Our father's stature as a man was constantly berated in front of our eyes, and if we ever did spring to his defense, we too were guilty of the same faults and inadequacies. She felt frustrated in getting what she wanted out of life, and it was always others who were to blame. My mother's mood, which could range from frigid to tempestuous on any given day, was the unstable atmosphere we all breathed.

There is no disputing that Patricia wanted the best for her children, and she worked hard to provide it. When the furies were calm, she could be filled with an uncommon grace and intelligence we were all too happy to share. "Kids! Let's go look at the stars," she'd sometimes proclaim on clear summer nights. Gathering her brood and a big picture book on astronomy, she'd troop out to the patch of wild grass that was our backyard. There we'd lie flat on our backs picking out the Big Dipper, Orion with his sword, and other constellations, laughing as only a family can.

But what the right hand provided, the left hand took away. My mother was as much the victim of a bad marriage and misogynistic times as she was of her own demons.

Kirk and I continued our intimacy during this period, although guilty shades of the incest taboo increasingly visited us in bed. In hindsight, there was no shame in what we did. In fact, we both later agreed that our bonding was essential to keeping some inner kernel of hope alive. But the risk of discovery and opprobrium took its toll. After a while, we stopped having sex and grew distant from one another: gay love cheated once again by the forces of social sanction.

Given the chaos of life at home, I was surprised when my father invited me out to the garage one night for a talk—just "man to man." I was in a rush to attend a rehearsal of a play at the local theater company but agreed to stay. I didn't want to miss this rare occasion, even though our last try at father-son sharing had been an abysmal failure. He had been embarrassed that I threw like a girl, so we marched outside where he hurled baseballs at me with mounting ferocity until my hands blistered. The episode ended only when it grew too dark to see. That was some years before, but I could tell there was now something even more pressing on his mind.

"I hear you've been going downtown and hanging out with that theater crowd," he said, once the door was closed behind us. I was speechless, more from dread than lack of words, for I knew where the conversation was headed. In fact, I had been spending a great deal of time lately working on both sides of the footlights—as a stagehand, bit player, whatever was needed. The community theater troupe felt more like a family than my real family did.

For one production I devised an ingenious multimedia backdrop of film and slide images. The play was John Dos Passos's *U.S.A.*, a galloping review of seminal people and events in the first decades of the century. I culled hundreds of pictures from old history books and in the process learned that the real engine of life in America is war. I decided then that I would have none of that. My brightest moment, though, was playing the lead in *Butterflies Are Free,* a drama about a blind boy struggling to escape the clutches of a domineering mother. It was typecasting, for sure: All the reviews praised my ability to act as if I could not see. Odd that my father never came to watch me perform. So why his interest now?

"Well, you must know some of the things that can happen," he said, toeing an imaginary line on the cement floor. "They haven't happened to you, have they?"

I pondered his query in embarrassed silence for a minute or two. Nothing of what he was implying had ever occurred; except for one performance when, as a member of the musical chorus, I was caught putting too much eyeliner on. Finally, I feebly replied, "I don't think so."

My father stood in the dim garage light, surrounded by the bins of gleaming copper pipe fittings that marked his trade. Like his own dad, he was a plumber, too. "I just want you to take care of yourself, son," he said, looking me straight in the eye.

I noticed how tired and haggard he looked. The never-ending battle with my mother was taking its toll. Yet, somehow, he was wanting to say or do the right thing. We stared at each other for a while longer, tension crackling between us. Then he spoke out again, telling me about a job he had just completed. He had been repairing pipes up the valley, he explained, at the old Tantamount Theatre, and heard that it was in need of a weekend assistant. He had volunteered me, my father said, for that very Saturday night.

I was stunned. Any pretense between us had just been stripped bare. Queasy with panic, I wanted nothing more than to run out of the garage. Instead, I remained motionless, determined not to betray any emotion. My father looked relieved at the decision that apparently had just been made. "I know you'll do well there," he quietly said, his eyes downcast. That was the end of our conversation.

As I drove the family's big-finned station wagon up Carmel Valley Road that fogbound evening, I reflected on all that had happened the past few years. Carefully steering past headlights on the winding country highway, I thought about my father, too. I knew he was there for me, however distant he appeared. After all, he *had* given me the keys to the car. Still, it must be difficult for him, I admitted, knowing his son was gay. And, of course, it was no secret to either one of us by now that he knew.

The Tantamount was treasured by everyone in the valley, and its proprietors were equally held in esteem. François Martin and John Ralph Geddis had come to Carmel a decade before, creative bohemians looking for a place to land. They had met in 1931, and had remained collaborators in life and art over the years. During the Depression, they operated a puppet theater on Boston's Beacon Hill.

They later toured the nation with a company of actors and masterfully carved stick-and-rod puppets, performing diminutive versions of the classics—everything from Shakespeare to *Alice in Wonderland.* After years of performing, they settled in Carmel Valley and rebuilt an old barn into a theater and home.

The Tantamount was a magical place; every board and batten was soaked with the spirit of its builders. Dramatically set on a grassy slope, sheltered by craggy white oaks, the theater had a soaring roof framed by the steep valley walls behind it. At night the trees were artfully lit by low soft lamps, and fanciful shadows played against the leaves and weathered sides of the building. People from miles around would drive down the theater's long gravel drive on Friday and Saturday nights and find François motioning them onward with a flashlight. An elfin but distinguished man, often cloaked in some garment he had woven himself, François greeted each arrival with a smile. Meanwhile, Ralph was busy in the theater's cramped balcony loading that evening's featured presentation into the projector.

Having grown older, they reserved their puppets for special occasions only. Now, their main bill of fare was classic films from the "golden age of cinema," as François would declaim. *Dinner at Eight, Los Olvidados,* musicals, *La Belle et la Bête,* the films of Keaton and Chaplin, *Rules of the Game, Les Enfants du Paradis, Camille*—each was offered up as the exquisite work of art it was, lovingly introduced to the motley audience of valley folk and village sophisticates.

After ushering in the last carload, François would shut the Tantamount's redwood doors and rush to the front of the intimate hall to explain, breathless but with perfect diction, the nuances of that night's double bill. Then, after the slightest bow, he would excuse himself and exit through a side door and behind the illustrated curtain, a scene from Molière's *Bourgeois Gentilhomme,* which he had painted himself. A second or two passed before the sonorous tones of a gong were heard throughout the room. This was Ralph's cue to lower the lights and start up the film.

There, seated in the back row, my romance with the movies was rekindled. More important, it was where my true and lasting romance with self began. Ralph and François were the first great teachers I had in life. Indeed, they offered the best lessons any young gay man could wish to have.

It was my job to assist people, once they had parked, through the dark to the theater. During intermission, outdoors among the oaks, I helped serve coffee in white demitasse cups. If Ralph was busy mending a broken reel, I was asked to take tickets at the door. After the last patron had left, the three of us would sit and review the evening's program. Their knowledge of world cinema was encyclopedic, but it was their opinion of one actress, in particular, that remains indelibly impressed on me. It was Garbo, and Garbo alone, who shined above all the others, they said. I was caught up by their enthusiasm and agreed. Her androgynous mystery was somehow confirming of feelings beyond my words.

Some evenings after the show they would take me on a tour of the theater and its adjoining studio. Fine art prints, Oriental antiques, and shelves of books were carefully displayed. A loom, carving blades, paintbrushes, and other well-worn tools littered their private quarters. They were the creators of a special universe—especially of their own lives—and who they were, and what they said, was in marked contrast to what I had previously observed about gay men. As we grew to know one another better, they told me more stories.

"In thirty-one, you could very easily live off five dollars a week," Ralph would begin one such conversation. "Food was cheap and tomato soup that could eat the tin off the can was plentiful." François would chuckle in reply. "Oh, yes, you could make a little go a long way. When we reached a starving point, there was always a watch we could pawn. The only problem with that was that they gave less for it each time!"

The men would continue with their tales, often past midnight; love clearly expressed for the other. During the late 1930s, went another story, they designed Macy's windows in New York City each Christmas. It took a year to create the dozens of mechanical figures that filled the windows, all brought to life by an intricate system of pulleys and gears. When they finished, "we would go up to the top of the Empire State Building and look down on Thirty-fourth Street where the Macy's Thanksgiving Day parade would end," François proudly recalled.

"The parade would stop in front of the vast window covered by great curtains. Thousands of people were there as the curtains were drawn and they cheered our work," continued Ralph. That was a long time ago, but "our standards will never change. We try to inject a human quality in everything we do."

These words were infectious. They were still ringing in my ears twenty years later when I came to sit at François's feet for the very last time. The theater had burned to the ground in 1978, destroying nearly all of the eight hundred puppets he had carved throughout the years. Harlequin, Polichinelle, Angelica and Orlando with his magic sword, the Little Mermaid, Don Quixote, Alice and her Wonderland cast, plus a childhood treasury of others, reduced to cinders and ash. Ralph had died soon after, as much from a broken heart as infirmity, people said, and now François himself was ailing, assigned to a bed in a nursing home, no other place to go.

The few possessions that had survived the flames were arranged on a bedside table and shelf. Drawings, postcards, and old theater notices were tacked to the wall, a plucky rebuff to the cold sterility of the place. While François's speech now rambled, his eyes still sparkled with the love that had once been so instrumental in guiding me on, in giving me hope. Our queer bond remained unbroken.

When I stood up to take my leave, François reached out, clasped my hand, and put something in it. It was a small wooden object, about the size of a playing card. Upon closer inspection I could see that it was a type block from an old hand-operated press, the very one, in fact, he had printed the theater's elegant bills of fare on. It was an engraving of Puck, the mischievous sprite of English folklore, who had also served as the Tantamount's beckoning emblem. "Take this now, I want you to have it," François tenderly said. "It is one of the last things to be saved from the fire."

François died several years later, peacefully in his sleep, I was told by friends who sent me the notice of his passing. As I read the clipping, I reflected on the stories he and Ralph had regaled me with on many a midsummer's eve. They were lessons about life and how to live it: without apology and always with gusto.

Through them, dim memories had found new meaning. I remembered the brisk autumn morning when, at age six, I marched down Lighthouse Avenue dressed as a splendiferous monarch butterfly. It was a children's parade in celebration of the butterflies' annual return to Pacific Grove. But, for me, with wire and tissue paper wings held high, that day was surely an inauguration of my gay path.

Be true to yourself, the two wise queers of the Tantamount Theatre taught me. My apprenticeship with them was a crucial juncture in my life, a turning point I would never forget. My father had been right about the job: I would do well. Long after words had failed, we both knew this to be his lasting gift to me.

Gay Body

Archetype of the Sames

My secret sexual bonding with Kirk and the partnership of François and Ralph, so publicly witnessed, awakened a deep instinct within me, the archetype of queer love itself—the Double. What inquisitive gay boys seek is an unfailing mirror in which to see themselves. But what sensitive gay men desire is the ideal companion with whom they may share that reflection. So we search for someone just like us, a twin or double self.

Pioneering gay psychologist Mitch Walker has identified the Double as a "soul-figure with all the erotic and spiritual significance attached to anima/animus, but of the same sex, and yet not a shadow." The Double, says Walker, "embodies the *spirit* of love between those of the same sex [and] fuses the fate of two into one."[8]

As an archetype of sames, the Double is the source of democracy, justice, and equality in the world, transcending boundaries of age, class, and nationality. This is what Walt Whitman implied when he talked about "adhesive" love, one celebrating "the need of comrades."[9]

We see the Double overtly reflected in the deeds of men who have bonded together for the sake of achievement, whether in the fields of science, art, or empire-building. We can sense its presence in stories about male friendship, the language of romance covertly expressed in terms of loyalty, adventure, and collaboration. It is pictured throughout mythology, too: in the legends of Castor and Pollux, Jonathan and David, Gilgamesh and Enkidu, to name a few.

The Double is one of the most important and ascendant elements within a gay male psyche. We feel its presence erotically, and project it—in ways both direct and subliminal—on the men we encounter and the work we do in the world. It is the wellspring of our creativity and endurance; it is the very root, in fact, of our modern gay identity.

Men who do not regard themselves as homosexual experience this archetype, too. For them the Double is not as prominently situated in the anatomy of the soul, or else its libidinal charge has been devalued and contained in hollow ritual, or even made taboo. For these reasons, the Double is one of the most thwarted archetypes in modern Western society, having been perverted from the enabling of loving comradeship to purposes of competition, envy, and war.

The Double is obviously oppressed in the world we inhabit today—as are we. Gay men are stigmatized, in large part, because this archetype plays such an obvious role in our psychology. Still, it vitalizes our global community of men loving men in ways that escape the tactics of our oppressors.

The imago or form of the Double is readily seen in pictures of heroic twins—from Huck Finn and Jim on their raft, to the soldiers of Sparta on a field of war, to clones in love on Castro Street. But the actual content of the archetype—its imperative or "will"—is better grasped through the myths which have been constructed from it.

"Myths are pertinent to psychological understanding because they are symbolic discourse about psychic processes—and because symbols are the psyche's native language about itself," explains Christine Downing, a scholar of religion. "To uncover the archetypal significance, the still relevant symbolic meaning of ancient mythological material, is thus healing and transformative."[10]

Myths are sacred time. They transcend the daily condition of our life and take us to another world. When we read a great myth, we are taken out of time. There, beyond what is known as reality, we discover an endless land; a great myth awakens and reminds us of who we really are. Sometimes, it even holds promise of a better way. For the journey of a king is no different from our own.

One of the most enduring myths of same-sex love and perhaps the most useful in understanding the energetic properties of the Double is the epic story of Gilgamesh. Often mentioned in discussions of Western literature alongside the *Odyssey* and *Beowulf*, *Gilgamesh* actually predates either of these more commonly studied legends. In fact, it is one of the oldest recorded stories in history, emerging from the Middle East region known as Mesopotamia over four thousand years ago. Apart from its historical importance, there are few myths which describe with such grand sweep and passion the redeeming power of Double love.

While the Gilgamesh epic has echoed down through the millennia, the story itself was discovered only in the mid-nineteenth century by British archeologists digging through huge earthen mounds. The mounds were all that remained of ancient cities; as the excavators dug deep into their core, they discovered numerous clay tablets, many of them broken and in pieces. Each tablet was inscribed with hundreds of sharp, angular markings in vertical columns that had been made by a wood stylus pressed into wet clay. This earliest form of writing was practically all that remained of the once-thriving civilization of Sumer.[11]

For contemporary gay men, interest in a tale about an ancient Sumerian warrior-king seems obscure, at best. Yet the myth has much to say to us today. In *Gilgamesh*, we are introduced to a man who is divorced from himself, who lacks understanding of others and meaning in his own life. And, reading on, we learn that these things, and more, are won through union with another man. Whether retracing the well-traveled markers of a timeless legend, or using signposts found on one's own path, seeking stories in which we can truthfully see ourselves is liberating.

The story begins by describing the mighty deeds of the king, who rules the thriving city-state of Uruk. Yet, even though he is partly descended from the gods, Gilgamesh does not govern his people all that well. They lament bitterly to the gods who respond by creating Enkidu, a man as big and hairy as a bull. Enkidu is sent to Earth in the form of a shooting star and lives wild among the animals of the plains, which he frees from the traps of hunters.

Days pass until one hunter finally decides to go to the king and ask for his help in dealing with this terrifying stranger. "There is a man who has come from the hills," the man reports. "In all the land he is the most powerful."[12]

Gilgamesh listens to the hunter's complaint and then commands that a temple priestess return to the countryside with him. There they patiently wait, until Enkidu shows up one afternoon at a watering hole. The priestess immediately steps forward and draws the wild man near. Enkidu is seduced by her unfamiliar charms, and seven nights go by while the woman initiates Enkidu in the ways of love and civilization. She tells him of many things, but when he hears about Gilgamesh's misrule Enkidu becomes angry and demands to be led to Uruk. Shortly after his arrival in the city, Enkidu encounters Gilgamesh on a street.

The king is on his way to the city's brides' house, where he violates the women who go there to offer vows the night before their wedding. Outraged by this indecency, Enkidu blocks the king's passage and a terrible battle ensues. Enormously strong and equally matched, the two men wrestle with one another "like bulls."[13] They struggle so hard that even the massive walls of the city shake.

Just when it appears that Gilgamesh might be the victor, his eyes gaze deep into those of his opponent and the king is overcome with feelings of profound recognition and love. The men stop and kiss one another like brothers. "Friend, a wail has choked my throat,"

Enkidu declares, "my arms are slack and my strength has turned to weakness."[14]

From then on, Gilgamesh and Enkidu are inseparable soul mates. They spend their days and nights together, and undertake a number of adventures devised by the gods. They march many days to the Cedar Forest, where they slay the demon Humbaba. Later, they overcome the terrible Bull of Heaven sent to destroy Uruk by the vengeful goddess Ishtar. This seals the bond of their friendship even closer, and the men are proclaimed great heroes of the land.

But in their hubris, they offend the gods, who now decree that Enkidu must die. The king's lover falls mysteriously ill and, after a long and feverish spell, Enkidu dies in his comrade's arms. Gilgamesh is stricken with grief and refuses to leave Enkidu's side. "Why am I left to live while my brother dies?" he weeps.[15] Many days go by, but finally Gilgamesh allows the priests to come and bury the body of his beloved friend.

Heartbroken, the king decides to leave Uruk. Clothed only in the unshorn skins of dogs, he sets out through uncharted land on a long quest. Gilgamesh is determined to find Utnapishtim, a man made immortal by the gods, who possesses the secret of eternal life.

Gilgamesh undergoes much hardship, including defending himself from a pack of hungry lions, but at last he comes to the edge of a vast sea, "the waters of death." He talks a boatman into ferrying him across the ocean to the island where Utnapishtim lives. After a difficult passage, they safely arrive. The ancient seer greets Gilgamesh, comments on his sorrowful look, and asks why he roams the wilderness.

The wanderer tells the old man about the death of Enkidu and how grief lives constantly in his heart. "Must I die, too?" he asks.

"How long is the eye able to look at the sun?" Utnapishtim responds. "From the very beginning nothing at all has lasted. See how the dead and the sleeping resemble each other."[16] He then proceeds to tell Gilgamesh a long story about a flood that once inundated the surfaces of the earth.

After reciting his tale, Utnapishtim presents the king with the test of staying awake for seven nights. Gilgamesh fails the challenge, but the seer takes pity on the king and tells him what he seeks to know. Under the water, says the old man, grows a thorny plant that endows everlasting life.

Gilgamesh plunges into the depths of the ocean and retrieves the plant. He embarks for Uruk, but just before his arrival at the city he stops to bathe in a pool. As he washes, a snake living at the bottom of the water comes up and eats the plant, shedding its skin. Gilgamesh mourns his loss, but nevertheless returns to Uruk. There he lives out the rest of his days a wiser man, aided by the spirit of Enkidu who joyously reappears to him in a vision from the underworld.[17]

While this is the briefest synopsis of a multifaceted story that has many interpretations, its basic theme is clear: how a man out of touch with his own feelings and better nature becomes more whole through the love of another man—a man, in fact, who represents his equal self, his Double. And how the imagined loss of that double-self sends the king on a hazardous journey into the darkest recesses of his soul, where what is perceived as lost is found and integrated into his being.

One way to read the Gilgamesh story is as a myth of gay male individuation. Any man's soul-making journey must necessarily involve the integration of opposites; the inner masculine and inner feminine, among other disparate elements. But for gay men, there are other potentialities of the soul to be realized. Our quest for wholeness requires the marriage of *sames*. "The union of opposites—male with female—is not the only union for which we long and is not the only union which redeems. There is also the union of the sames, the reunion of the vertical axis which would heal the split spirit," comments psychologist James Hillman.[18]

Gay men are led to the center of their souls—to a true Self—by the Double, who appears in our lives as if he is a gift from the gods. He can take many forms: as a lover, mentor, surrogate son, father figure, or ideal friend. In whatever guise, one recognizes the Double by the romantic feelings he stirs, Eros being the language of relationship. It is the archetype of the *sames* that engages our soul. And men touched by the presence of this "secret sharer" experience a different mythology.

When two gay men spiritually and erotically bond, they create a supplementary relationship. When heterosexual couples unite, they come together as dissimilar and complementary opposites. Gay men do inside themselves what heterosexual people must do outside. Psychologically, a man and a women weave their life together through a horizontal axis; each mirrors the absent qualities of an unlike other and seeks to compensate for what is not found.

Two partners of the same sex bring wholeness to the *alike* other by enhancing qualities which are perceived as being already there. They stand more like twin pillars than buttressing beams. Forging a loving relation to this magical twin image of ourself—one just like us—results in kinships of remarkable felicity and strength.

A divided psyche triumphantly united is what all men seek, yet so few obtain. It is what we pray and make magic to. This is the alchemical gold that medieval philosophers sought. It is the Holy Grail, the truest meaning of Jesus, Buddha, and all myths of perfection on earth. For queer men, it is the numinous power of Double love which mends us whole.

We, Two Brothers Clinging

Companion to the Center

Something powerful within me had been awakened. But what? And how was I to deal with it? Whatever it was, I could feel it rumbling, like some long-dormant god stirring from a deep slumber. If only he could speak more directly. His growing presence was like distant thunder, but what I really wanted to experience was the spark and burn.

And no wonder. My sole concern in life to that point had been survival. I was still hanging tight onto dullness, as one would cling to flotsam in a disastrous sea. Maybe it was the only tactic possible in a rapidly fragmenting world. My nuclear family had exploded, the radiation of failure seeping into every member. There was angry despair and shortcoming amply demonstrated in the greater society, too.

Students only a few years older than myself were rising up across the land and had been gassed or shot for their efforts. The media were filled daily with news about assassinations, cities on fire, and deadly racial tension. My greatest worry, though, was the war in Vietnam. I could be taken there any day and, like the elder brothers of certain classmates, never return. I was prepared to file as a conscientious objector or even flee to Canada if necessary, but a high lottery number and enrollment at the local junior college kept the draft at bay.

There was no money for full-fledged university studies, so I had decided to stay at home awhile after graduation, in order to work and save a bit before moving on. I got a job writing copy for the local weekly, *The Carmel Pine Cone,* and planned on attending classes and editing the college paper. I had edited the high school paper for a couple of years. Yet, despite my considerable involvement in life on that campus, departing from there was anticlimactic, a passage noteworthy only for what it was not.

I was spending graduation day painting flats at the Golden Bough when a chance glance at my watch reminded me of the ceremony about to happen. I dashed out the theater and up the hill to the high school gymnasium where the last of the senior class was exiting. The school secretary hurriedly stuffed me in a cap and gown and shoved me out the door toward the waiting assembly. Impatient to return downtown, I perfunctorily completed the ritual. Only when I was departing did the hollowness of the day strike home.

This was supposed to be a signal event in a young man's life. The field around me was testament to that: It teemed with dozens of beaming grads and their proud families bearing gifts and congratulations. But, as I pushed through the festive crowd, I realized that not one person from my family had bothered to attend. I kept on walking, with nary a backward look, until I reached the theater. Picking up a paintbrush, I resumed my work on the set.

"Where have you been?" asked someone who had noticed my absence.

"Oh, no place special," I tersely replied. How little did they know how much I meant it.

My life as a budding gay man felt no less pinched. I had dared to risk a certain degree of openness—at least within myself—during the previous few years. And with that exploration had come some expectation: Maybe it *was* possible to live happily as a homosexual. Still, the preponderance of available evidence spoke otherwise.

The healthy image of gay twinning projected by my mentors at the Tantamount was an anomaly. That I knew. Elsewhere the culture was saturated with negative myths and stereotypes. All of the Clifton Webbs of Carmel and the world beyond seemed to be living out some awful self-fulfilling prophecy. My generation of gay men wasn't helped much either by hateful books such as Dr. David Reuben's *Everything You Wanted to Know About Sex But Were Afraid to Ask* or depressing movies like *The Boys in the Band.* I returned home late after seeing the film one night, feeling deflated by its morbid portrayals, only to find my parents waiting up for me with quizzical stares. At least they weren't fighting for once.

The counterculture's representation of gay life wasn't much better. I was no stranger to the underground press, purchasing copies of Bay Area rags like the *Oracle* and *Berkeley Barb* at Carmel's one head shop, a dingy basement located near the firehouse. The gay riots in Greenwich Village the previous year had passed with scant mention anywhere on the West Coast, but one could find other gleanings of queer life in the pages of the alternative papers. Photos of naked male bodies at pansexual "be-ins" were commonplace, but the *Barb* had the audacity to run a regular column about gay concerns. Unfortunately, what the writer seemed most concerned with was seedy tearooms. A cartoon of him sitting on a toilet waiting for fresh meat to be shoved through a hole in the stall door was as scarring to my impressionable mind as was Reuben's assertion that queers screw in lightbulbs where they shouldn't.

These disingenuous images, real and imagined, presented the shadow side of being gay. The unsavory, sad, and suicidal was about all the mainstream would allow in its depictions of homosexuality. Dismissing a part of life to the unconscious or shadow realm is to demonize it. Therefore, society's intolerance of same-sex love could only result in its queer folk being cast as carriers of sin and sickness.

I had no trouble seeing society's culpability. But understanding the dark side of homosexuality as it lived within gay men themselves was more perplexing. I learned that individuals, like the collective, also have a shadow. It's where we stuff all the things about ourselves we're too loath, humiliated, or disinclined to see. If we don't bring these buried aspects of self into the light of awareness, they function as demons, gnawing away in our guts as bad feeling or erupting in ill will toward others. No matter how suave or randy, closeted or flaming, gay men are bound to possess society's homophobia within their own shadows. There is no escaping that fate, I concluded.

But there's something else contained within the shadow aside from self-hatred and other remnants of a negated Self, something vitally important to us. It lives there, yet really isn't of it. One spring morning it emerged more clearly, as if drawn out by enticing scents, while I lay on my bed reading a book. The text was John Rechy's recently published *City of Night*. Although it had been banned from most homes and libraries, I had nevertheless managed to get my hands on a copy of the controversial novel, which describes in raw detail the adventures of a Los Angeles hustler.

Johnny Rio was not like any gay man I knew, and his journey through the surreal underworld of big city queer life was foreign to my experience. Rechy's antihero was shady enough to qualify as a shadow figure, yet I instinctively knew he wasn't. Johnny was too hot and alive and sexy for that. He was his own man. Although he was as different from me as night from day, I knew he was my kind of guy. Johnny pulled me after him into my own depths. He was the Double personified.

As my brother had done in real life, this fictional character had aroused powerful feelings. One had crawled into my bed, the other into my head, and I would never be the same for having had contact with either. Still, neither really existed. Kirk and I now exchanged few words because of a fallout due to our family's painful fracture. And, once I finished *City of Night*, Johnny, too, was gone. What they had stirred inside, and even had come to outwardly embody, had to become more acknowledged within. I could no longer ignore this inner figure, or simply project him on convenient others, but see him as a living part of my own psyche.

The lesson put before me, I intuited, was one of psychological integration. We can flirt with a lover as easily as we can flatter a mentor, but until we learn to honor the inner lover and inner elder equally well, then all we're doing is pointless entertaining. Our feelings about ourselves and others are not ethereal wisps of passing emotion, but actual facts: the prima materia or building blocks of consciousness.

Learning to work with psyche's intangible forces with awareness is a difficult task, however, and one of the functions of mythology is to illustrate a way. The myth of Gilgamesh is an especially useful metaphor for these times. While its message is universal, seeing Gilgamesh's struggle as like our own can assist gay men in dealing with the daunting challenges we face. Conspiracy over our right to exist, slaughter by a lethal virus, harm on the streets, and hate in our hearts have erased the ground of certainty from beneath our feet. Those who have spiritually arisen from the shadow world are literally returning there. Wanted or not, we have no choice but to acknowledge the descent and learn from it. As Gilgamesh discovered, integrating the content of one's unconscious helps to restore balance to living.

When the gods create Enkidu, they first present the vision of him to Gilgamesh in a dream. The king is awakened by an image of a stone ax falling from the sky. He takes the dream to his mother, a wise prophet, who tells Gilgamesh that the dream marks the arrival of a companion whom he must love.

The appearance of the warrior from the sky marks the beginning of Gilgamesh's separation from the Mother. Like a sword, the ax is a symbol of a discriminating mind. It is a necessary instrument in the creation of consciousness, clearing a way through the dark and allowing light to penetrate.[19]

Although he is not quite the shadow, Enkidu reflects to Gilgamesh an unconscious aspect of himself. The king must embrace this "primitive" side of psyche, or he will never be whole. With Enkidu's help, the king can cut through the repression which keeps him from achieving his full virtue. For without inner knowing, his strength would remain an oppressive force. In time, his might would fail even him.

The two men seal their bond through adventure and risk. Together they journey to a distant forest and confront a demon who guards its treasure, which we can read as an exploration into the unconscious being made and won. Later, they defeat a jealous goddess, who does not want to relinquish her power over the king. Both acts hasten Gilgamesh in his individuation journey.

Enkidu's final blessing to Gilgamesh—his ultimate meaning—is to die. The king's soul has been infected by the love he feels for Enkidu; their romance has indelibly inscribed upon Gilgamesh a yearning for wholeness. There can be no retreat now. Gilgamesh has no choice but to go forward alone. The spirit of the Double must live within.

Beckoned by the image of the Double, the path that Gilgamesh must take is downward, a descent into his grief and loss. The story reveals that before he can find the answer to his suffering, Gilgamesh must adbicate his kingdom and journey into the wilderness that lies beyond. The city-state he leaves behind is symbolic of a false self: his persona.

Functioning as a "skin or hide," the persona is that which shields and protects. It is the mask we wear, our "personality," the medium between the ego and the environment.[20] But any man who is unable to distinguish his persona from a true Self is living superficially, at best. His actions are governed by unexamined and, more often than not, destructive impulses. He rules his kingdom, as did Gilgamesh, less than wisely. But, as Gilgamesh learned, no matter how formidable the city gates appear, there are disruptive forces on the other side. Invariably, suppressed feeling will arise out of the unconscious and challenge him, as did Enkidu confront the king.

Gilgamesh's first response was to fight this embodiment of his unknown Self. But the two warriors' battle, waged on the threshold of a brides' house, ends with their conciliation and ecstatic merging. Only a decree by the gods is capable of separating the two men. Enkidu's death is required before Gilgamesh can set forth on his quest: naked, alone, stripped of all hubris and guile.

Enkidu's death necessitates Gilgamesh's descent into the unconscious: a world not of projection or masks, but a domain of feeling. When Enkidu is taken to the underworld, Gilgamesh, bound by his love, has no choice but to follow. Love, here, is a prerequisite to his ultimate surrender. The knowledge Gilgamesh seeks—the secret of "everlasting life"—is there revealed to him most completely. Indeed, he is rewarded.

The final lines of the myth, which exist as no more than a fragmented coda, reiterate a crucial message. In these few words, the king pleads with the gods to release his beloved from the underworld. The gods eventually open a hole in the earth so that Enkidu's spirit may rise before Gilgamesh and instruct him in the mysteries of life and death. The reunion of *sames* is here literally pictured.

While Enkidu is not the shadow, he has led the king to confront the shadow within his own psyche. As Gilgamesh discovers, the struggle to assimilate the contents of the shadow involves anguish, fortitude, and letting go. At the conclusion of his lonely pilgrimage, Gilgamesh has gained wisdom as much by taking the journey as by what he finds at its end.

Every man must take a hero's quest to find the salvation that lies beneath the mask he wears. Authentic masculinity is forged not just by engagement in the conscious "aboveworld," but in the immaterial "underworld" as well. It is there, in the world that lies deep within every man, where the Hero Twins must live eternally united.

And so I, too, came to realize that what had been awakened was not just another "lifestyle" choice, an appetite for homo sex and all its trappings. But that there was an actual diety, a God-like presence living in my soul. Shy and even stunted, but alive in every cell of my being.

I quietly made that discovery a few days before leaving home for good. I was departing the peninsula to begin life anew in San Francisco. Like the snake at the bottom of Gilgamesh's pond, it was time to shed my skin and, with it, all the lingering doubts and unhappy family drama.

I meditated on all that I had come to accept about myself as I walked the windswept shore of Bixby Creek Beach. The cement span of the bridge hundreds of feet above me vaulted like the beams of some great church. Soon the trail of footprints left in the sand would be washed away, leaving no trace of the fact that I had once been here. Not a moment too soon, I thought. Because now, at last, it was time for joy.

3

Wounded Healer

My escape from the peninsula was launched one August day, with my possessions piled high in the back of my sister's boyfriend's truck. Never had the two-hour trek northward seemed so slow. I had just turned twenty-one, and time was not to be wasted. As with any young man leaving home for the big city, the first order of business was to get laid. Aside from my brother, I had not had sex with any other person—a situation I was intent on remedying at once.

We arrived by nightfall at the small apartment I'd found the previous week, not too far from the San Francisco State University campus, where I was registered for classes. That night, with farewells done and boxes unpacked, I set out on my horny quest. The means of my hoped-for assignation was a bar picked from the pages of *The Gay Insider: USA,* a first-ever assessment of the nation's queer subculture by activist-author John Paul Hudson. Considering the dearth of good gay books at the time, it was as inspiring as it was handy.

I had happened to find Hudson's work stuck among a shelf of feminist literature at Carmel's one liberal bookstore, its back cover censored by strips of wide black tape. I trepidly hid the book between two paperback novels and prayed that the plump clerk working the register wouldn't notice. He did at once, acknowledging my purchase with a conspiratorial wink. I fumbled the change and fled.

Entering the Stud was a daunting experience, but there could be no retreat once past its redwood portal. The bar was a vortex of infectious energy, and one couldn't resist being pulled deeper into its smoky core. I jostled among the stoned and raucous crowd, finally spotting a seat on a ledge near the back wall. There I plunked, releasing a sigh of relief. My first rite of passage into gay life had been successfully maneuvered. Now if only my luck would hold until the next goal was achieved. It did not take long.

I forget the man's name, but do remember that his fingers were as thick as rope when he tapped me on the arm, asking if I'd like a beer. We talked awhile: He said he was a merchant marine. Then we went back to his place, where he demonstrated his knot-tying skills and fucked me hard while shoving a tiny brown bottle of foul-smelling liquid under my nose. The evening couldn't have been more rapturous.

I stumbled home the next morning, the idiot grin of the well-screwed plastered on my face, not a thought in my head except for what had just happened—not even when I might see my new friend again. I never did. Not that it mattered. We all acted like kids running berserk in a candy store from Nirvana.

The aura of romance, of unfettered hope and freedom, was palpable. Each day was an open ticket to our reinvention. The San Francisco sun burned away more than just another morning's dank and predictable fog: burdensome inhibitions were likewise consumed. By the time of my arrival that summer of 1973, the queerification of the city was already in full swing. Young people from all over the nation, indeed the world, were showing up to stake their claim on truth.

Although fewer in number, preceding waves of gay seekers had done much the same. From its known beginnings the San Francisco Bay Area has been an ideal incubator of queer dreams and desire. The Ohlone, the principal tribe indigenous to the region, accorded a special role to their "two-spirited" ones. Initial accounts made by white invaders over four hundred years ago most certainly describe the area as a queer-friendly place: They reported that it was an island inhabited by fierce Amazonian women.

This part of the world has always seemed to inspire the fantastical, no less so than in Walt Whitman, who saw it as the seedbed for a new kind of civilization in which the loving comradeship that "waits, and has always been waiting, latent in all man" would hold sway. His vision was borne by some of his contemporaries; those lovers of "manly friendship" who arrived to pan for gold in the mid–nineteenth century and stayed to build a city especially conducive to homosexual activity.

By the 1930s, a thriving, if sub rosa, circuit of queer nightspots, bars, even a bathhouse or two, had taken hold. But the city's gay community didn't visibly solidify until the period following the Second World War, polarizing around artsy bohemians and a newly landed gay bourgeoisie. Somewhere in between were the queens, a cross-dressed caste rallied by José Sarria, husky chanteuse of the Black Cat Café, everybody's favorite North Beach boîte where consciousness-raising renditions of "God Bless Us Nellie Queens" were conducted every Sunday night. Poetry nor propriety particularly mattered to those in drag: They were there to poke fun at all kinds of role-playing and maybe through their absurdity and humor help engender a larger consensus of community.[1]

Schisms of the fifties eventually gave way to the sexual revolution of the sixties. While the ragtag arrivers of that era did much to further knock down the doors of perception and the closet, they accomplished little that could be tangibly built on: too much drugs and free love, and too few summers to parlay the knowledge distilled from them before dissipation set in. What they put in motion, however, was the full-blown liberation of the next generation. Those postwar pioneers who had established the city's burgeoning homosexual infrastructure, and the queer flower children who later came to redecorate it, created powerful precedents for the mass gay movement soon to come.

By the early seventies we were arriving in droves, refugees from a homophobic America. The sheer force of our presence began to change the city in innumerable ways, no less so than in the Castro district, a shabby-genteel neighborhood of second- and third-generation Irish and Italian workers. The four nondescript gay bars in the vicinity seemed to multiply overnight, and other establishments catering to an eager gay citizenry opened as well. Gentrification began to rapidly transform the sleepy streets of the Castro, and none were more taken by surprise than the housewives in hair nets who still conducted their daily regimen amidst the vastly more colorful wave of new settlers.

If any one place served as a symbolic halfway house between the two ways of life in the neighborhood, it was Andy's Donuts, the prototypical urban greasy spoon. Like its customers, Andy's was a survivor: plain and without pretense. The frayed Naugahyde stools lined up before the counter, the chipped ceramic mugs, even the food itself, were as utilitarian as its longtime patrons.

The immigrant crowd brought their own touches, of course, mainly in the tone of daily banter. Late at night, the place provided safe haven for struggling poets, artists, and revolutionaries. But old habitué or new, none could deny the café's one shared pleasure—its donuts.

The grease-soaked cakes were made in a stainless steel contraption that could have been designed by Rube Goldberg himself. On display in the diner's front window, the machine was a marvel of odd gauges and intricate gears, with a funnel-like port out of which the hot rings of dough plopped one at a time. They were then either glazed, dusted, or sprinkled with various sugary coatings and set before the passersby. Andy's donut machine provided one of the best shows in town, and not just because of the confection it made. No matter what time of night or day, a ravenous throng was sure to assemble on the sidewalk when the donuts came rolling out. It was the neighborhood's cruisiest spot, and one could just as easily bring home a boyfriend as a bag of fresh dunkers—oftentimes both.

Appetites of all kinds were insatiable, and day by day the street took on a carnival-like atmosphere. The entire city was a perfect container for a social experiment that appeared to have no constraints; unlike the place itself, a virtual island surrounded by water and hills. The possibilities of life in this gay mecca imbued everything with a magical quality. I even found the sidewalks there covered with glitter. It was an ephemeral trail, but one that promised to lead somewhere better, especially for those who landed there daily. We were all striving to reconstitute ourselves, and celebrated that promise in ways previously unimagined.

It was an awakening of historic proportion, and I was proud to be a part of it: this first generation to come out after Stonewall. With that foundational benchmark behind me, I adapted to post-modern gay life with relative ease. Aside from delving into the life of the city, I joined a coalition of fellow queer students which met at the university. We organized rap groups and on-campus socials, although the announcements for these events were usually ripped off the bulletin boards as soon as they were posted. Even in such liberal environs, homophobia had no bounds. By the following spring, the decision was made to participate that June in the fourth local parade commemorating Stonewall.

Putting the tricks learned in summer stock to use one more time, I made myself over in flamboyant thrift-store drag, with hair hennaed and eyes lined in cheap Egyptian kohl. We had all dressed as psychedelic pranksters and traipsed alongside civic leaders in cars—commerce on the march—while boys disco-danced on floats, sassily playing the role of fools. We imagined ourselves rebels against the city's gay commercial establishment, who appeared less interested in reordering the status quo than seducing a piece of it. The contradiction of sending up something that had given us the security to be there at all escaped us.

That afternoon, after the parade had wended its way through the sparsely populated avenues of the business district, the attending horde adjourned to the nearby Civic Center plaza for a political rally. The droning speeches in progress there were in marked contrast to the events of the previous year's celebration, which had been more show than tell. Those festivities had wrapped up on a sunny meadow in Golden Gate Park where men and women alike stripped to the waist, some going even further by dropping all their clothes on the rolling green.

As if that wasn't scandalous enough to the park keepers, a sprightly group of naked men had formed a circle jerk in a stand of eucalyptus trees adjoining the field. Rhetoric of any kind seemed pointless in the face of so many men with erections caressing and carrying on with such egalitarian tenderness. For one brief spell, a tiny bit of turf had been transformed by the living spirit of gay love, unadorned and truly set free. Somehow, I think the kind of magic exhibited that day is always here for us. If only what was revealed could grow beyond such rare happenings. But that was seldom to be the case.

My cohorts and I had done well in shucking the polite, assimilatory posture adopted by many queers before us, rightly assuming there is nothing to apologize for and everything to defend in being homosexual. Yet we failed to question our own attitudes about gayness as the new decade was entered pell-mell. At ease in nature, unbound by heterosexual strictures—as during that afternoon in the park—we could let down our masks and authentically relate. But we were too full of our poisonous selves to see that, for the most part, we were still using sex as a weapon—not against the enemy, but toward each other.

Our sexuality is one of the most important tools at our disposal: We can flaunt it, and use it to incite and goad the opposing forces to reveal their true colors even more than they dare. An enemy so unmasked is easier to vanquish. Then we can employ our sexuality as a healing instrument, a way to love, self-knowledge, and fortitude. There is no denying that these two functions of queer libido were clearly in view during those incandescent times.

We were in heat, emboldened by our lust: as naked in the streets as when in communion with one another. But while we paraded and demonstrated and fucked our way through the city like the hotshot kids we were, the crushed children we had once been still raged inside. Unfortunately, introspection was not our game. How like refugees we really were: in desperate search of asylum from the stultifying law of a homophobic and gender-bound land.

But at that crucial point ours was still mainly an outward crusade toward a saner place. We had not yet arrived powerfully enough to admit to the devastation wrought by the homo-holocaust that had occurred within our souls. How could we possibly own up to so much horror inside, without letting it fall onto the others around us? Our romp on the playground was clouded with shadows of our own projection.

Disregard for the self, an almost overwhelming sense of being less than fully human, is a condition endemic to gay lives. It is the price we pay for being "other" in a society of calculated sameness. "It is virtually impossible to be different, particularly in this culture, and not feel deficient for the difference, because any awareness of difference inevitably translates into a devalued comparison," state Gershen Kaufman and Lev Raphael, life partners who have written extensively about the crippling effects of shame in gay people. "First we are devalued by others, and then we devalue ourselves."[2]

Sociologist Carlton Cornett observes that because we are continually bombarded by negative evaluations, "many gay men internalize representations of themselves as inadequate or morally bad. However, there is also a realization that there is no other way to be. The only compromise available in many cases is to maintain an alienation from the self."[3]

Once this damaged self is set in place, the tragedy is compounded by its projection onto similar others. We are destined to fall short in one another's eyes because the deficiencies seen in friends and lovers are usually our own. The disagreeable aspects of one's negated self is time and again cast onto these convenient living screens. This is why the theater of all possiblity I thought I had moved to soon regressed to the haunted house of my youth. Rather than remain a land of milk and honey, mecca began to sour.

Wounded Healer

The San Francisco of my wishful dreaming was in actuality a hall of mirrors in which not only hopeful aspirations but monstrous encumbrances from the past were magnified. It was hard not to see the bad among all the potential good, but like most others newly arrived, I was looking through only one side of a lens—the one that seemed to promise salvation.

I remember one muggy night on Castro Street when the bars were just letting out, the usual sidewalk scrabble soon to begin. There is always a poignant scent of chance in the air that hour of the morning. I was drifting about outside as picking up men in bars was not my forte, my one lucky strike at the Stud notwithstanding. Besides, I rationalized to myself, who in their right mind would want to be shut up with all that rancid smoke? My meandering eventually took me past a crowded stoop where a handsome man was picking candidates for an orgy soon to commence in a nearby apartment.

"You, you over there," he said, pointing to one man attired in tight-fitting jeans and construction boots. "You'll do." He continued his survey of the other men like a general sizing up recruits. "Okay, you're in, too," he told a bearded hunk without a shirt. After another pick or two, the ringleader turned his attention toward me. Our eyes momentarily met, and with an imperial wave of a hand he indicated that I, too, had passed muster.

A few more guys were chosen, and then the captain of the stoop came back round to me. "No, I don't think you'll do after all," he coldly announced. Our eyes connected again. There was some strange flicker of vengeance in his. "Oh, come now. Don't look so sad," he caustically said after noticing my fallen expression. In truth, I wanted to rip his face off.

I was not bad looking, yet there was probably something in my look that had betrayed me to him. I certainly wasn't of a type—

wasn't in fact, of any type but my own: Maybe the Nebraska pedigree was showing too much for his comfort. His rude dismissal of me in front of the others came as a crushing blow, nonetheless. I was instantly transported back to those hated mornings in the high school gym when I was deemed not butch enough: I was always among the last three or four sad sacks nobody wanted for their team.

The cruelty of those days was no less felt than now. Furthermore, I knew that the big queen arbitrating our fate tonight had been among those left standing by the final draw. That kind of humiliation quickly grows into hate, a type of hatred that knows no boundary of time and place: a disgust of self and kindred others that feeds upon itself. That monster was being fed again, here tonight.

I retreated down the street, trying not to let the man's witless rejection overwhelm me. I knew the prickly flush of shame he'd raised had also breached a far more complex emotion: My body had been judged as a sexual object. And I felt violated as a result. I had always been uncomfortable in my body, removed from its reality as if the "me" part of myself were floating just a few inches above this stocky framework of skin and bones, meat and muscle. Now it was being objectified by others, transformed into a commodity, a thing to be desired, or maybe not, like a vase in a museum or a new toy on the playground.

Just the thought of it laid bare all my barely repressed anxiety about my physique: shoulders not broad enough, ass too big. All that was left for me to do was to take hold of my wounded inner kid and accompany him home to bed. I wasn't ready to put myself on an auction block in the gay sexual marketplace—not this night at least, maybe never.

The objectification of our lives was growing exponentially every day: images in ads, ever-new fashion statements, an amazing array of venues in which to vent our lust, even the window displays in downtown shops. All sought our attention while defining us in the process. It was as curious a feedback loop as any devised and, of course, we participated in its invention each step of the way. On one level, the wholesale visibility was providing the mirroring we never received as children. But, if one looked critically enough, the shadow side of all this modeling, posturing, and easy sex was just as clear.

Thus, while it was certainly advantageous to picture the many bathhouses in town as wellsprings of community, incubators of intimacy and mutual trust, in reality that was often not the case. To be sure, these erotic outposts—which ranged from seedy to opulent—could be likened to healing kivas, underground temples where societies of men share their mysteries. Indeed, many saw and used the bathhouses in just this way.

But the floors of such places were usually sticky, and beneath the dim lights was dirt, a perfect breeding ground for contagion: all those men sweating and shitting, coughing and coming, in such tight proximity. The commonality and closeness provided by being there was fine enough, yet it was a pale glimmer of what is truly possible when gay men gather as a tribe. Buying admittance into any part of the gay commercial culture meant playing by the house rules. As was the case far too often, our pride was exchanged for their profits.

Myth or Meaning

The problem underlying the dichotomous nature of queer life in the city—the reality of the self versus collective fabrication—was the basic myth out of which modern gay identity had been constructed. It was dramatically enlarged, as we know, one June night in 1969 with the sound of shattering glass. Someone had finally got fed up enough to take a rock and smash it through a window.

Beer cans, bottles, and other debris quickly followed. Angry words were also hurled in the early morning air: "Police brutality!" "Pigs!" The fury and force of the crowd grew by the second. The men in uniform who had come to knock doors down were now trapped behind them. A parking meter was uprooted and heaved through yet another window. One person cried, "Let's get some gas." Somebody else lit a match.[4]

The riot against routine harassment of the Stonewall Inn, a motley bar off New York's Sheridan Square, was led by street kids, dykes, and men in dresses. It did not take long for others to follow. News of the uprising was quickly carried by one person to the next across the nation: one long daisy chain of hope and aspiration stitched from Manhattan to California. Soon it watered the seeds of queer revolt wherever they were sown. In many cities and towns, however, talk was not limited to the condition of gay people alone but encompassed all who are oppressed by strangling roles and simplistic definitions.

"We want a new society," a spokesperson for the nascent movement said. "We bring to the world not only our love for people of the same sex, but also the cultures and strength we have developed in affirming and fighting for that love." The impulse of the moment was revolution, not assimilation. "We are not the same as straights," said another leader, "we are better."[5]

But the call for deep and lasting social change for all people soon dissipated: Infighting and violent backlash dulled the zeal.[6] Gay liberation's original vision was gone. It was replaced by another view, one less percussive and more palatable to the increasing numbers of people coming out. By the time I came to San Francisco, many of the old revolutionaries had already faded from view, supplanted by an up-and-coming generation of professional achievers. Homophobia was named, prejudice somewhat changed, and gay people once again learned the price of getting along.[7]

The impulse fueling gay liberation's fiery first years was about more than changing unjust laws and awkward labels; it was meant to challenge the entire myth system these things had sprung from. It was not enough to merely reform and redeem. One had to go to the very root of the source itself and, if necessary, pull it up. Because we cannot see the myths that substantiate our lives any more than a fish can notice the water in which it swims, finding the basis of belief is an elusive task. In this way, too, did early gay liberationists fall short in comprehending how insidious the myths they were revolting against really were.

Like a brick through glass, those revolutionaries rudely assailed society's homophobia. Drawing energy from concomitant struggles for peace and justice, they generated new ideology to counter the old dogma of sin and sickness. Yet, as important as messages of pride and self-determination are, the notion of a "liberated" gay person is still an historical construction—spun from the same basic system of values which oppress us. The falsity of that underlying invention has kept us false to ourselves to this day.

It's important to realize how integral myths are to our lives, for they are the building blocks of daily reality. Scholars of comparative religion, such as Mircea Eliade and Joseph Campbell, have shown how different societies use archetypes to create myth and tradition in their own distinctive way, and yet how these myths transcend the particularity of their origin. Spun out of bits and pieces of personal revelation, myths are distilled over time and by numerous retellings until only the universal remains. Like a river flowing to the sea, a myth is destined to become part of a greater whole as it wends its way through history.

Myths are the metaphors of the collective unconscious, and are ideally meant to instruct, inspire, and transform. They are "clues to the spiritual potentialities of the human life," says Campbell.[8] But if they are to serve us meaningfully, myths must be continually re-evaluated, discarded or translated into modern metaphorical language, and then read anew. The notion of a modern homosexual—or "gay person"—is one myth that warrants our reexamination.

The word *homosexual* was coined over a hundred years ago by a European physician, during a time when many forms of human experience were being categorized and contained.[9] It was the ultimate rational conceit: As if the seizing and maiming of the earth wasn't enough, the vast and still uncharted landscape of the soul had to be dissected, too. Needless to say, those responsible were sexist, racist men intent on propagating a patriarchal order in which sex, women, and nature are seen objectively: as objects and therefore as exploitable commodities.

Now the world of humans was halved, divided into categories of two opposite sexual types as well as genders. Overlooked were the many of earth's cultures which had long honored their third and fourth gender people, the kinds of individuals whom we'd recognize today as "queens" and "dykes." These "intermediate types," to use Edward Carpenter's phrase, occupied meaningful social roles which functioned to the benefit of the entire society.[10] How unlike our own culture where any individual who transgresses rigid gender and sexual categories is considered to have little social value, if any.

With the notion of *homosexual* firmly rooted, a long derivation of words followed—some created by ourselves, most by others—to describe those who inhabited this new colony of human desire: *invert, uranian, isophyl, homophile,* and recently, *gay.* There is a baser list as well: *sodomite, degenerate, homo, pansy, faggot,* are among the pejoratives with which we've been labeled.

In a world ruled through the reapportionment of language, words themselves become powerful political tools: If you name something, you control it, or at least have a way of defining its life energy. Therefore, to be a homosexual was to suffer the fate of being a "bad" heterosexual. In this way we became a deviation from a correct model: a perversion to either extinguish or cure.[11] It is here, at the level of the so-called perverse, that we first come to know our name. How could it not be otherwise? For in establishing a false category, enforced by righteous code, modern Western society can only reflect back a warped vision of our soul.

The populist slogan, "Gay is good," is a bald rebuttal to the construct of a good-versus-bad sexual identity. Still, the very idea of that "goodness" remains within the domain of the central governing myth of homosexuality itself. Communicating the truths of so-called gay people, a people whose place in the world has been largely self-won and whose culture today is undeniably real, does not rectify the problem. Resolving the paradox of what we've been labeled and who we might intuit ourselves to actually be is one of the great moral challenges yet before us.

Certainly, the word *gay* provides a useful, if expedient, prefix to our lives: It bolsters self-worth, defines space within a pluralistic society. A word gives life. But words, like anything else, become used up: They can lose their ability to imbue meaning. Once acquired and deployed in the outer world, what does this word signify within? Present-day gay identity is like a tool one uses to open a can, but in no way is it the actual contents. We must always be rejuvenating the language of self.

Sorting out fact from fiction, true meaning from a false myth, is trickier than it would first appear, however. Where and to whom do we look for answers? The morally charged dynamic of good or bad is just one dualism that gay people find themselves dangled between. The argument of nature versus nurture is also waged about our lives. Are we "essentially" gay—that is, born this way? Or has our identity as homosexuals been "made," mandated by society as a means to control its gender-variant members?

Cases for both points of view have been well established. Differences of the brain, in chemistry and organic matter, have been cited for the former.[12] A thorough deconstruction of gender roles and other modes around which personal identity forms has substantiated the latter.[13] But the debate will remain unresolved as long as a dualistic, either/or containment of the issue prevails.

Answers exist outside the argument of nature versus nurture, labels of either one thing or only another. It is simply shortsighted, for instance, to identify too closely with the various forms of homosexuality that have preceded our own: whether in ancient Greece, the pre-Columbian Americas, or Renaissance Europe, among the many places we have looked hoping to gather clues, or even justification, for our present-day existence. Although the sentimental assumption of shared behavior across time and various cultures may soothe the itch for self-knowing, it can hardly remedy the deeper question.

So, too, does the idea of same-sex love as a cultural creation, a juncture of polymorphous sexuality and historical circumstance, offer only part of the solution. How ironic that the discourse about homosexuality—and *which* homosexuality, at that—is mired in the very system of perception which oppresses us. As long as the critical queries about our lives—Who are we? Where did we come from? What are we for?—remain in orbit around the false myth of the homosexual, we'll be at loggerheads in the dialectic of good/bad, hetero/homo, born this way/constructed.

The arguments of either/or are waged on a horizontal plane; there is nowhere to go but forward or backward or to remain in the same stuck place. But by tipping the inquiry over into a third direction—the realm of both/and—it's possible to accept the fact that we are socially constructed while also acknowledging there have always been the kinds of people we today label as gay. The philosophical stance of both/and destabilizes the impasse of opposites abutted and steers thought into a vertical axis: that is, up and down as a metaphor for going inside oneself. For, I believe, the answers we seek are to be found in the domain of shadow.

Because we live in a time when the objectivistic values of the Industrial Revolution and a Newtonian-Cartesian worldview (which separated the mind from the body) are rapidly giving way, some people are realizing that meaning in life can be found through subjective experience rather than from something that is externally ordered. One possibility this presents is an ecology of associated differences: a world consisting of interdependent and multilevel realities in contrast to the monolithic model of superiority, conflict, and exclusion which still binds most people to their outworn cultural myths today.

Queer people are harbingers of this new way of seeing and being in the world: an ascending consciousness that can help carry the world of the old, dying myths we now live in toward a more inclusive reality. As traditional systems of belief are forced to change, it will be recognized that we intermediate types play a vital role in effecting that change. When acting from our authentic selves, we evolve definitions of family, community, caregiving, of culture itself, even as that change continues to be resisted with an equal force.

Creation of the new out of the debris of the old is usually difficult, even dangerous. So how can those whose function it is to mediate between the worlds of past and present, the seen and unseen, assume greater awareness about the tasks and trials ahead? I found that it usually takes a crisis of faith, a dark passage of the soul, a feeling of being trammeled by forces beyond control to break through to this deeper level of knowing.

The accepted role of shamans in various native cultures offers one clue about who we may really be, as tenuous as that comparison may seem at first. Shamans are initiated into their work as mediators, healers, and soul guides through a ritual descent into the underworld, where they are symbolically dismembered and their bones scraped of flesh. Shamans are mortally wounded, and thus after their resurrection are endowed with the capacity to perceive the wounds of others. In our complex, post-modern era, that signifies the wounds not only of individuals, but of groups of people and the societies they form.

What queer person who has struggled to gain consciousness about his or her true Self has not felt the scrape of flesh from bone? It is a soul-making process sadly without context, perhaps not even wanted, but encountered nevertheless. When we descend through the wound, a part of who we think we are—or have been taught to be—dies in the process. Through this transmutational act, the archetype of the wounded healer is brought to the fore. So, too, is the discovery of the gifts and powers that await those who live out its myth. Claiming the wound is our spiritual occasion: the royal road to coming out inside as the transformers, healers, and workers of wonder we have the potential to be.

The deep well of feeling into which I had tumbled affected me soon enough. Even though I couldn't say why or how, I could feel the changes stirring beneath my defended hide. I gradually perceived that not all that's stuffed in the shadow is dark and negative—far from it. Much about ourselves which is beneficial lives there, too. Because I hadn't been properly seen for who I truly was, I couldn't recognize my potential for wholeness—until now.

If my first year in gay mecca showed me anything, it's that pride alone is not enough. Indeed, I began to wonder, when does too much pride become hubris: a preening satisfaction with the self which ultimately defeats it. To come out to a world of gay affect is hardly a salvation when the inner world has been as devastated as it's been in nearly every queer life. What we can't see is exactly what hurts us the most. Not claiming the wound means abandoning it to shadow, and thus we are fated for failure time and again.

The gay pride movement has worked hard at rebuking bad fathers: from the sins of the patriarchy to the deficiencies of personal dads who didn't provide the nurturing we needed. Those bad fathers live within us still, but we're too shielded against all the rage and pain that poor parenting wreaked to see it. We look for this lost love in others who are similarly wounded and therefore are just as blind, only to wonder why it so often doesn't work out. And we clamor for acceptance by using the very myth that was devised to demonize us while secretly asking: Is that all? Bad fathers, bad myth: It's no accident that we gay people have the awful tendency to self-destruct and eat our own.

It is no longer enough to bargain for small favors, a bit of ghetto sidewalk, a new way to name the same old lie. Advancing conditions in the modern West have allowed us to come out this moment in time, yet have also defined us in the process: This, in ways we have scarcely begun to know, in a world where every gay person who dares to love is made a politician. Only by risking to come out inside can we ever hope to keep on evolving our own myth.

Gay Body

Scary Monsters

If living well is the best revenge, then an inordinate number of gay men were spending their lives getting even. Our consumption of drugs, sex, and alcohol would exhaust the most dedicated of hedonists, yet we never seemed to tire in search of new highs. The motor driving this frenetic pace was a pubescence once stalled and now kick-started into a full-throttled roar. Men in their forties were acting like they had just turned sixteen, and those of us who had only recently turned that awkward bend from the teens to manhood behaved no better.

No matter what our age, we were all siblings living out the same adolescent flings missed the first time around. There wasn't a grown-up in sight, and if one did appear in the form of a scolding mayor, a disapproving newspaper columnist, or a fundamentalist preacher, we just thumbed our noses and merrily let the party roar.

After a while, though, a part of me felt like it was being left out—and deliberately so. Not by others, such as that jerk on the Castro Street stoop, but by unseen hands with their own volition. My initial adventures had been liberating enough, to be sure: They had put me back into my body; revealed what a transformative force my sexuality could be. Like everyone else, I, too, was experiencing psychic rebirth, a much delayed coming-of-age. But my inner censor still lived as it always had, curled up and watching from some part of my soul, so old that it was beyond reforming.

I have always carried a sense of gravity with me wherever I go, and have been told more than once what an "old soul" I possess. I'd always shrugged such remarks off, figuring it was more a comment on my implicit weariness as parental peacemaker than on any real sagacity. But now I began to wonder differently. Many gay boys are precocious and old-acting before their time, like the Patrick Dennis character in *Auntie Mame* who knows how to stir the perfect martini before age twelve. It sounds fun, but such glibness disguises the sad loss of innocence most queer boys endure when we subconsciously realize we are not going to get validated by the right kind of loving. A childhood so stolen makes us wise about some things, foolish about a great deal else.

I could whitewash my gay wound with more coatings of pride and rebellion or continue to regard it, as I had seen I could: as an opening or conduit through which I could grasp and develop stunted aspects of Self. Maybe that mean-spirited Jeremiah who sat in judgment wagging his finger inside wasn't so bad after all. Perhaps all he was really trying to say was for me to take more responsibilty rather than to abdicate it further. One result of my gay wounding was my capacity to listen, to provide attentive witness to other people's words and actions. Now I was becoming savvy to the fact that I could listen to myself.

Because I lacked the ability to have an empathetic response to my own pain and suffering while growing up, I had an abundance of empathy to share elsewhere. In fact, it was this penchant to watch and weigh, to diligently digest life around me and then disseminate that information to whoever was in need of it that led me to my chosen profession as a journalist. It had also produced a lifelong pattern of ubiquitous self-compromise, a tendency to dissemble whenever a situation got too close in exposing some guarded inner truth. Being clued about other people's reality but clueless about one's own is another example of how the shadow contains potential for the beneficial as much as the bad.

Coming out of the closet was my first step forward in consciously owning the contents of this unknown self. Admitting to being gay in the locked vault of one's head is progress of sorts; revealing it to strangers as I did during that night at the Stud advances the truth yet another degree. But somehow one is still colluding with the shadow until the secret can be universally proclaimed as the good news it is. My epiphany of openness happened about a month after my arrival in town. The place was a roomful of peers, fellow queer students at San Francisco State, who had gathered to form a common, united front.

I had not originally planned to be so bold. Agitated rumors about the new organization had made their way to the campus newspaper onto which I'd just signed. With the suspect reasoning of one afraid, I figured I'd better uncover the story before it exposed me. So, in my best offhand manner, I volunteered to track the controversy down. It was easy feigning routine interest to my editor. After all, I was the paper's feature writer, oddity my beat.

I was steeped in journalistic remove and felt protected by it, having chronicled everything from births to deaths for my hometown weekly the previous two years. Being a newspaper reporter, even one as tyro as me, agreed with my carefully husbanded persona just fine. I could blend in wherever I went; be there, yet remain invisible at the same time, like a black-clad stagehand. In much the same way, I could interrelate with action and adventure without incurring risk to myself. Or so I thought.

But as life is about so much more than moving props from one scene to the next, or noting if the actors remembered their lines, it did not take long for the real story beneath the story to surface. Once I stepped into the meeting place—a circle of young people, gay like me—it was clear that I was there to tell the story of my own life as much as other people's. I blurred the line between passive watcher and active doer the moment I put my notebook down, walked to the front of the room, and honestly declared what I had been hiding all those years.

One of the first contributions I made to the group was to suggest that we have a publication of our own. Sympathetic mention in the campus press was all well and fine, I argued, but we have a distinctive voice that needs to be separated out and amplified beyond what the mainstream can allow. The idea that gay people comprise an indigenous culture—that we think and act differently from nongays beyond our sexual preference—had not yet dawned in my head. But some nascent spark of queer consciousness must have ignited my proposal, for it was accepted by the other members of the circle at once.

I immediately got to work, assigning articles and finding typesetters and a printer. I wanted our effort to be as polished as possible and went before the student council demanding funds. After some heated discussion, the money was allotted and in December 1973 five thousand copies of our tabloid-sized newspaper were distributed on campus and at various points around the city. Appropriately enough, the publication was entitled *The Voice.*

By then, the core group had expanded to include students from other colleges, a Bay Area–wide coalition announced in the lead article. Other pieces dealt with the struggle to form an identity as queer students ("We have to educate people so they don't feel threatened by our lifestyles," said one freshman), and the need for courses addressing specific gay and lesbian concerns. One teacher bravely came out in an essay, and a fund-raising dance was advertised on the back page. All told, the first edition wasn't bad, even though a small block of type had fallen off the front page layout somewhere en route from my kitchen table to the printer's.

Enough money was raised to publish a second issue the following

May, and we were able to expand our range in size—from four to twelve pages—as well as content. Articles on what it was like to be black and gay ("I take great pleasure in screwing white men as they take every opportunity to screw me . . .") or a radical-lesbian-feminist-separatist ("You have to remove the people presently in power [and] I don't see doing it any way but with a gun . . .") challenged the pat notions of many readers. Homos in the dorms, myths about masculinity and gays as child molesters, and the American Psychiatric Association's declassification of homosexuality as a mental illness were among the topical issues covered.

People off campus were beginning to take notice of *The Voice*, too, and after our colorful participation in that June's Stonewall parade the Gay Students Coalition had no trouble mustering support for a third and final edition. Castro camera shop owner and political hopeful Harvey Milk was among those outsiders encouraging the paper, and frankly I needed all the kind words offered. With three part-time jobs and a full class load, I was barely making it through the days. My grades were suffering as a result, but somehow editing and publishing *The Voice* was the most important thing I could be doing. Besides, I had ink in my blood, an intoxication explainable only to those similarly afflicted.

I had grown up hearing tales about my grandfather's yeoman duty on his small-town paper and how my mother had worked summers and after school by reading galleys to the blind editor-in-chief. When I was thirteen, she purchased a pawnshop typewriter so I could type out the junior high newsletter on thick carbon sheets before mimeographing it for the rest of the class. That's when I got hooked, I think. The other kids might have thought me a nerd, but there was power to be had in the press: not only by learning how to mechanically manipulate it, but in deciding who and what got covered within its pages.

On the outside, I pretty well pretended that all my hard work was of selfless intent but, deep down, I knew that being a newspaperman was probably my best chance at gaining power in life. The subject of coming to power, especially for gays, was therefore of particular fascination to me, and I stressed it in the pages of *The Voice.* Queer people were just arriving at a time when they could seriously consider running openly for political office, and so I asked Harvey and would-be gay power broker David B. Goodstein to comment. Milk, a ponytailed grassroots liberal, and Goodstein, a former Wall Street investment banker, could not have been further apart on the political spectrum. But their contrasting views made for lively copy in *The Voice,* probably inflaming what was soon to become a bitter public feud.

I had heavily edited Goodstein's rambling remarks before publication, a show of audaciousness he was not used to, and after the final issue of *The Voice* hit the stands in April 1975, I received a call from the businessman summoning me to his office. He had just bought *The Advocate,* a Southern California–based gay newspaper with national reach, the previous November for a princely sum. The purchase had been a controversial one, and many gay community leaders' worst fears were confirmed when Goodstein replaced the old staff with a fresh crew more in sync with his ambitions. The new owner considered the majority of movement spokespeople to be scrappy losers, and that they and their principal mouthpiece were badly in need of upgrading.

Goodstein wasted no time in wrenching *The Advocate* from its provincial roots, moving the paper lock, stock, and barrel to sleek corporate headquarters located in a suburb twenty-five miles south of San Francisco. The paint was barely dry on the walls the morning I walked in for my appointment. I was completing my final term at State and didn't have much time for ersatz press lords. Still, I couldn't help but be curious.

Goodstein's office was shrouded with thick paisley drapes, and despite painter Paul Cadmus's impressive allegorical canvas, *Study for a David and Goliath,* hanging on one wall, I thought the room in terrible taste. Much to my surprise, I received a job offer instead of a chewing out for my unsolicited cuts to his article. The fact that I was going to take a pauper's tour of Europe right after graduation did not deter the publisher's proposal. It seemed to make him all the more insistent, and with no other prospects in sight I could hardly refuse. In truth, I was thrilled with the opportunity. It gave me an excellent chance to continue what I had already set out to do: Reflect back to my own community its worthy act of becoming.

We sealed our pact with a handshake over Goodstein's enormous mahogany desk, after which he called in John Preston, *The Advocate*'s new editor, who arrived with a thin file of clippings. They discussed a number of assignments with me—an interview with artist David Hockney in Paris, profiles on gay life in Amsterdam and other popular destinations—but it was the contents of the folder, which they saved until the last, that piqued my interest the most. It was a jumbled collection of foreign dispatches and a handwritten note or two claiming that Spanish homosexuals were being incarcerated in prison camps and cruelly tortured.

As in the United States, news of the Stonewall rebellion had inspired many previously apathetic gays in Europe to organize. By 1971, a Spanish movement for gay liberation had arisen in Barcelona, capital of the freedom-loving Catalonia region, but the watchdogs of Generalissimo Francisco Franco's fascist regime wasted no time in undermining it. Within a few years, the once-thriving movement there had been completely squashed, subjected to censorship and far more brutal repressions. Whether the reports about concentration camp–like prisons were true or a product of exacerbated rumor was not known. But whatever the case, Goodstein and Preston wanted me to travel to Barcelona and find what was really happening.

The request was easier issued than done, for the only available lead was the address of someone in the Netherlands. I wrote the person asking for help at once, and began to make what preparations I could for the rest of the trip. I embarked several weeks later, a single bag flung over my shoulder, camera and notebook in hand. I spent a day with Hockney, tagging along as he made the rounds of his Left Bank neighborhood, and then quickly continued northward. I had managed to establish contact with a member of the by-now-underground Spanish group just a few days prior to my departure. My letter had been forwarded to him, but his only response was for me to wait in Amsterdam until receiving further instruction.

I had grown restless by the fourth day there; my other research was completed and even a roll on the nude beach outside of town with a hirsute professor from Brooklyn couldn't calm me. That evening, just as I was beginning to think about moving on, the phone rang at the hotel I was staying in. It was for me. "Come at once," the voice on the raspy line said. The caller stated a time and place to meet—a park bench on Las Ramblas, Barcelona's most fashionable boulevard—and then he hung up. With nary a second to waste, I packed my bag and left that night.

The train was crammed with students on their way to the Mediterranean, not one seat left empty. So I spent much of the next twenty-four hours camped out on the floor, the stench of overused toilets and the constant babble of kids in heat leaving me quite miserable. Sleep was impossible, and the odor of smoke, urine, and spoiled food was glued to every pore by the time the train pulled into the Barcelona station. A glance at my watch told me I had just enough time before my assignation to check into a pension and splash some cold water on my face. I found the bench by the appointed time, though, and sat down not knowing what next to expect.

As I nervously waited, the colorful stream of humanity passing by belied any immediate concerns I had about visiting a totalitarian dictatorship. The milling crowds seemed happy enough; nearby cafés were full and vendors circulated freely, hawking everything from exotic birds to cups of a sweet, milky drink known as *horchata.* It took me a while before noticing that I was being watched by an intense, wiry man some distance away. Was this a member of the secret police or my informant? I matched his gaze, and after another moment or two he approached the bench. The man was nicely dressed and in his early forties, I surmised, but visibly anxious. When he spoke, I recognized his voice; he was the caller on the phone.

He uttered only a few words of greeting and, with a wary look around, indicated that I was to follow him. We didn't have far to go down the tree-lined street before turning a corner and entering a spacious, antique-filled apartment. Once the door had closed behind us, my guide relaxed and broke out into a welcoming grin. Yes, indeed, he was my correspondent, the "Señor Fluvia" I had traveled thousands of miles to meet. He was one of only six people reputedly left in his country's movement for gay equality.

That evening, I met the other five. We were standing on the terrace of a high-rise apartment overlooking the jagged alleys of the city's ancient Barri Gòtic, the setting sun painting everything with russet hues. Aside from my host, who I learned was a scholar of genealogy, the other surviving activists included a young journalism student, an insurance clerk, the son of a wealthy Spanish industrialist whose apartment this was, and two women, lovers who worked in a factory by day and attended school at night. Dozens of their colleagues had been arrested, harassed, or otherwise scared off when the group's activities, mainly regular meetings and the publication of a newsletter, became known to the authorities.

While a gay tourist to Barcelona could easily find a dozen bars, several saunas, and other established cruising spots, most of the action was contained within the walls of the barrio and subject to periodic sweeps by the police. Political organizing of any kind was heavily discouraged under Franco's iron-fisted rule. "We are not citizens," stated Fluvia, who had twice been imprisoned for his outspoken views. "*You* are a citizen. *We* are subjects. I have lived under a dictatorship all my life, and by now I wear it like a second skin."

As we continued to talk through the night, I began to grasp how entrenched their repression really was. The situation seemed particularly grim for the lesbian couple, who struggled not only with homophobia but with sexism. "Our society doesn't like women," said one. "And the women here don't even recognize it as a problem for themselves. That's the sad thing." There was very little that any of them could actually do to address these problems, explained the student, without facing severe reprisals. "We're just waiting, preparing ourselves to act until there's a change of regime or until Franco dies. It's not much, but it's the only thing we can do."

Fortunately, they did not have too much longer to wait. That November, shortly after my piece about the group appeared in *The Advocate*, Franco died, bringing a thirty-nine-year reign of terror to an end. A more democratic society soon rose up instead, but the terrible toll of repression, which I had witnessed firsthand, made an indelible impression on me. That fall, after I had returned from Europe and began filing my various stories, I knew that the subject of liberation for gay people, wherever they were, would from then on be the primary focus of my journalism. My report on the oppression of gays in Spain began a nineteen-year relationship with the newsmagazine that encompassed many tasks and duties—from reporter, photographer, and graphic artist to featured writer, cultural editor, and, eventually, Senior Editor.[14]

I had learned two important lessons during my trip abroad. The first, of course, was the plight of queer people in other places around the world, and how their struggle was similar to, yet different from, ours in the United States. The American model of gay activism had been fairly well exported to other lands, but the understanding that homophobia is but one symptom of an intermeshed culture of oppression seemed better understood there than here. Many times it appeared we were concentrating on this one issue at the expense of other concerns equally important to our lives.

Of course, it was not unusual to perceive Americans of whatever ilk having their heads stuck in the sand. Arbiters of trend were calling us seventies boomers the "Me Generation," and being gay or straight had nothing to do with this massive case of myopia. Now, my eyes were a little more opened. As I went about my daily business on San Francisco's busy streets, I couldn't help noticing how dubious people of all persuasions seemed beneath their placid, self-assured masks. On an unconscious level, I think most realized how tenuous their perceptions of stability and security really were.

It was a revealing time, in so many ways. Not only had the sexual revolution upset gender norms, but the hegemony of the state and other powerful institutions was being undercut and questioned as well. An American president had resigned in disgrace the previous year, the war in Vietnam had concluded in infamy, and the ugly costs of profligate consumption as a national way of life had finally come due. Unsure of the moment and nervous about the future, people adopted various strategies to cope with their anxiety.

One response was to recycle the past. Old movies were revived, music and styles from previous decades taken out and dusted off. Nostalgia merchants had a field day and, of course, those having the most fun with it all were gay. Rather than rework remnants of past culture solely as a mass-market balm for contemporary angst, many of the queer artists in town saw the reaching back as a forward opportunity.

Groups like the Cockettes—an anarchical gender-fuck theater troupe founded on the last day of 1969 when gay flower-child Hibiscus and a friend mounted a New Year's Eve entertainment on the stage of a funky North Beach movie house—had paved the way by turning myths of glamour and romance on their heels. The absurdities of other worn-out ideas and binding attractions were likewise exploded in an age bankrupt of real meaning.

"We were trying to create a new culture," one veteran of the group told me. "We were all very young and doing something that has never been done before. Stonewall had happened the year before and we were just realizing that gays even had a culture. We were liberating ourselves on stage while also battling a lot of external forces. Namely, a whole cultural tradition." In life as in art, the Cockettes' outrageous queer sensibility was cloaked in radical drag.

"The dress was part of our everyday existence. Going down to the welfare office or to the bus would end up in the newspaper the next day because no one had seen anything like it before. Two men walking down the street in dresses and beards and singing was incomprehensible at the time. That's a political act when you challenge the sexual ethics of a society at large—that's a threat. Mainly, though, we were putting out the message that being gay is fantastic."

The troupe grew to consist of about thirty core members who scripted and performed, midnight on Saturdays at the Palace Theatre, imaginatively conceived, campy shows with titles like *Journey to the Center of Uranus, Gone with the Showboat to Oklahoma, Tinsel Tarts in a Hot Coma,* and *Myth Thing.* One night the curtain opened to reveal bearded gossip queen Vedda Viper hooting, "All the dirt, all the stars, no matter whose life I fuck up." The show on Halloween night 1970 featured a spectacular pyramid of naked boys. The cultural clichés and fables exposed in the Cockettes' glittering, widely publicized productions drew audiences in the thousands, providing ready fodder for a host of other interpreters—those who had little to lose in saying that the king, too, wore no clothes.[15]

Social commentator Charles Reich points out that most people living today are burdened by a false map of reality. "Our society no longer works the way it is supposed to," he says. "We find ourselves in the position of the baffled child in a dysfunctional family."[16] The displacement and alienation so widely felt in recent years is our culture's contextualizing web of myth coming unwoven.

Politicians and pundits struggle to infuse fresh meaning into our depleted stories: myths such as the infallibility of democracy or the sanctity of the nuclear family. But such myths are like containers with too many cracks. No matter how much we revive and recirculate them, they fail to stay whole and provide much sustenance. Cowards will say this isn't so, or cynics try to save the last scraps for their own self-serving purposes. But either way, it amounts to the same thing: the desperate perpetration of an exhausted vision.

One of the key roles that queer people play in any society is to preserve, refurbish, and expand its cultural values. The tasks of a wounded healer are many: to teach and inspire, providing a prophetic voice for all; to observe and uphold the rituals of birth and death and other life passages; and to create new ideas and forms of expression by which that society can evolve. Dag Hammarskjöld, Margaret Mead, Allen Ginsberg, Tennessee Williams, Aaron Copland, and Bayard Rustin are among those intermediate types whose lives and work have made an important contribution within my lifetime. The list of other such artists, writers, inventors, priests, healers, teachers, mythmakers, and community builders who have invested an often hostile world with ameliorant vision is a long one, indeed.

These individuals can be characterized as shadow workers; those who elucidate the mysterious, speak the unspeakable, make real what is shunned or not seen by others. It has been a traditional queer function performed throughout history. It's no wonder, then, that two of the most darkly potent pop myths of our time, the stories of Dracula and Frankenstein, have derived from the depths of queer consciousness. Here, the hidden monsters of gay shadow have been transmogrified and set loose upon an even more monstrous world. As cautionary tales about the dead that have not really died, they illustrate the consequence of private demons left denied; how buried feelings inevitably arise from the grave and take form as inner figures with a will and a want of their own.

The story of Dracula was penned by Englishman Bram Stoker one month after Oscar Wilde's sensational trials and subsequent conviction in 1895 on charges of sodomy.[17] Stoker's ghoulish tale reflects his own anxiety as a closeted homosexual during an era when same-sex love was near universally reviled. Despite his loving correspondence and three visits to Walt Whitman in America, Stoker couldn't resist modeling Dracula's character after a fellow gay man, Wilde, whom he had long known but now portrayed as a repulsive, preying monster. Stoker's horrific creation was born out of the horror of his own emotional repression.

Mary Shelley's myth of Frankenstein was similarly created in an atmosphere of homosexual oppression. She conceived the idea in 1816 during a summer sojourn on the shores of Lake Geneva, where she was staying with her husband, the poet Percy Bysshe Shelley, and his friend, the notoriously famous author Lord Byron. Both men were bisexual, and felt the effects of England's virulent homophobia which then sanctioned public executions of gays. Percy boldly wrote about homosexuality, as did Mary's mother, Mary Wollstonecraft, a radical feminist writer who documented her own lesbian love affair. Her father, William Godwin, was a writer who also explored homoerotic themes in his work.

Given this queer family context, it is not surprising what Mary came up with when Byron suggested a ghost story competition to bide their time while on retreat. Could her monster be the homosexuality so prevalent yet persecuted around her? Beneath her creature's dull yellow eyes gleams the desire for relationship, a need for his maker's love, while Frankenstein is so obsessed with the monster he's created but loses to an intolerant society that he follows him to the end of the earth.

The piecemeal man that Frankenstein, the scientist, cobbles together is the nameless other—the masculine double—which lives inside him. How could Mary Shelley not portray this figure, which she must have observed living a tortured existence within Byron himself, as anything but miserable and scary? *Frankenstein; or, The Modern Prometheus* is the story of every gay man and his homosexual soul. A man, who in the eyes of the world, pursues a hideous creation that is in actuality (and as Shelley herself describes it) a thing of great beauty without which he cannot live but must all too often languish deformed, defeated, or deadened inside. In an almost eerie precursor to the modern gay movement, Shelley unleashed this monster full-blown upon an unsuspecting world.

As for Lord Byron, that summer by the lake he dreamed up what is regarded as the first vampire story in literature; a story that no doubt influenced Stoker's work eighty years later. In the myths that Byron and Mary Shelley concocted, what each creature wants more than anything else is friendship: the vampire, a male companion for a long trip, whose life-blood he will never suck; the monster, understanding embrace from another man. Denied this basic acceptance, both creatures turn grotesquely unnatural.[18]

Life during my first two years away from home had been instructive about so many things. Gay mecca had seemed like such a wonderful playground when first glimpsed, but now I could see that it was the inner playing field where the real action was. I had stumbled and fallen, bruised my ego enough times to learn that how things are on the outside are usually their opposite within. There were more than enough scary monsters to go around in real life without having to conjure them up in the movies or from the pages of a book.

In short order, the dysfunctional family system—with all its dynamics of shame, secrets, and acting out—that most gay people had come from was being re-created here on these very streets. No matter how gay we got, the familiar old nightmares were still inhabiting our heads. Feelings as facts: What were we to do with that?

Nor could I excuse my own family and my relationship to it as being any better. My parents were scary monsters, too, a fact made abundantly clear the previous fall when I was called back to Monterey to testify at their divorce trial. Their long-overdue separation was the predictable mess of bilious lawyers, tearful relatives, and ripping accusations. My sister, my brother, and I were kept waiting on a bench and then called up to the witness box one at a time and asked strongly worded questions about our mother's sanity. My father was trying to claim her "emotional instability" as valid reason to take custody of his third and youngest son.

It was an all-American tragedy, so pathetically sordid that even the judge looked away in embarrassment. We three witnesses were reduced to a sobbing Greek chorus by the end of the day, trying not to feel traitorous but left definitely asunder. The judge ruled in favor of my mother, but the real payoff came for me in the public exposition of my parents' marital drama: Dad was weak, Mom castrated him. Their inner monsters had been put on the table and viciously splayed, a prelude to the sadomasochism soon to surface in my own life.

I observed my survival and ongoing struggle a few weeks after returning from Europe by going deep into the mountain woods north of the city. I hiked a good part of the day until arriving at a secluded river gorge so perfectly serene I could go no farther. I took off my clothes and sat down on a bank of pure white sand, then took a small piece of psilocybin mushroom out of my backpack and thoughtfully chewed it. Maybe it would assist me in experiencing some of the great peace I hoped to find.

Wounded Healer

Using a broken willow stick, I drew a magic circle of protection around me in the sand. Inhaling big draughts of the clear autumn air, I began a low singing chant, calling for the strength of every guiding spirit in the forest. "Help me," I said.

And, in due time, they answered back: Wounded healer, heal thyself.

4

Tricksters in a Mirror

On sultry spring nights the plaintive tones of Billie Holiday's "Strange Fruit" or some equally soulful tune wafted, like ethereal smoke, over the close quarters of the Castro. For once, the neighborhood was hushed; everyone at home, taking a collective breather. With every bay window flung wide open, it was easy eavesdropping into each other's lives. There is no curiosity as intense as the voyeurism we had, for it was about much more than catching a peek of the nude Adonis next door. Having no precedent with which to compare, maybe, just maybe, we might learn something new about how to simply be ourselves.

Of all the various characters now crowded into the district, none fascinated me more than the queens—those who bore their effeminacy as a badge of honor, an indicator of true strength. They were well outnumbered by plentiful examples of gender's polar opposite: would-be lumberjacks, construction workers, roughriders of many types walking around, not entirely unlike the men who settled the place a century before. This was the West, after all, and bristling displays of testosterone could not be unexpected.

We were reclaiming our masculinity, wholly and without doubt. After an interminable drought of eviscerated, mincing stereotypes, who could argue with that? Homo-masculinity was now being pushed to its logical extreme; as lovers of the same, the outward manifestions of that sameness were intensified, doubly charged by romantic myth and sexual musk. We were presenting to others what we hoped to find for ourselves: a man, a *real* man—the man we really needed when growing up. Given the limited menu of choices about what masculinity means in America, it's no wonder that the macho swagger on display was usually over the top; like performances in a play the actors are not quite sure they know the meaning of.

All men are ultimately betrayed by the hollowness of the script on how to become a man, especially when acted by rote, which is nearly always the case. For the traditional signifiers of masculinity—the artifacts, emblems, poses, its drag—are pretty suspect, whether modeled by straight men or fags. But at least gay men mean it—or think we do—when donning the vestments of American manhood. As I stood on Castro Street on any given night, I could see that sincerity proudly, if naively, displayed as my contemporaries ambled by.

Still, it was the queens in the 'hood, I concluded, who possessed the real power of their convictions. Despite the soft ambiguities of their appearance, they were never afraid to speak their minds, no matter what it cost them in lost opportunity. "To me gay liberation doesn't mean being synthesized into a culture I think is sick," said Michael, a member of the Sissy Caucus, an offshoot of Bay Area Gay Liberation (BAGL). "The trend of masculinity in the gay community is almost like a religion, a cult." A cogender activist group with strong socialist leanings, BAGL was founded in January 1975, partly in response to the cloning of the gay look as well as mind-set.

My friend had strongly held views, yet admitted to a contradictory pull of emotion. "When I see men parading around the Castro trying to convince everyone that they look sexy and attractive, my first reaction is to give them that validation," he sighed, labeling the "straight-identified faggots" on the street with the acronym STIFS. "I buy into that, but I don't feel good about it. I'm trying to work through the internalization of hate I have for myself for being a sissy."

Even though wearing a dress or some other piece of feminine clothing meant "giving up the tickets" into the privileged male world, another sissy-identified man explained that androgyny had opened him up to another kind of power. "Sex roles are one of the primary ways in which we identify ourselves. If you can break out of that, it would be easy to see how you could break out of other restraints—to think that there is more to the world than what we see."

"I'm learning to trust my feelings," Michael softly said as he sat before an ornate oval mirror combing his long brown hair. "And that's a spiritual development. For me, that's what magic is."

While my friend and fellow sissies had the courage to make their opinions known in an erotic milieu where the reticent were rewarded, they were not the first generation of gay men in town to pin vulnerability on a dress. In another, older quarter of the city, the Tenderloin, the original mother lode of drag still thrived. Sometimes, my friend told me, he liked to put on a dress simply to express his kinship to "those people I have learned from." But for the longtime cross-dressers, many of whom were old enough to be his father, cognizance beyond the confines of the small world they occupied appeared about as low as their hemlines. This did not make them any less giving—

and to others they gave a lot—but they did not seem as able to name the internalized negativity which frequently flummoxed their lives.

The new breed of queens was an awfully sharp bunch, not hesitant in the least to put streetwise politics back into drag, using it as a confrontational ploy to deflect society's bullshit. I usually felt stung when one of my more gender-liberated friends hurled back some of mine—my stodginess or refusal to look at some aspect of the bigger picture. The older queens could be just as snappish, but usually about other things—like not getting laid enough or in their critique of one another. They came off more as provisionally kind, somewhat dysphoric aunts than right-on comrades who just happened to wear skirts. Still, I found the queens of the Tenderloin hard to resist.

First was their historical importance. Many were the queens who thrived as part indefatigable cheerleader, part knowing sibyl; entertainers and truth-tellers to the troops of the terminally afraid. It was queer men in dresses who stood in the formative front lines of forging a gay-identity politic. José Sarria, for instance, holds the distinction of being the first person in the United States to run for public office as an openly gay candidate. His 1961 bid for a seat on the San Francisco's governing council netted 5,600 votes and sent shock waves through the city's political establishment. (The campaign also necessitated José's first suit of men's clothing.) More than just admonishing downcast gays to stick up for their rights, Sarria had the tenacity to go out and actually do something about it.

The seeds of a tangible gay power were sprinkled elsewhere by the queens, too. In 1946, an old honky-tonk tavern in a Seattle hotel was converted into one of the country's first gay-owned nightspots, the Garden of Allah, an everyone-invited, anything-goes kind of place where during the next decade men in high drag used song, dance, and bawdy humor to inspire, tease, and goad the clientele into making a lasting gay and lesbian community in the Pacific Northwest. "The Garden was a real underground decadent cabaret straight out of Toulouse-Lautrec and you loved it. It was daring and romantic . . . it was 'our place,' " one longtime patron there recalls.[1]

Back East, flamboyant drag balls were an important feature of Manhattan gay life in the first decades of the century, creating community for the hundreds of gay men and lesbians who regularly attended them. "The 'drag queens' or 'fairies' on display at the balls . . . symbolized the continuing centrality of gender inversion to gay culture, much as ethnic parades and festivals helped establish the solidarity of the ethnic community by bringing people together and constructing a sense of common culture," observes historian George Chauncey. "The organized programs of the drags served to emphasize even further the role of the 'queen' as the symbolic embodiment of gay culture."[2]

Some balls in the 1920s brought thousands together in the Village, fostering a shared identity in a world where the chances for queer people to assemble, be seen, and celebrate were slim. Police crackdowns and draconian measures to legislate morality during the Depression years squelched this means of socializing, however, paving the way for a post–World War II era in which sexual paranoia became the sub rosa rule of the land.

A sense of gay kinship and culture was nevertheless kept alive by Minette and other cross-dressed performers who went on the road caravaning from one dingy club to another, lighting nascent sparks of queer consciousness as they went through the moves of their fabulously campy routines. "The only way to get out of the darkness is to want to be liberated and try for something beautiful," the resilient entertainer said after a lifetime in drag. "If you do things ugly, people treat you ugly."[3] His remarks, recorded a few years after Stonewall had forever changed the way gay people saw themselves, cannily reflect the attitude of the queens who were on the scene of that historic rebellion.[4]

"We are the Stonewall girls,/We wear our hair in curls. . . . We wear our dungarees,/Above our nelly knees!" a chorus line of singing, step-kicking queens mocked the cops who had been brought out to quell the riot.[5] Many observers of the three-day melee noted that it was those usually put down as sissies or swishes who showed the most courage and sense during the uprising. "I'm not missing a minute of this—it's the *revolution*!" said Sylvia Rivera, one of the brave cross-dressed activists leading the action.[6]

Like many travelers in New York's gay world, Rivera had long despised the cozy relationship between the police and the mafia, whose payoffs to the authorities allowed them to control the bar scene with impunity.[7] Exploitive, substandard conditions were the result, with periodic raids tolerated as a way to quell any criticism that the police were not doing their job in curbing the perverts. But it was all a sham, no matter how one looked at it, and it was the queens, more than most, who finally said, "Enough!" They had received the brunt of the damage and had long ceased worrying what others might think.

Glamorous sissies like Sarria, Minette, and Rivera stand out as totemic figures within their communities, but there is the work of hundreds of other queens in cities big and small around the country to consider as well. Larger-than-life beacons in a dismal landscape, they projected humor, hope, and enough bitchy innuendo to turn the tide on any repressive force. The queens knew how to put a good face on just about anything. If nothing else, they shined a bright light on the dark corners within, where every faggot hides his denial.

The queens were exemplars, the gutsy champions of Mother

Camp, that sardonic, irrational method of coaxing the truth out of any situation. They were quick and smart about so many things, including the fact that where there is Mother Camp, there is Father Camp, too.

The swift retooling of gay men's self-image—from nellie swish to hypermasculine stud—is a daring leap for one generation to have taken. Still, no matter how relieving the transition has been for many, it is the sissies who realize how preposterous the affectations of gender, male or female, really are to queer nature. One can act manly and bold or be sensitive and pliant, even congruently, but these things are not the same as putting on a butch or femme veil: That is about the wearing of disguise rather than letting whoever lives inside be revealed as he completely is.

Drag queens know they are not really trying to be women. They may borrow a lot, but they invent even more than they take, enlarging everyone's common notion of womanliness and, in the process, our ideas of how a man should be. In taking the expectations of gendered identity at face value and then blowing them up—to extremes and with sly panache—queens young and old demonstrate how caught we are by them. That is, if we're watching.

The outline of a man, whether gaily colored or left starkly blank, is still just that—a mere parameter. Beyond the surface boundaries of the body exists a truer self. And for us queer men, as the queens among us so abundantly reveal, that self consists of elements both masculine and feminine and of something else, too, that is neither. Maybe that is the figure of the inner queen: the wisecracking, tough and tender survivor that lives in every gay man's heart. The governing figure that mediates the dreamiest yet deepest part of ourselves. Like Ozma of Oz—once a boy, not quite a girl—someone, somewhere in between.

San Francisco's drag queens were like the costumed, clowning mascots on the sidelines of a fierce game where opposing teams grimly struggle to score. It didn't matter at all to them who won; they were just there for the fun of it. They took great pleasure in being their outlandish selves, and if that happened to benefit others, so much the better.

When one is dubbed a queen, why not seize the crown and run with it? Thus most older queens in town were members of a charitable guild known as the Royal Court, organized like any other group of civic benefactors—only with more flair. Since its inception in 1966, when José Sarria proclaimed himself First Empress, the Court had raised tens of thousands of dollars for gay and needy causes through its annual balls and other extravagant functions.[8]

The coronation night of 1977 was one such affair to remember, a vast glittering pageant entailing the efforts of hundreds. I arrived early in the evening, feeling a little sheepish about being in attendance at an event I thought antiquated despite its noble aims. Once in the building, a five-story glass atrium connecting two brick showhouses in the design district, my curmudgeonly mood didn't last long. My senses were instantly barraged by a phantasmagorical whorl of glittering tinsel, bright feathers, and fabric of every imaginable sheen. The theme of the night was "Land of the Pharaohs," which gave the twelve hundred people in attendance permission to drape or undrape themselves as far as their whimsy allowed.

I was immediately pushed aside by a solemn group of thickly robed men bearing an Egyptian sarcophagus. Farther down the hall I could see other men in gold lamé loincloths hoist a giant replica of some odd white bird onto the towering, Mylar-covered stage. The multileveled edifice fairly glowed in the smoky air, a supernal setting for the strange grand opera about to commence.

My dumbfounded gaze was interrupted by a Liz-Taylor-as-Cleopatra lookalike, who hissed to no one in particular as he swept by, "The one in the blue just *has* to go." In another moment, I too was swept up in the passing stream of ersatz goddesses, gladiators, and guys in scarves and Bakelite bracelets. "You look gorgeous! You should be a chick all the time," one Nile princess complimented another as they jostled past. "I am," the young woman warily replied.

Once everybody was seated, the evening began with a blare of trumpets and with Flame, the outgoing sovereign, bursting through the wrappings of a mummy stationed high above the audience. Loudly, lest anyone forget, the entrance was proclaimed "Flame's Dream" as the Empress XI de San Francisco descended to thunderous applause. The fanfare was well earned: Flame had been a strong, hardworking representative of his community, and pride beamed from his face as he introduced the other members of his royal court with regal pomp and circumstance.

I had interviewed Flame the week before as a mild-mannered, plainly dressed white-collar worker in a downtown restaurant. Chuck had grown up in a rural suburb not far away and married his childhood sweetheart. Two kids soon followed, but even then he realized that something was missing. In due time, he separated from a life that lacked meaning and moved to San Francisco, where he became involved in the drag scene. "I went to the old Fantasy Club," he said, "and got to know some of the female impersonators there quite well. I liked the illusion they came across in."

Two years previous to becoming Empress, Chuck entered the "royalty trip" and spent over fourteen thousand dollars in the succeeding months to realize his goal. He thought Chuck lacked the drive that Flame seemed to always find. "We're two different people. When I'm in boy's clothes, Chuck is very down-to-earth, charming.

When I go into drag as Flame, there is an air of bitchiness. I become very forceful, flashy, dynamic, and center of the stage."

Flame won the citywide Empress race by a landslide. Messages from the Mayor and other elected officials were among the congratulatory calls. "Suddenly, playing the part no longer meant just running home to put on a dress for a bar opening," Flame said. "The costumes, the flash, the funk electrify people. If you can turn them on, you can get them to be a little more knowledgeable about the issues you support. To a certain degree, I consider myself a political activist. I'm proud and work hard for the betterment of the community. I may not have much power, but I do think I have influence."

A lot of money for good causes was, in fact, raised and important civic ties strengthened during Flame's reign, as the presence of a state senator and other local politicians at the coronation visibly attested. They took on the role of sympathetic citizens by being there, and were rewarded with the pocketing of needed votes in return. Furthermore, all the *frou-frou* and fantasy needed a straight man, as it were, someone to feed the joke and recoil ever so slightly from the laughter. Without their justifying presence, the evening might have been in danger of going flat like an overbaked soufflé.

As the ceremony lumbered on with assorted entertainments and the presentation of drag dignitaries visiting from other cities, I couldn't help reminiscing about the times my brother and sister and I played dress-up, too. It was usually on a Saturday afternoon when Mom and Dad were away on errands and we were left temporarily on our own. The house would be scoured for dime-store beads and old towels, which we fashioned into turbans, after having first stripped down to our Skivvies. Then out came the albums of Broadway show tunes, played at full throttle as we bounced on the furniture in delirious glee like little eunuchs on dope.

The magic words repeatedly rang out—"There's nothing like a dame . . . Some enchanted evening . . . I'm going to wash that man right out of my hair . . . Let me entertain you . . . I enjoy being a girl . . ."—until we were too exhausted to go on, or the crunch of returning tires on gravel was heard. For once, I could wiggle and prance—be a sissy and enjoy it. But that sweet innocence was lost soon enough to the glum recognition that real boys don't act that way.

I had dabbled a bit with flash and glitter after leaving home as a way to reconnect with my inner queen, but he/she got buried too far, too fast, for complete recovery. That part of myself seems destined to live vicariously through the antics of others, like the big queens in bugle-beads at Flame's coronation ball. But by one in the morning even they had had enough. The new Empress now crowned, they took their aching feet and drooping wigs off home to bed, this feast of fops, fools, and forgotten boys at last come to an end.

It was fun sampling the gala happenings, but my fascination with the drag set did not last long. I could see what the queens were up to in a public way, and unlike many gays my age did not scorn it. Putting on pretend royal trappings was one way of making their oppression bearable, even presentable to the world. But beneath the blond headdresses and pancake makeup, I could see the private suffering still simmer and eat away. Not surprisingly, much of the court scene operated in and around the gay bars of the Tenderloin and adjoining Polk Gulch area, where the coin of the realm was the price of a drink.[9]

I recall sitting on a barstool in the back of one such place, the 222 Club, one Sunday afternoon in late November. Thanksgiving was soon approaching, the beginning of the dread holiday season when so many gays, outcast from their families, had no place to go. The bartender was a good-hearted man who, in his off hours and high finery, was otherwise known as Tenderloin Tessie. He'd long led an effort to provide for the forgotten and elderly, gay and non-gay alike, who lived in the rooming houses and run-down hotels of the neighborhood. In the week ahead, over two thousand would be fed and nurtured. "What we do should be respected," he said, referring to himself and his cross-dressing cohorts. "Our gifts are enormous."

Of course, I agreed. I had come to the Tenderloin in the first place as a curious explorer of gay life in all its variation, and, as a journalist, I had written supportively of the generous things that he and the other queens had done. But as I sat listening, nursing my second Bloody Mary of the day, I knew there had been another, more secretive attraction to gay life as found on this side of town.

Like everyone else occupying a barstool in the city that afternoon, I, too, harbored a taste for booze. It was partly inherited: my father, like his father before him, had been an alcoholic. Now I was third in line for this addiction. I struggled to keep it under control. Still, the temptation to self-obliterate was great, and I could easily sense the same urge in others. One could almost hear the copious slapping of change on counters in the vicinity, bars with names like the Fickle Fox, the Vagabond, the Trapp, the Kokpit, and Lonely Bull. As showy and fun as the queens tried to make them be, the bars in the Tenderloin were for the most part depressing places. Spiritually speaking, they were houses of the dead—or, perhaps, the living embalmed.

Nor could their put-on gaiety and calls to muster disguise the fact that the queens, too, were drowning their sorrow. The construction of glamorous personas was their way to cover up the rage felt by nearly every sissy boy. What the alcohol didn't numb, the elaborate gowns neutered. It wasn't just their sex that was being erased, it was their considerable feeling as well. Castration of self as a coping mechanism: That's one way to get through the days and even longer nights when the cold, hard facts of life threaten the tenuous balance between total annihilation and a reason for being. It's not easy growing up as a nellie fag, and by hanging out with the queens, I could see how some survived by sacrificing a part of themselves while decorating the rest.

In the Castro, we were dressing up like our absent fathers; the powerful men we hoped to find or needed to be for others. In the Tenderloin, gay men dressed as mothers: great, goddamned, or otherwise. It's the way the powers known as masculinity first came to many of us—through our mothers. The strength and forbearance of mind channeled through them was not all of the feminine domain; there were the teachings of fathers and brothers, and the masculine aspects of a mother's own psyche to be passed on, too. In the conspicuous absence of true male authority, where else was our libido to go?

The old Freudian saw which claims that weak fathers and possessive mothers cause homosexuality in men could not be further from the truth. This imbalanced axis of the masculine and feminine creates nothing but sadness and loss in men who need other men for wholeness. The all-too-frequent case of missing fathers and overly present mothers in our lives is more a result of, rather than the cause of, being gay. Dad absconds or simply doesn't know what to do when faced with the fact of his queer son. And Mom, in ways she doesn't even fathom, steps into the breach.

Strange fruit, strange fate. Instead of being cultivated as the natural wonders we are, we're left hanging to wither and rot, or to gather life in any way we best can. Certainly, the queens of the town taught me that. In their own peculiar way, they also showed me how.

Gay Body

Meditating Madness

By now, I knew I was publicly swift but personally slow. For all that I had learned, I was still dragging my feet. What was the problem, the resistance to knowing myself better? I felt stymied, as if a tangled ball of emotion was clotting the way. Whatever the matter was, it bubbled just beneath my unfailing niceness. That much I figured. An awkward ambivalence about my body and a marked thirst for escapism were symptoms. But what was the underlying conflict? It was the queens in their gowns who finally offered a clue.

I could see the transformations wrought by the appropriation of femininity: If we could not be powerful men, then why not be powerful women? The resulting collision opened up a kind of third, or neither, place in many gay men's psyche, not quite androygnous in the sense of male and female blurred into a mushy middle, but a whole separate category. I certainly noticed the great vitality and spiritual truth there, and how wearing a dress helped some to find it. Yet, more often than not, it seemed that something crucial was being covered up in queer lives, costumed or not.

I had been drawn into the orbit of the queens for much the same reason I sought solace in nature: as a way to connect with positive aspects of the Great Mother. My experience of this primal archetype had been contaminated by the distress and unhappiness that had accrued in my own mother's soul. Reaching out to fellow gay men with maternal-like qualities and to the earth itself were compensatory moves to right the imbalance. But as contents of the shadow will, the negative feminine soon enough crept into my perceptions of these gentle men. Owning these projections became, in due time, an important part of my inner work. Still, I saw how these men, too, struggled with the dark and destructive side of the feminine.

We had acquired strength and brilliance vis-à-vis our mothers, but so, too, had we inherited their considerable rage. I was now aware of that fury as a systemic reality, a nasty backwash of feeling that circulated throughout my entire being. Not just the rage of having grown up a sissy boy, or having been dumped by Dad and slighted by society, but the rage stemming from a mother's struggle for success and honor.

My mother was trapped in a misogynistic culture and, like most women, she hated it. And there was her personal madness to consider, too: the polar moods, self-centeredness, and anger brewing from childhood on. She had raised her voice to a constant, bitter harangue as a way to cope with frustration and failure—and vent it. But it was her raging, as it lived internalized in me, that was the most inescapable voice of all.

Venting rage on the streets is a good thing for queer men to do; expressing the hurt of rejections past is a healthy and necessary preamble to creating a better tomorrow. But it's much easier to nail a discriminatory practice in public than it is to go ferreting about in the depths of one's personal shadow. On that level, our rage is well insulated and difficult to find. Without grabbing it hard and bringing it to the surface, gay men will continue to flail about in the mire of rage. One friend says it's like being "stuck at the bottom of a well." Another confesses that the rage festering inside him is akin to "being coated with mud."

The covering up of gay rage takes many forms. Dressing in drag appears to vent it, but usually in a hysterical way that reveals the anxiety and secret resentment harbored in the relationship that a lot of gay men keep with their mothers. We would be the last to deny that such grievance exists, however, as so many gay boys are raised to be willing slaves to a mother's needs at the expense of their own autonomy. Drag is less an expulsion of rage than a repudiation of it;

all too often it's used as a form of denying rage and, actually, as a way of colluding with it.

We can adopt attitudes and mental pictures of ourselves just as well as dressing up to pretend we're somebody else. Depression, dullness, vituperation, manic behavior, addiction to food, drugs, or sex, are among the ways we learn to cloak the rage. In whatever single way or multiple forms it takes, our ego merges with this overwhelming yet repressed feeling, and we become it. Rage split off and unintegrated into psychic wholeness evolves into organisms within the soul, becoming the source for the scary monsters we call our maladies and neuroses.

And what a rogues' gallery they are: There's the lumbering one, the creature with a wooden head, definitely retarded and maddeningly slow. With too much self-effacement, one runs the danger of becoming an invisible man. There are the vampiric kind who prey on the life force of others, having no sense of life on their own. There are all manner of other beasts, including those who are always on the prowl, appetites never slaked. So they go, on and on. As they press their needs upon us, we fall helplessly in their thrall, acting out as if these monsters were actually the sum of us.

Education regarding the self is the answer, so we do not mindlessly merge with these thoughts, impulses, and disorders but rather have viable relationships with them. One can learn to talk with them as one would speak to needy offspring—these raging, hurting kids inside. Some are mama's boys, others are tough punks and father's dolts. But whether they are benign or dangerous, we must see them for what they really are: inner voices largely born of and fed by our gay rage.

Beneath this level of psyche exist more archaic figures, less local, one might say, and more universal in their origin. They are potentially helpful forces in dealing with the squabbling in our minds. The archetype of the Trickster is one such figure.

Trickster takes many forms, as he's a mercurial force with the power to change shape and upset any situation by his rougish pranks. Native Americans saw Trickster as representing the way things are in nature before social taboos arose to inhibit man's natural instincts. "In many cultures his figure seems like an old river-bed in which the water still flows," says Jung.[10]

Because he is so deeply ingrained in the collective unconscious, Trickster is both subhuman and superhuman: animal, man, and divine being all at once. Even his sex is malleable. Native American stories are filled with accounts of how Trickster detached his penis and carried it in a box, or employed it to make useful plants. He could remove his anus and entrust it with a special task, too, or turn himself into a woman and bear children. His body's lack of unity reveals a primitive unawareness, though, which gets Trickster into one ridiculous entanglement after another. Like the antics of a carnival clown or drunken buffoon, Trickster elicits our laughter, thereby exposing guarded feelings or fears about our own unrelatedness.

More than anything else, Trickster is a shadow figure, betraying the formal order of life to better reveal the uncivilized, chaotic depths that exist beneath. Trickster helps us to get around the psychological defenses we've built to protect ourselves against the irrational and unpleasant, those painful aspects of the self we don't want to see. His swift kick in the ass is always called for when we avoid facing the unconscious.

You can bet that Trickster is in the room whenever an embarrassing gaffe or slip of the tongue occurs. As such, there is something of the savior in the Trickster, a companionate figure to any shaman or wounded healer, who employ pain and peril and therefore must undergo it themselves, in order to do their work. Trickster suffers as much as he inflicts, as a means to take the suffering itself away.

I see the Trickster in almost every gay man I meet, and certainly in every queen. Cross-dressed men, and gay men in general, are good at revealing the margins of things only to transgress them. Showing society's shortcomings and going around them is one of our cultural roles, an indisputable function of the Trickster. He is a savior of our survival.

Yet because of his undifferentiated consciousness—one which has hardly left the animal level—Trickster also plays tricks on himself. As a collective shadow figure, Trickster is "an epitome of all the inferior traits of character in individuals."[11] Thus he lives for making mischief onto us as much as he does for others. Trickster is no one's fool and, at the same time, the biggest fool there is.

No greater was the trick than the one he played on young Narcissus, one of the most handsome men to ever walk the earth. Everyone who saw Narcissus was smitten by his beauty. Yet he would have nothing to do with the youths and maidens who sought his attention. Such was the plight of the wood nymph Echo. No one loved Narcissus more than she, but because of a curse put upon her by a jealous goddess, Echo could not speak to Narcissus or anybody else directly. The nymph was doomed to repeat only the last words spoken to her.

One day, while in the woods, Narcissus became separated from his faithful band of male companions and cried out, "Is there anyone there?" Echo replied, "There!" Narcissus was amazed and looked about in all directions. Then he shouted out, "Come!" Echo called back to him with the same word, but Narcissus could see no one approaching. "Let us get together," the gorgeous youth persisted.

Echo repeated his words and then rushed out of the woods with open arms.

Narcissus recoiled at once. "Take your hands off me, I would die before I let you possess me," he said with disdain. Echo replied with only the last words, "Possess me," then turned and fled into the woods where she was never seen again. Narcissus's cruel rebuff of Echo was just one of the many callous rejections he'd made. Finally, one of the young men whose love Narcissus had scorned cried out to the gods: "So may he himself fall in love, so may he not be able to possess his beloved!" The young man's plea was heard.

Soon after, Narcissus came across a clear pool of water, glistening like silver. As he bent down to take a drink, he saw his own reflection and immediately fell in love with it. Narcissus was so transfixed by the beautiful image he was unable to move. He stared at his eyes, like glittering twin stars, and the smooth white skin on his perfect face. "What am I to do?" he asked himself. "Should I be the one to be asked or to ask? Oh, how I wish that I could escape my body!"

Narcissus cried and cried, with nothing to console him except his own adored reflection. His tears disturbed the waters, and he grieved even more over the disappearing image. "Do not desert me," he exclaimed. And Echo repeated his words. Wasting with despair over not being able to reach the depths of his love for his own image, Narcissus finally tumbled into the pool and drowned. On the place where he had pined, an exquisite flower grows, beloved by all who see it.

When looking into a mirror, no one takes his image as being someone else. But Narcissus's punishment—his madness—demands that he does. I can't help thinking of his dilemma every time I recall watching one majesterial queen or another prepare for a public appearance. All that plucking and primping, the expert application of powder and paint, until some idealized person is found—an image of someone else.

Then, I must confess, there are my own hours before the mirror; less an exercise in outright fabrication, I suppose, than an attempt to bolster and rearrange a flawed self-image by will. Either way, there's a burning need to put on a new face in order to confront the world as someone other, yet the same; a person we desire to be one with, but cannot otherwise attain. Narcissus's plight lives in us when we attempt to possess the self through a reflection of self, rather than find salvation through the breaking of the illusion.

Gay men, who've been deficiently mirrored by parents and society in their youthful years, have nothing but their own reflection to confirm existence. When young, we come to define ourselves through others: a mother's unconditional love, a father's acceptance. But in a culture blighted of positive gay modeling, what's a parent to do with a child who is subtly perceived as being different from the others? All too often, they absent themselves, or distort and deflect.

Many are those who've been psychologically cut adrift through parental neglect and homophobia, their authentic Self not affirmed: Whoever really lives inside must therefore not exist. Years later, when hoping to rediscover the one who was left behind by using the mirror of self-absorption, we behold an image distorted by tears, and hear echoes of grief. Yet we delude ourselves into believing otherwise.

What madness this is: For the self we see is the self as the ego wishes it. We are captivated by its selfish designs, its supreme conceitedness. It's for this reason that Narcissus is haughty and impervious to anything but his own beauty. To find the center of the whole personality, rather than merely its affects, would mean claiming the damage of the past and the despair grown from it—the Self buried in shadow. But Narcisssus has no taste for this. He is a boy with a most beautiful illusion—his grave error is to believe that this seductive image of himself is his true being.

If Narcissus were to be completely honest, he would have to admit that he holds himself in very low regard, despite his imperious airs. His aloofness and disdain for intimacy with others is a hedge against admitting this low self-esteem. Gay men live Narcissus's myth each time we try to cover up our own intrinsic insecurity with behavior that's contemptuous of others. There are other telltale signs of his madness, too.

After a lifetime of devaluation, it is not unexpected for gay men to express ambivalence about life or to mistrust its potential fortunes. "After repeated instances of hoping, which lead to disappointment, one learns to keep careful hold of the propensity to hope," says Carlton Cornett. "Gay men are generally particularly guarded in their willingness to hope (and often staunchly determined not to hope)."[12] Like any queer before a mirror, Narcissus needs to be reassured with the sight of himself because he doubts his own existence.

Being deficient of hope often means that one does not feel worthy of love. It's hard to accept a compliment or praise for a task well done, a narcissistic wound I've known all my life. Sometimes it's even impossible to accept love when it does arrive: One may suspect the bearer of life's finest gift of harboring a spurious motive. Or one may spurn it altogether. Many are those who reject what they most desire because of their *own* inadequacies, rather than anyone else's. Narcissus is secretive and alone, his solitude deepened each time Echo sends him back his own voice.

The need to be the center of attention, the focus of others' undying admiration, is another sign of Narcissus's plight. No one is as clever, talented, and fabulous as he. But beneath the grandiosity lurks depression. Alice Miller points out that "grandiosity itself is the defense against depression, and depression is the defense against the deep pain over the loss of the self."[13] Covering up the pain, and the rage born of it, is Narcissus's biggest talent of all.

When Narcissus was born, his mother asked the seer Tiresias if her infant son would live long. "Yes, if he will not have come to know himself," she was told. The prophecy holds true only as long as Narcissus does not recognize the one he loves. He must first believe that he loves another in order to be able to love himself. This is why, I think, Narcissus's dilemma promises hope despite his folly. For he does finally come to possess himself.

I don't believe Narcissus's story ends with his tumble into the pool. Instead, it continues anew. (The blooming of his namesake flower seems to tell us this.) It is exactly this kind of death—the dying one feels when owning shadow—that ensures *knowing* the love of true Self. Narcissus died in those depths. And it was Trickster who pulled him in.

It is Trickster who pulls any queen deeper into his mirror, and hopefully into his truth. It's the madness of Narcissus that keeps us resistant to being penetrated by that truth. The silvery surface of his pool betrays more than it reveals. Beneath those waters bubble our rage, our hurt, the scary monsters we strive to avoid. But with luck, and maybe a helping hand, pitiful fascination ends with our fateful submersion, too. Lucky, indeed. And another myth gay men are familiar with tells us why.

Myth of the Twice-Born

Gay men can see another important part of their psychology reflected in images of the Divine Child: from mythological Narcissus, and Michelangelo's Ganymede, to such modern-day incarnations as Peter Pan. Here, gay spirit is pictured in one of its most transcendent roles: as the embodiment of ecstasy in a utilitarian society disallowed much joy.

Like Narcissus, gay men are among any era's golden few. More than most, we've been handed the keys to life's great vault of mystery, which contains, among other treasure, the knowledge that life and death are but opposite sides of one thing. We are the gatekeepers to the adventure of life and its final mystery, death. Our knowledge of the opposites, and our propensity for traveling between them, enables us to bridge the seen and unseen, the past and the yet-to-be-formed.

This puts us in a place invisible to the dualistic worldview held in the West, although Western society has long used our mercurial aptitude for perceiving the hidden to its advantage, albeit unawares. As intuitive seekers of mystery and wonder, we dispense the secrets such vast and sadly removed storehouses of human emotion contain. By taking fanciful flights and daring leaps of faith—often into faith itself—we serve the world.

But the question remains: How to identify oneself and kindred others along the margins of the unknown? Our course in life is seldom straightforward, but is made of sharp angles and twists—as if our only map were the fracture lines embedded in our soul. Along this vertiginous path we find bits and pieces of self, confirmation found in random shards rather than whole vessels. It is in these places of contradiction and opposites united that we find many things. Perhaps even religion itself, which in its oldest sense means to *rebind.*

As an ageless wunderkind, the Divine Child does not grow into adulthood. This eternal youth, or *puer aeternus,* flies irreverently in the face of death and decay. Gay men know this elevated figure well.

Psychologist Edward F. Edinger illumines the archetype's beneficial quality when he explains that "to become like children is to revert to the undifferentiated state of the *prima materia* [first matter], which is a prerequisite of transformation."[14]

Like all archetypal forces, the Divine Child has a dichotomous nature: a dark as well as a light side. This complexity is well illustrated in the classic Greek figure of the Divine Child whom we know as Dionysus. The god of life, Dionysus was the last and most androgynous of deities to be admitted into the Hellenic pantheon of immortal archetypes. Close to women and nature, Dionysus was usually aligned with various forms of the Great Mother, acting as her consort. The story of Dionysus is particularly relevant to gay men living today because his myth is one of the twice-born.

Dionysus was the son of Zeus, ruler of the gods, and Semele, a mortal woman. Semele was tricked into extracting an oath from Zeus to reveal himself in his original form, the Lord of Lightning, in whose presence no mortal could live. Bound by his promise, Zeus transformed himself before Semele, killing her with the fire of his thunderbolts. At the moment of her death, Zeus plucked Dionysus from Semele's womb and sewed the infant into his own thigh. Now made immortal, this divine child was carried by Zeus until he was ready to be born. Hermes, the messenger god and another of Zeus's sons, assisted with this unusual male birth, or rebirth.

The spirit of this god within inspires aliveness, encouraging all who would joyously dare. He is meant to lead us, via fervent excess, to the liquescent depths of original being. Knowing Dionysus as an active part of one's psychology means being open to emotion, the senses, and the highs and lows of life. Dionysus is a bringer of laughter. But being an archetype of extreme opposites, he is also the most tragic and persecuted god of all. People suffused with Dionysian energy come as easily to suffering and madness as to deliverance and ecstasy.[15]

Any man favoring this god experiences contradictory pulls of mood and behavior. Although he expresses his passions intensely, he is prone to periods of depression. He tends toward the exploration of altered consciousness, yet may have problems in establishing appropriate limits. His thirst for the transcendent makes him an indiscriminate consumer of earthly experience. A man with Dionysian tendencies often has difficulty taking responsibility for his actions, feeling out of step with the "real world."

It's easy to see how the Divine Child archetype functions within the psyche of gay men and the subculture we have formed. The roots of our present-day identity are Dionysian to their very core. Although we seemed to emerge sudden and remarkable from the side of the patriarchal, our allegiance to the Great Mother was unquestionable. We lived in a state of protracted adolescence, with all its wildness and curiosity. Our innocence emboldened us. Invulnerability was never doubted. And, to a point, we were transformed. But then we were confronted with mortal reality, including death in the form of an unstoppable virus.

To accept the reality of death is a part of Dionysus's story, however. At one point in his life he was dismembered, torn to pieces by the Titans. While he remained the suffering god, Dionysus also became a symbol of resurrection. He came back to life. Later, Dionysus was called to descend into the underworld, the domain of shadow, to search for his mother and release her from her imprisonment. Here again, the myth shows a way.

If he is called to explore the unconscious, a man with Dionysian tendencies must pay particular attention to bringing the puer-mother complex to the surface. "If he is to grow psychologically," explains

Jean Shinoda Bolen, "the Dionysus man must leave behind his identification with the Divine Child and eternal adolescent, and become the hero."[16] A man under the influence of the Divine Child easily falters in his reach for new psychological ground, however. His efforts lack conviction because he doesn't really want to grow up and assume adult responsibility. His soul is stagnant, dominated by the complex of a possessive, even wrathful mother.

Dispelling Dionysus's mystique of eternal youth is an important task for gay men; the Divine Child must seek its own maturity and sense of groundedness. But Dionysus is a willful, mischievous god, who stirs feelings of panic at having to leave adolescence behind. He leads us back to the Great Mother. Entranced by her favor, we forget the inner work that must be done. Like Narcissus, we're caught in illusion. The silvery pool into which he stares is a fragile mirror, yet no stone in the forest seems big enough to break its surface.

During my years in San Francisco, I met many golden boys lost in self-absorption. The city was an ideal refuge for those with no other place to go, an alluring beacon at continent's end. When the chemistry of that charm faded, this fabulous and moody habitat for the disattached became a jumping-off place into curious and tragic places within the soul, sometimes even into death itself.

No wonder gay men, prone as we are to intense self-gazing and the coveting of hidden things, sought the city out, making it their own. Dionysus, with the masks of high drama and low comedy always in hand, licentiously prowled its streets. It is he, not the temperate Saint Francis, who ruled as the city's patron keeper. Dionysus is a deity of folly, but unfortunately he is also a god with no compassion. His mixed blessings were bestowed upon every person entering this city of the Golden Gate.

As the 1970s continued to roll on by, it was clear that of all the world's golden children, it was my generation of ageless travelers who invited the spirit of Dionysus to rise the highest. The observant few prospered by loving the god wisely, if not too well. For when the play was done, it was the indiscriminate many who fell the hardest. How like the myth to be ripped apart in the midst of heady glee.

I remember the orgies of sensual consumption, all-night revels prodded on by giddy queens, that were the talk of the town. These enormous disco parties drew hundreds, all drugged to the tits, stomping through the night to the sounds of Sylvester. He had got his start as an opening act for the Cockettes, claiming he was Billie Holiday's cousin. Whatever the truth was, it didn't matter. He was a big black diva, an outrageous goddess, pumping out benedictions of love: heated, heartfelt chants for our queer tribe. Never had it felt so good to be young and gay.

Such was the case one Halloween night in the ballroom of an old Victorian house inhabited by a collective of queer, cross-dressing tricksters, members of the Angels of Light. A successor to the Cockettes, the theatrical troupe had enchanted the city for years with their grand, magical productions in which global myths were combined with plucky sensibility to make shows the likes of which have seldom been seen. E. M. Forster defines "plucky" as the "one queer victory over cruelty and chaos." The credo of the Angels of Light, in the words of Angels' playwright Adrian Brooks, was "the fascination with everything incandescent and luminous, the glorification of the present tense."

The walls of the room were lined with dozens of discarded mirrors, cracks and broken edges refracting the light in shimmering patchwork patterns. A bowl of punch in the next room had been spiked with acid. The sexy beat never ceased, and who in their right mind could not help surrendering to what appeared to be utter freedom?

Around and around we twirled, time as meaningless as the outside world. We seemed safe in our fey cocoon, safe to be anything we wanted, anyone but ourselves.

As I danced before the mirrors, I caught odd glimpses of wild eyes, electric hair, and gyrating bodies in the florid swirl. It was hard not to stop and just look at the spectacle of it all. But I couldn't. Not with Trickster pulling me deeper and the Divine Child keeping me high in the air. Balanced between these contradictory spirits, I found it impossible to stay observant of anything else but my own fractured image.

Queer men, guardians of entrances and exits, are fated to traverse the world of paradox, forever reaching upward to better stake our claim on the heavens. With any grace, we may also find a way to keep our feet on the ground, rooted in the hard clay of unshakable reality. If life has any lesson to yield, I believe it's that everything is eventually transformed into its opposite. That night, little did I realize how soon this golden moment in time would seek its own dramatic revolution.

5

Burning Times

The summer of 1979 was a critical milestone, marked by three hundred thousand queers, their families, and friends who gave witness on Market Street the last Sunday in June.[1] It was the biggest showing of gay pride on record and one of the largest civic gatherings in the United States that year, although one would have to look pretty hard in the mainstream media to find it so reported. Despite the progress made in the decade since Stonewall, much uneasiness about gay and lesbian people persisted in the nation; we were either goblins from the collective id, let loose to prowl, or alien invaders. Yet, no matter what others might think, the day offered no better proof that we, too, had been cut out of America's whole cloth.

We did not have to be kings or their lovers, endowed with genius or a trust fund, to own our feelings. Gay history as popularly writ is but a list of such privileged people. In post-modern America, it's the sons and daughters of the working class who've defined the margins of otherness. It's been an unique experiment in democracy—one that's offered real possibility for real people—and it was the partaking in that common trust we celebrated. "I feel free to be anything I want here," one marcher from Iowa said.

I found a spot on a curb near the beginning of the parade route early in the morning and sat there for the next five hours as contingent, after group, after thousands of queers representing nothing but themselves, passed by. A thunderous phalanx of dykes on bikes led off, followed by a brass band oozing oomph. Then came waves of ordinary folk: athletes to zoologists, and every occupation in between, parents of gays and gay parents. The religious were quite on view, from Episcopalians to pagans, including a rowdy convent of male nuns vowing perpetual indulgence. Hedonists of all kinds were in their glory, from bare-bottomed boys to lesbians in leather, and, of course, tarted-up queens as far as the eye could see. Plain or fancy, humanity in its fullness was on display that day. It would be hard not to feel proud just from sharing in the sheer nerve of it all.

Beneath the exuberance and cocky strutting, and the sense of history being made, another realization stirred, however dormant, as if admitting it too fully would ambush our gains. We were growing up fast, getting older, and there wasn't a man among us who wanted to let the endless summer of his refound youth slip away. Like it or not, though, adulthood and its responsibilities had been thrust upon us. It was time to step back and take stock, maybe slow down a little from the frenzied pace of San Francisco's gayest era. A decade of incessant partying and insistent politicking was beginning to take its toll. Even the shape of the city itself was bending to accommodate emergent interests.[2]

Supervisor Harvey Milk had been shot to death in his office the previous November by colleague and rival Dan White, a political naif put up for the job (and some say the assassination itself) by the vested downtown power brokers "Manhattanizing" the city. Towering new developments and other boondoggles displaced the poor, while gentrification discouraged the rest. As a result of the greed, rents and the price of just about everything else were skyrocketing. Soon, only the rich or very clever would be able to live in San Francisco. Harvey, ever the uppity queer, had spoken up loudly against the rapid change and its consequences.

"It's a scandal of human nature to rip down sixty-seven housing units in this day so that the wealthy can have a place to rest their cars," he lectured, taking on the real estate speculators and other venture capitalists who, in his view, were ruining the city. "A place for an auto to rest is not as important as the need for a place for people to rest." On another occasion, he held fast against reductions in city library services and schools, saying that in tight times this amounted to cutting "the bone, not the fat" in government.[3] Harvey paid for his candor with his life.

Forty thousand mourners held lit candles in front of City Hall the night of Harvey's death. They were not only commemorating the demise of a gallant leader, but the passing of an age of innocence in the life of a gracious city. Six months later, a stunned community reacted again when a jury of White's carefully picked, conservative peers found him guilty of manslaughter rather than cold-blooded murder. The lenient sentence shocked and outraged nearly every citizen, no matter what their sexual stripe, and a major riot broke out on the evening of the jury's knee-jerk pronouncement.[4]

An enraged crowd quickly assembled in the Castro and marched toward City Hall, furiously chanting "Avenge Harvey Milk." Soon they were a mob of five thousand. Hundreds stormed up the steps of the building while the rest screamed for Dan White's blood. The ornamental ironwork on the front doors was pried off and used to smash through the thick glass panes. Stones rained from all directions, breaking every first-floor window. Flaming newspapers were then thrown in the basement in an effort to set the building on fire. City officials meeting inside were trapped.

Demonstrators ignored calls for peace, even taunted them. Arriving police were assaulted with chunks of broken concrete and asphalt ripped from the streets. The fury of the mob swelled as the stench of tear gas filled the air. One young man kicked in the window of a squad car, threw in a lit book of matches, and fanned the fire. Once the car was ablaze, he moved on to the next. Within minutes, a block-long line of police cars had burst into flame, their gas tanks exploding with loud thuds. The screech of melting sirens grated like banshees in the night.

"Fuck you! Let em' burn," cried one protestor, a raging trickster in the flames. The man picked up a rock and hurled it toward an advancing line of policemen with batons. "Dan White got away with murder," he shouted over the noise of the mob.

"Don't worry," yelled one of the cops in return. "We'll get ours." Which, of course, they did.[5]

I was out of town when the jury's verdict was read that late May afternoon. But by nightfall, as I reentered the city after a long day at work, I saw gray plumes of smoke ringing the great Beaux Arts dome of the building where Milk and his sympathetic ally, Mayor George Moscone, had been shot dead. As I made my way near, it felt like the whole of San Francisco was gripped in a frenzy beyond anything imaginable. The apocalyptic sight of a night sky lit by fire, the wailing sound of bombed-out police cars, would be forever recorded in our collective memory. Those dying howls and the mob's angry screams created a baleful yet appropriate soundtrack for the end of a truly ingenuous age.

I had seen Harvey for the last time just a few months prior to his death on the very spot now covered with flaming debris. It was Gay Pride Day, 1978, during the post-parade rally held on the stately plaza at the city's center, and Harvey had been his customary ebullient self. His flair and sense of the ridiculous were infectious. These endearing traits were no doubt cultivated by a love of opera and friendships within the world of off-Broadway theater.

Harvey was a natural-born showman, but I think it was only after his trek from New York to the West Coast in 1970 that he found his ideal stage. Now, after several hard-run political campaigns, he was one of the town's major players. Although Harvey reveled in his newly won post as supervisor, he had not forgotten in the least his role as paterfamilias to a generation of younger gay men following in his footsteps.

Despite the joviality of the day as well as the attempts of a friend to cheer me up, I was in a despondent mood. My friend, more of an intimate of Harvey's than I, called him over when we happened to pass in the milling crowd. Harvey took one look at my dour expression and burst out laughing.

"Look, nothing can be that awful," Harvey grinned. "See this?" he exclaimed, pointing to a large pimple on the end of his nose. It was a real shiner, impossible to ignore. "Well, it doesn't matter one bit."

Somehow, the Zen-like message contained in his declaration got through. Staring at the ugly-looking bump, I immediately began to feel the gloom lighten. I smiled in spite of myself, a change of spirit Harvey acknowledged with a sly wink before he bounced back into the throng.

I thought about Harvey and his simple teaching a year later while boarding another plane to Europe. This time I was venturing abroad for my own reasons, determined that nothing would blemish the need to spend some time alone. It had been seven years since I had left home, but somehow, the ponderousness that had infused so much of my life there refused to lift. A black cloud had settled over my heart. Neither time nor any number of escapades seemed capable of dispelling it. Perhaps putting even more distance between me and its originating source would provide a way to see clear.

I spent a week in Hungary, touring the country with some Carmel friends who had relatives there. The famous waters of the region's many natural springs are reputedly capable of curing all manner of ailments, but not, it seemed, my misery. I left for Athens, but there was nothing there among its dirty streets to help either. It was not until I was on a boat to Crete that I felt some lifting of spirit.

The afternoon was bright and sparkling, as only light reflecting off the waters of the Mediterranean can be. I was sitting on the ferry's top deck, a copy of James Barrie's *Peter Pan* in hand. It had been a going-away present from a friend whose sense of whimsy was more cultivated than mine, and who had once been foolish enough to profess his love. Silly Bill, little could he know how impossible it was for me to reciprocate that love; like Peter himself, I just flew away.

I was on the last page of the book when tears began to roll down my face. There was something about Barrie's tender fable that had struck a deep chord: in Peter, the consummate puer, I had seen the promise as well as the pathos of myself. Not wanting to let the other passengers on deck notice me cry, I turned and looked out across the azure sea. In a flash, a school of dolphins leapt out of the water, glinting in the sun as if they were Neverland's lost boys themselves. It was an exuberant sign. For the first time in my life, I felt less the orphan, claimed by some force other than steadfast sorrow.

It was not until breakfast the next day that the significance of this omen revealed itself. I had arrived in Iráklion, site of Minoan ruins on the island's northern shore. The morning was fresh. I felt present and alive. Walking to a sidewalk café, eager to spread out my guidebooks and plan the day, I noticed that all the tables were covered with crumbs.

With ceremonious moves befitting a dandy, I took out the white handkerchief I always carried and grandly dusted away the offending scraps. I didn't notice myself being observed from the far end of the otherwise deserted café until after I had sat down. When I looked up and spotted the fellow traveler, I could scarcely avert my eyes.

He was a gay man, all my senses told me that, and probably an American as well. His boyish but handsome face was topped with a mop of curly blond hair. He was solidly built and very tanned, and fit into his black leather jacket with practiced nonchalance. As clichéd as it was to think it, the image of an affable yet sexy farmhand came to mind; an all-American rebel, with or without a cause, yet nice guy, all rolled up into one Tom-of-Finland-esque archetype.

We sat in silence, studying each other over cups of steaming coffee. His gaze was bolder than mine. I was not used to asking for what I wanted, let alone getting it, but I was determined not to leave without at least a greeting. He must have been reading my mind when he stood up, ambled his way over, and sat across the table from me. His round blue eyes told me he was amused.

"I couldn't help notice how you brushed away those crumbs," he said, barely suppressing a smile.

I had been caught in an act of high queenery, and he knew it. Before I could offer a word in defense, my visitor picked up one of the tour books. Like myself, he had traveled across Europe to see the ruins, once the palace of Minos, King of Crete, where the mythical Minotaur stalked. After a few minutes of genial chitchat we decided to spend the day together exploring the local sights.

The afternoon was spent picking our way through stony mounds, the rubble of a once-great civilization. Our enthusiasm for what we were seeing, and delight in being able to share it with each other, energized the day. Every so often, we'd find a large rock to perch on and share more of our personal pasts. Gary and I both had strong Midwestern roots and had spent our adult lives in pursuit of an antidote to the dullness of that tie.

He was more of a risk taker, though, having roamed nearly every continent in search of adventure. Gary had managed to simplify his life to the contents of his backpack, the next destination on his map his only goal. I felt hopelessly complicated sitting next to him, yet as the day progressed, I began to sense that things were not as facile as they seemed beneath Gary's bright surface. The more intimate our conversation became, the more I could begin to see the dark currents beneath.

Both of us, it seemed, had been failed by our fathers. In my case, it was the failure of neglect. But Gary had been outright rejected by his dad to the point of having been regularly beaten for imagined sins. Neither of us had been properly seen and reflected back to ourselves by the primary men in our lives. As a consequence, both Gary and I suffered a damaged self-image. While there had been no mirror held up for me, the mirror of masculinity made available to Gary was deeply marred, even shattered.

We were wanting our manhood, a search that had taken us to similar places. It was no accident, I thought to myself toward the end of the day, that Gary and I should happen to meet where the Minotaur had once lived in the minds of men. This potent symbol of masculinity had fascinated us both since childhood. It was no coincidence, either, to learn that we'd gone looking for the Minotaur in other ways, too—especially in the underground leather worlds of New York and San Francisco. No doubt about it, we were fellow travelers.

Raging Bull

The legend of the Minotaur was born when Minos prays to Poseidon, god of the sea, to send him a bull to sacrifice. A magnificent snow-white bull appears from the waves, but Minos is so covetous of its beauty he decides to sacrifice a lesser animal instead. Poseidon is offended and as punishment the god causes Minos's wife, Pasiphaë, to fall in love with the bull and bear him a son, the Minotaur. Half-man and half-bull, the monstrous creature feeds exclusively on human flesh.

Ashamed by all that's happened, Minos commands the inventor Daedalus to build a place for the Minotaur to live, and so the Labyrinth, a deep underground maze from which no mortal can find exit, is constructed. Each year, the city of Athens is required by treaty to send seven young men and seven young women to the Labyrinth, where they are devoured by the beast. One year, Theseus, the son of King Aegeus of Athens, volunteers for the ordeal. With the help of Minos's clever daughter, Ariadne, Theseus ventures to the center of the Labyrinth, kills the Minotaur in its lair, and finds his way back out of the maze.[6]

The story of Theseus, as an adventurer and future king, is a far-reaching one. But his encounter with the Minotaur surely stands as the defining moment of his manhood. Like all myths involving tributes, monsters, and victorious heroes, Theseus's slaying of the Minotaur illustrates man's need to overcome base instincts within himself before establishing higher spiritual ground. The Minotaur, with its bull-like head and body of a man, represents these two conflicting sides of self. Its ferocity and need for sacrifice, its origins from the ocean's depth (the collective unconscious) and the womb of a queen (the matriarchy), further signify the Minotaur's archaic roots within psyche.

Gay men go searching for the Minotaur when they stalk the corridors of their own mazelike, otherworldly temples: those places we call bathhouses. There, at water's edge, we, too, seek fateful encounter: hunting it down one dimly lit path to another, wending our way ever closer to the center, to an inner sanctum where connection is nakedly made. We are not looking to slay the primitive, however, but long to embrace it there instead. This is one bull we want to take literally by the horns.

The essential function of a labyrinth—be it the one at Knossos, on the floor of the cathedral at Chartres, or anywhere else—is to defend the center. That is, to provide an initiation into sanctity, a way toward fullness of spirit. To retrace the path of labyrinthic patterns on the ground of many medieval structures, for instance, was once thought of as a symbolic substitute for a pilgrimage to the Holy Land.[7]

Many queer men come to spirit through the body, traveling its labyrinthine paths of instinct and emotion guided by the divining rod of phallos. Phallos is directive, possessing the power to differentiate and move us forward. It is the hardness beneath our grip, the determination behind our stride. "Phallos is the fundamental mark of maleness, its stamp, its impression," comments psychologist Eugene Monick. "No man has to learn phallos. It presents itself to him, as a god does."[8]

There is not a man alive who, at one point or another, has not stood naked before a mirror to wondrously behold this god rise. The poet James Broughton puts it this way:

This is the secret that will not stay hidden
this secret that is no secret
Such power thrives against every denial . . .
Here is the wonder of the god in man
Here is the dangling flower of Eros
This is He who awaits his ecstasy.[9]

Phallos as guiding instrument, healing wand, and joyful stick is a reality known to every man.

Like the biformed Minotaur, the archetype of masculinity has two sides: solar and lunar. Sky-reaching solar phallos obviously dominates where unchecked aggression and ceaseless acquisition is the rule of the land. Earth-centered lunar phallos, intuitive and prescient, works to lead men toward a world of reflection and refinement. Lunar phallos "is the hidden source of masculine power, dark because of its hiddenness, capable of catastrophic rage, but capable also of tender love and keen attention, based upon instinctual nature and need," says Monick.[10]

Darkness is not the same as shadow, for what happens in the dark often reveals the finest measure of a man. We encounter our dreams and the divine in the dark. But when not properly claimed, the part of masculinity that finds its fullest expression in the dark—lunar phallos—is relinquished to shadow. There, the nurturing masculine is confused with femininity, typically in its most negative forms. While lunar phallos can be expressed through the language of femininity, in no way is it feminine.

Queer men tend to discover masculinity's lunar polarity early in life, left little choice in childhood but to adapt and borrow from the feminine world. If, later in life, we are able to rescue this receptive masculine source from shadow (where, like so many things deemed feminine, it often lies diminished), we can find sustenance in what other men reject. But failing to retrieve lunar phallos from the domain of the negative feminine means a further susceptibility to soul sickness. Feelings turn ever more moody, brittle, and sterile. It's no wonder that so many gay men personify the stereotype of doomed, irritable queen.

Not honoring the two-sided spirit of phallos in its wholeness results in our masculinity becoming—like the Minotaur—a creation at odds with itself. Our betrayed feelings thrash about and bellow, demanding bloody sacrifice from others. The Minotaur's fearsomeness as well as his predicament are contained in gay men. Maybe when we seek him out, we hope to free the frustrated masculinity that's been created within ourselves.

At Knossos, I began to understand at last what makes the Minotaur rage: He was a child born in shame and shunted away. How like this beast my own masculinity was: never rescued, never prized. Never nurtured by the man I called father. My father's humiliation about his own mishappened son, I realized, remained buried deep inside the core of me. What a monstrous thing, imprisoned and angry, waiting to die by the hand of some savior king—a hero like Theseus who one day might come calling. Perhaps he was the one I was with.

As uneducated about our personal mythology as both Gary and I were, a sensibility of injured masculinity most certainly drew us closer as we clambered over the ruins of ancient Crete. By dusk, we were definitely bonded, like brothers from the same dysfunctional family of many children. We decided to pool resources and get a room together for the night, with him to go his way in the morning and me on mine. At least, that was the plan. Neither one of us honestly counted on that one night becoming a week of nights, one of the most memorable weeks of my life.

I was in love by the next morning, but had neither the mental acumen or sexual assuredness to admit it. Instead, I played the game of new best buddy, a macho sport if ever there was one. We slowly made our way along the coast of the island, traveling west toward the town of Khaniá, where I was scheduled to meet the poet and filmmaker Charles Henri Ford and Gary had plans to hike a well-known gorge located in the mountains nearby.

Ford had been a famous queer presence in the international avant-garde since the early thirties when he and critic Parker Tyler penned *The Young and Evil,* a novel about Greenwich Village's gay scene of the time.[11] He much later dabbled in experimental film; *Johnny Minotaur,* his best-known work, features a scene in which a beautiful youth on a beach fucks a ripe melon. I happened to see the film one night at the San Francisco Art Institute and was determined thereafter to meet the creator of this audaciously erotic image.

The work of Ford and other queer visionaries of the cinema, such as James Broughton, Jean Cocteau, and Kenneth Anger had provided me with my first introduction to the notion of "the Homintern," a term the poet Harold Norse coined in 1939. A takeoff on Comintern, or Communist International, it was meant to suggest a global homosexual network. Norse conveyed the phrase in a conversation to W. H. Auden, who used it a few years later in an article written for the *Partisan Review.*[12]

Feeling connected to a circle of wily queer sages, past and present, was part of my spiritual search, I carefully explained to Gary one evening over a dinner of roast lamb and feta salad. Being gay was about a lot more than what two men do in bed. Although that night, looking at each other through the flames of a flickering candle, I think it was hard for both of us to imagine what could be more important than that.

Our days were idyllic. Most mornings we'd stop to swim naked in the sea, sunning ourselves among dunes unfortunately pocked with foul patches of oil jettisoned by passing tankers. In a world so perfect as this, we asked, who could be so thoughtless?

One afternoon found us stranded in a small mountain town; the last bus of the day had left and few words of English were spoken by the villagers. Not many travelers made it to this remote corner of the island, and soon we were invited to share a bottle of wine with a couple of curious local elders. In due time, and over many flowing but barely comprehended words, we were invited to share a lift into Khaniá in the back of a hearse driven by one of their sons. Gary and I completed our journey flat on our backs, as much from laughing as from being crammed next to the ornate coffin filling the vehicle.

The evening was spent visiting Ford in the renovated sixteenth-century Venetian sea captain's house he made his summer residence. Ford was charmingly avuncular, pleased with my flattery and even more delighted by Gary's good looks. But we couldn't wait to return to our drab pension. There we made love for the last time, any further thought of death banished or treated like the joke it had become that day. It was unimaginable to think that, back home, death had already arrived like a poisonous tide.

As we lay interwined on the threadbare sheets, eyes droopy with sleep and blissful contentment, I took care to take a mental snapshot of the moment. The whitewashed walls and blue shutters of the spartan room glowed supernally in the light of the kerosene latern. The blond hairs on Gary's sun-burnished limbs fairly glistened. His entire body looked as if it had been carved out of one giant block of amber. He noticed my rumination and rolled over to face me head-on.

"Who do ya think you're looking at," he teased, pushing me lightly on the shoulder. I didn't reply and merely smiled back. I had never felt so good in my life and, for once, words seemed unnecessary. Suddenly, though, I could detect turbulent clouds pass behind his normally clear and playful eyes.

"Whatever is the matter?" I inquired, brushing my fingertips across the soft stubble on his cheek.

Gary fell back on the bed and reached for a cigarette. "Oh, I don't know," he wearily sighed. "I guess I've been feeling very confused and frightened over the decision of what next to do with my life. I'm tired of constantly having to make fresh starts from nothing in order to give my life meaning. Inevitably, I'm always coming face-to-face with myself and asking, 'Now what do you do?' "

I could provide no other answer but to reach out and hold him tight. His open questioning made me realize that Gary's peripatetic ways were less about discovery than escape—but from what dreaded thing I could only begin to imagine as the nighttime hours slipped by.

We awoke early, having to make our separate connections; Gary on a bus to the gorge and me back to the mainland. We walked slowly through town to the square where buses sat in jumbled rows. The streets were crowded with scurrying passengers and women on their way to market. Choking updrafts of hot dust swirled through the air. Gary's bus was almost full, and the driver impatiently waved the last riders aboard. There was just a minute and not much to say, really, other than good-bye and that we had no idea when we might see each other again.

We stood oblivious to the frantic scene around us, then embraced and passionately kissed. The horn sounded; the engine started up with a guttural roar. Gary lifted his pack, climbed aboard, and shouldered his way to the back of the bus, where I stood waiting on the outside. The last sight I had of Gary as the bus pulled away was of him trying to wipe the grimy window clean. He wanted a better view of our final seconds, but forgot that the dirt was on the pane's outer side.

The bus disappeared in a cloud of dust and I remained standing, dumbstruck and scarcely breathing for the longest time. Then, in a sudden rush, I ran between a row of buses and began to sob. The tears seemed without end and I didn't care if anyone heard me weep. I had lost more than a lover, an ideal friend, I had lost an indispensable piece of myself: a piece missing for so many years, found for a week, only to be taken again.

The absence was huge, the pain too familiar not to shamelessly cry. By that evening, I was miles away in high Delphi, sitting on another ancient stone, alone, asking the oracle: What now?

Sons and Lovers

The next five weeks were spent traipsing through Italy and France, forlornly at first, a battered volume of Lawrence Durrell's *The Alexandria Quartet* my only companion. But as the days sped toward summer's end, my spirits began to noticeably lighten. I had a new, clear destination in mind: a remote oasis in the Arizona desert where I hoped to find the spiritual cleansing I had gone in search of. Life seemed simple enough while on the road, but the austerity imposed by my vagabonding ways did little to ease the churning inside. Perhaps a clean sweep of empty land would provide relief.

There was another reason for traveling to the Arizona outback, actually. It had been chosen some months before as a favorable location for a conference of spiritually seeking gay men. The planners of the event, self-dubbed "radical fairies," wanted the gathering to be as far away from the heterosexual hegemony and its perceived ills as possible. I had promoted the upcoming retreat in the pages of *The Advocate* by interviewing gay visionary Harry Hay, who was organizing the event with longtime social activist Don Kilhefner and psychologist Mitch Walker.[13]

Hay was already well-known as the outspoken founder of the Mattachine Society, the first ongoing organization of politicized homosexuals in the nation. Since those initial efforts in the early fifties, Hay had watched the movement for gay liberation take an increasingly assimilationist stance. He was critical of this advancing conservative guard and saw the desert conclave as an important opportunity for queer men to reclaim their radical roots. In sum, to experiment with the advancement of a certain mythology.

Central to Hay's vision was the theory of gay men as a third-gender people: "not men" in the traditional sense, but not exactly womanlike either. In other words, a distinctly different ethnic class. "We Homosexuals are a Minority, who share each other's Dream whether we speak the same language or not, who share a common psychic vision whether we share the same cultural make-up or not, all the days of our years," Hay wrote (in his typically idiosyncratic fashion) in a speech delivered at the 1970 Western Homophile Conference in Los Angeles. "This shared commonality of outlook is a world-view totally unfamiliar to the accrued experience of our Parent Society. It is a view of the life experience *through a different window*."[14]

Hay was not claiming gay superiority, but merely a way of being in the world that is "neither better nor inferior—but *athwart*." As such, the "gay window" had something to offer to humanity at large. Our gender variance is meant to be a contributive factor to the human story, not a detriment. Accumulated centuries of homophobic stereotypes and lies have denied us that naturally selected function as spiritual healers and cultural mediators, however. Lacking this correct social context, we've been rendered powerless or, worse, nonexistent.

Hay explained: "For three hundred years, our useful contributive past in Western Culture has been pulverized and effaced by deliberate politically motivated Conspiracies of Silence. In this hell of Anomie, we of the Homosexual Minority have been reduced to semiconscious rudderless wanderers, driven like sheep to conform to social patterns which atrophied our perceptions and shredded our souls."

Hay's thinking was as prophetic then as it proved to be a decade later. It's not only time to reclaim gay spirit within ourselves, he continued to expound throughout the 1970s, but our rightful spiritual place in society. The way to do this is by "maximizing our differences" with the heterosexual majority. Hay's ideology was powerfully seductive, especially to the post-Stonewall generation of younger queers. By the time I arrived for the first-ever Spiritual Conference for Radical Fairies, nearly two hundred gay men, mostly in their twenties and thirties, had shown up at the isolated encampment.

The three-day gathering went by in a flash. Indeed, it was a flash: an explosion of repressed feeling and need that would reverberate for years to come. I cannot think of one man whose life was not changed in some seminal way by the brave acts of reinvention that occurred on those reddish sands. We talked a lot and held each other more, and made our serious business playful. The mere acknowledgment that queer men possess a reason and purpose for existing beyond society's false constructs meant everything.

It was a breakthrough time, soul curing on the deepest level, as words and actions were matched to emotions suppressed for lifetimes. The first fairie gathering was as historically important to the development of gay male consciousness as the Stonewall riots had been a decade before.

Like those activists who had spontaneously acted up during the first days of the revolution, we shared an urgent belief that old values and views had to be erased clean. For an earlier generation, that meant exorcising—at least publicly—the terrible demons of pathology from our lives. The Stonewall explosion and its fiery aftershocks signaled to the world the everlasting freedom of gay souls from exile. The intensity of that announcement drew new boundaries and lines of inquiry everywhere. Once at home, in the promised land that gay pride and separatism secured, we would continue to sort out fact from fiction; to see beyond defending ourselves from society's negating myths.

Or, at least, this is what some of us assumed. But pride can all too easily become hubris, and separatism its own rationale, if not assiduously tempered with the private inner revolution that true liberation requires.

Foremost in our minds was the question of leadership: Where was it? The clichéd feminist axiom that we were "leader full," meaning that each one of us held the potential to powerfully direct, was more problematic than real. The gay community had long had the habit of putting one straw man after another into the key light, only to see him go up in flames. A has-been jock or movie star, or discharged Air Force sergeant, or political hack does not a leader make. Even as role models for the young, these were tenuous figures. The message delivered is one of subterfuge, really: If you can hide out long enough to make it in the "real" world, then we'll take you on. But it was a fire-sale situation, at best.

Anyone who was someone in the gay community at that time seemed like damaged goods. There was certainly truth to be found in that. But the plain, awful facts about the damage were never completely disclosed. Coming out to gay life was treated like the ultimate win: a triumphant arrival rather than an admittance to the failure and heartbreak that had come before, and still percolated in the gut. Without absolute personal honesty encouraged and publicly shared, we were all doomed to suffer. This was by lack of example, the biggest lie of all: that coming out was somehow going to cure, in one magic stroke, all the covering up of the past. Somehow, the brokenness that stayed hidden in our so-called leaders was sensed.

For this very reason we never let anyone lead for long: We ripped apart, found fault, and betrayed without a moment's hesitation. How could we possibly trust any of them when we failed to trust ourselves? It takes a special kind of individual to inspire others with impunity, someone with just the right bag of tricks. Harvey Milk was possibly such a person. Perhaps he could have risen above the border wars and petty disputes that compromise any disenfranchised people and become a true national leader, given time. But he was slain before he had a chance. Now what? The burden of proof was now on each one of us, and for all our snappy banter and swell-headed opining, we were far from assuming any mantle of leadership.

Still, what we fairies in the desert had to say was not incorrect. Ten years after Stonewall, some of us looked around our newly gentrified gay neighborhoods and, except for fresh paint and cheerful signs, saw that the world had not changed as much as been given a makeover. Instead of a new reality, we were given over to a reservation filled with booze and pox—then conned into prettying it ourselves.

Critics called us cynical, impatient, even ungrateful, but, more than anything, we were spiritually dissatisfied, morally fed up. A decade of striving had resulted in a sidewalk or two to call our own, yet the license to roam those pavements did not mean more consciousness about who we queer men really are inside.

Assimilating into the mainstream invariably means playing—indeed, paying—by the rules dictated by those in power. To be well-adapted homosexuals in a maladjusted world wasn't answer enough. A few idealists struggled to make their objections known. However, more chants of pride, or Socialist dogma, or solidarity with other just causes could not possibly remedy the emptiness we felt. A further clearing, not yet more acquiring, was needed.

So when the call for Arizona was issued, we had come. No one knew what being a radical fairie was supposed to mean, not that it even really mattered. Somehow the words themselves seemed to fit into that hollow place of the heart. The point of our trek was to expose, without fear or judgment from others, that emptiness—as well as the longing for wholeness beneath. The first move toward recovery was to expunge the patriarchal ghosts that still rattled within our centers. To do this, we were told, meant returning to the nurturing arms of the Great Mother. Nowhere was this message made more manifest than during the mud ritual on the gathering's second day.

Men carried brimming pails of water to a clearing in the desert and mixed it with the dry soil there until a big pit of mud was formed. About forty fairies then stripped naked and sensuously covered themselves with the sepia ooze. No inch of flesh was left untouched. Bits of dry grass and chaparral were braided into hair. The earth-caked celebrants in this devotional orgy to Gaia became one tribe of men positively, irrevocably correct in their queerness. The scene was as atavistic as it was enlightened, an act of ultimate erasure and rebirth.

My own personal epiphany came a few hours later when I danced alone before a small audience, clad only in a loose pair of cerulean silk pants. For once the inner censor was not taking notes. It was such a modest act, especially within the day's larger context of revelation, but a daring one nevertheless. For just a minute, I had let my reserve down. However, it would take more, a great deal more, to slay the scary monsters that guarded my true Self.

During the next ten years, I made annual pilgrimages to fairie gatherings held on various western lands, while thousands of like fellows assembled in other secluded spots around the world; from New York City lofts to Australian beaches. It was a queer subculture in the making, although few gays in the mainstream allowed it much credence.

One late summer, a large group of us were caught in the rain in the mountains above Santa Fe. We persisted, forming healing "heart circles" in the mud, letting the drizzle mingle with tears of pent-up pain and the perspiration of neurotic purging. (Any fairie circling resulted in the releasing of both.) As we descended to the flatlands en route home, a few of us were lucky enough to stay over in a huge adobe dome sitting in the middle of the New Mexico desert. Built by a fairie and his friends and without electricity or running water, the building's interior spiraled deep into the earth. It was as if we were literally spending the night in Mother's embrace.

At a later gathering in the emerald hills near Sonoma, California, another fantastic structure was made by rigging enormous blue tarps between trees. It billowed and flapped in the breeze like the sails of a mighty ship; our own vessel prepared to move into the unknown. One night it was transformed into a makeshift theater by an earnest group of players putting on a camp version of Clare Boothe Luce's *The Women.* The satire got the added laughs expected from men, attired in hiking boots and chiffon, acting women's parts. But the guffaws also came from the recognition that fags and women have sharpened their collective wits on the same obstacle stone—the intransigence of straight men.

Maybe the answer really was to get away from such a brutish world, as far as possible. So, in Wolf Creek, Oregon, eighty acres of meadow and forest was acquired for use as a permanent fairie "homeland." Many gatherings were held there over the years, each one distinct in tone but linked by an emerging fairie mythos. One rite common to nearly every gathering was the Kali fire, a late-night ceremony devoted to the wrathful Hindu goddess of mysteries.

Sparks flew high as logs were thrown on the glowing pit to feed the rising flames. A circle was called and drums and rattles gathered. One by one, the men around the blaze stepped forward to burn their offering: an old love letter, a lock of hair, photographs of friends who'd died, scraps of paper inscribed with prayers for the living, a well-thumbed address book, a vial of AZT. Powerful music was made while some men stripped clean, others flaunted their drag. Some danced wildly before the inferno, running around the pit faster and faster as they chanted the name of the goddess: "Ayeee! Burn to Kali!"

My faith in the ability of gay men to meet in healing ways was renewed by these times with the fairies, but by the nineties my interest in the movement had waned. The group had lost its direction, I felt, becoming ever more fixated on the matrilineal. In my view, any man caught within the Great Mother's domain is fated to go round in circles.

At some point, the radical fairie movement changed for me. Now it seemed less about spiraling inward to tough new spiritual terrain and choices. It became a circuitous retreading of familiar laments. A lesson was learned. Men who remain exclusively in service to the Great Mother find she favors them most as impotent eunuchs—

psychologically or even physically castrated, as historical studies of third-gender castes such as the hijra in India bear out.[15]

Without phallos to guide the way, Mother-dominated men remain in thrall, powerless to anything but her whims and desires. The goddesses we chanted to during innumerable ritual nights—Kali, Hecate, Demeter, Isis, Astarte—are often more fearsome than benign. I discovered that we were unwitting in our obeisance, for nothing less than a pound of flesh is required for their blessings.

Although I departed, I continue to recognize the fairie movement as an invaluable means that has helped me and others peel back the skin of heterosexual conformity to better see our potential beneath. Fairie gatherings offer a unique rite of passage I still recommend: once come out a fairie, one is always a fairie. These spirited conclaves have crystallized the need for sanctuary acutely felt by so many gay men, past and present: from Edward Carpenter's Millthorpe farm a century ago to the fairie communities and other places for contemplation and retreat which have sprung up around the country in recent years.

Through my time with the fairies, I came to accept the radical, or root, reality of my queer life. And, of course, this involved reeducation about the Divine Mother, in all her aspects. On the positive side, I discovered that one can reclaim the matriarchy as a political act of defiance against the military state. I learned about the politics of gender; how one's gender identity is made to appear as if cast in stone but can actually be bent at our will, if we want. So, too, I was taught how to "lighten up," to literally embody my feyness as creative play. Mainly, though, I adopted a more compassionate attitude toward my own mother's plight: Patricia had done her best, acting tenaciously and with courageous brio in the face of almost overwhelming odds. What had been lost in her life were also those things denied her by an oppressive system extending over generations.

More than anything, this authentically queer movement—born out of indignation, angst, and faith in the impossible—was an attempt to retrieve what was taken from our lives. As queer boys, we had been left to imitate some ideal of manhood that was never true to begin with. Or worse, we were completely divorced from masculinity and its necessary initiations. As Great Mother's consorts, gay men bear her gifts and injury alike. Our task now is to find the Good Father and realize his favor within ourselves. And then, ultimately, for each other. For those of us whose masculinity has been denied and demeaned, nothing is more important than this.

In being distanced from good aspects of the Father, we've been alienated from the same qualities within ourselves. I keenly recognized this absence in my own life as well as the lives of other gay men who came together in fairie ritual to heal their split-off selves. Yet few of us knew how much diligent scrutiny, if not self-forgiveness, that task requires.

A decade after the initial Arizona gathering, I found myself once again with the fairies, but it was about the last time. Over two hundred men assembled, linking arms on a high Pacific plateau near Malibu. It was October, and a moist breeze stirred the boughs of great white oaks surrounding us, sentrylike, on tawny hills. Our circle was so large that those standing on its other side were barely visible in the lambent moonlight. Yet in our connection I could feel a steely, albeit sensuous current passing from hand to hand.

We stood in silence for a while. Then, out of the dark, arose a spontaneous homage to a screen legend recently departed. An amused, emphatic voice suddenly declared, "I'd love to kiss ya, but

I just washed my hair." Someone retorted with another line from one of her movies. "What a dump!" And then, from still elsewhere, came, "Fasten your seat belt—it's going to be a bumpy night."

The laughter that quickly followed was in acknowledgment of Bette Davis, a fellow survivor, a dark goddess that we had learned from. It was as irresistible as it was ironic. Our Dionysian rite was meant to affirm a connection to the earth and our rootedness to one another. In drawing down the moon, however, we could not help conjuring up a kindred spirit—in all her overdrawn glamour—to voice what perhaps would not be spoken otherwise. For there was something else about our midnight circling. The ritual was in remembrance of departed brothers, claimed by AIDS. Beyond the cohesion of this sacred circle stood *another* circle: a broken ring of those loved and now forever gone.

The sheltering sky was not big enough to contain our grief. If the earth were to shake, it would be a mere echo of our fury and dread. In making our public ritual, we privately asked: How do we empower ourselves—with what vital stuff—while we tend the sick, bury the dead, and go forward in life? The ground of certainty has split open beneath us. How do we make sense of what arises to confront us from unknown depths? How balance on the precarious brink between hope and despair, fulfillment and failure?

The alacrity of the moment was answer enough that night. However, the experience helped me realize we gay men are poised on the edge of two ways of being. One, where personal identity is sublimated within the collective. The other, where monuments are erected to the supremacy of the individual.

We've endured as acquiescent sons of the matriarchal age, which historically ended over four thousand years ago. At the same time, we're the sons of thoughtless fathers, whose current patriarchal age of miracles has been born out of plunder and destruction on a scale previously unimagined.

Perhaps we gay men stand on the frontier of some enlightened place now forming, a new epoch fusing the Matriarchy and Patriarchy into a more androgynous wholeness. Two epochs of the world, two realms of the soul, out of balance and lacking unity—except in the lives of those who already exist between them.

If there is a New Age dawning, who would be better harbingers of it than members of the world's first post-modern tribe? It is a tribe with no land to call its own, consisting of queer folk who have crafted themselves from particles of worlds now disappeared and ebbing.

Seekers without portfolio, we queer men are no strangers to the wilderness. But finding our way home, as I discovered soon enough, means leaving false sentiment behind: regret for fathers we never knew, longing for mothers who know us too well.

6

Shadow Play

Nestled in the center of San Francisco is an island of calm known for its natural beauty and serene vistas of the city's northern and eastern fronts. Named Buena Vista, which means "good view," the park encompasses the crown of a hill that towers above the surrounding neighborhoods like some wondrous cathedral constructed out of whole trees of cypress, pine, and eucalyptus.

Until the mid-eighties, the place was a luxurious secret garden known primarily to local residents and the queer cognoscenti. Its foliage had grown so thick that passage through some parts was near impossible. Secretive gnarled paths had been tunneled out of the dense growth by enterprising lovers and other seekers of reverie wanting privacy from the city's clang.

A couple of sanctioned trails twist their way to the apex of the peak, but back then it was the outlaw routes that offered the most fun. Gay men came to the hilltop from all over the city to cruise its hidden glades; during sunny afternoons no leaf was left unturned in pursuit of the hunt. But when the crisis of AIDS bloomed, the park was severely trimmed for purposes of ecology, or so the newspapers said. Only the queers knew that the drastic pruning had happened for another reason.

Over the years, I could not help becoming an astute observer of the droves among the grove. My apartment was situated on the top floor of a nine-story, Art Deco–era building overlooking the park and provided a ringside seat to the comings and goings below. The space, compact though it was, was an aerie among the clouds. From one corner window I could see the orange spires of the Golden Gate Bridge; the red beacons glowing atop each tower stood out above the thick white fog that usually swirled beneath like cherries on a bowl of cream. A bird's-eye vantage of downtown high-rises and the Bay Bridge stretching its way toward Oakland was possible if one stuck one's head through a window at the apartment's opposite end.

The most prized view, however, was from the middle window: an oceanic scene of lush treetops rippling in the Pacific winds. I never tired of looking at this vast, incessant movement of green. Sitting alone at night in a darkened apartment, with only moonbeams illuminating the sea of restless vegetation before me, I imagined myself a captain on a solemn ship going nowhere in particular, beautifully.

In the months following my summer excursion I was more pensive and apart than usual. Countless hours were spent meditating on the view from my room. The changing shapes and colors of the forest as the autumn season turned to winter held my interest as no other picture could. I considered my window landscape a perfect canvas upon which to project my own subtly shifting perceptions.

All around me, of course, life in the city was going full tilt. The erotic charge in the air was palpable as more and more gay men arrived to partake of the hedonistic freedoms so available to us. I sometimes wondered what effect the thousands of orgasms happening in such close proximity each day might be. Only seven miles square, San Francisco is actually a tiny place when compared with its fame. Sometimes the town seemed like one very sophisticated amusement park, with gay men not only inventing the rides but endlessly entertaining each other on them.

Castro Street, Polk Gulch, the Haight, North Beach, and Land's End: each in its way was treated as a theme area, with appropriate attire and attitude required of resident and tourist alike. Clones, queens, militants, aesthetes, and satyrs all had their own arena in which to play out the script they had been handed. For men whose childhood had been suppressed by censure and guilt, living on this stage of unfettered possibility meant indulging the adolescence they never had. Certainly, there was no lack of trying to make up for lost time and stolen promise.

From my tower on Buena Vista hill, I judged that we were loving one another a lot, but not always well. In my dark and critical mood, I wondered how long this gluttonous feeding could last. The desire to be touched, to be sexually healed, to perhaps even find true love, was not false. What wasn't right was the compulsion we brought to the appetite, as if skimming from one sensation after another could possibly fill the yawning chasm of our needy hearts.

Still, in the complexities of sex, are we gay men really that different from other Americans? We all live in a morally conflicted nation, hypocritical and nervous in the extreme about matters of libido. I saw this quandary especially well demonstrated by the magazine I worked for.

It had been politically expedient for many on the staff as well as in the community at large to pretend that the sexual marketplace aspect of *The Advocate* was not as important as its function as the primary mouthpiece of the gay movement. After all, why confound our process of assimilation into the mainstream with the bald facts: that gay men liked to fuck, apparently a lot, and often in unorthodox ways.

In fact, the classified personal ads, which had grown out of the back pages of the first edition (clandestinely printed in September 1967 in the basement of ABC Television's Los Angeles headquarters by gay men working there) into a separate pull-out section a decade later, were the economic mainstay of the operation. Easy removal meant easily out of mind, however, regardless of the central importance these copious columns of sexual advertisements had to both the publication and its readers.

The schism between truth and denial I witnessed at my workplace is typical in a society fed by decades of popular culture that has cynically used sex, mainly to sell things. Gay men are as captive to this calculated plan of neediness as anyone else. What is not false is our yearning to connect with the epic power that is hidden beneath the vapid pitches for mass consumption. The pages of any gay publication are filled with pictures of the gods we worship: deities of homo love, icons of the mystical twin that mends gay souls whole, provides *meaning* and *purpose* in the fullest, most religious sense.

The importance gay men place on sex is not wrong, just frequently misguided. We're constantly shopping—cruising and using, rejecting and renegotiating—for a living embodiment of gay love's archetypal god. Projecting the need to connect with the He who lives inside onto actual vessels of flesh and blood is a natural part of psyche's process. Yet the abiding satisfaction that comes from the two-as-one will elude us if we fail to first name and know the inner figure.

Great numbers of gay men cannot seem to escape the societal programming that seduces us to skip from one person to the next in search of perfection's symbol—an improbable attainment if only looked for in outer life. The man-of-our-dreams is invariably found to have feet of clay when he is mindlessly confused with the original ideal already living inside. Not owning our projection, not sorting out fact from fantasy, leaves us ever in want. In this, we are as much the heedless consumer as any other in a culture that must continually co-opt and dissemble so that appetites and desires are never really slaked.

Nowhere does this manipulation seem more apparent than in Los Angeles, where I had been regularly sent on assignment since my tenure at *The Advocate* began. There I was confronted with constant reminders about what is real—and what is not—as I whizzed at seventy miles per hour past the anonymous, drab warehouses where a nation's collective conscious is made.

It was hard to correlate the stuccoed fortresses of the entertainment industry with the escapist fantasies of my youth and, harder still, to reconcile grim outer reality with the permissive fictions that lingered on. What was more real: those fabulous illusions or life led in the fast lane?

Gay or straight, most Americans are confused about sex, and thus dishonest. We want too much fulfillment, with gloss and ease, without paying the price: which is to take responsibility for our yearnings, less tidy in real life than in the nonsensical propaganda implanted in our heads.

So, too, I had lost myself at the movies long ago. With a fantasy life as big as a Cinerama screen, I was more interested in the escapist scenarios possible in San Francisco's back-lot by-the-bay than in facing up to reality. My own adventure land of choice was South of Market, a picturesque district of tenement slums, railway yards, and old brick buildings housing everything from leather bars to fish markets. The main street is Folsom, a virtuous-looking artery in most parts except for its disreputable end.

The boulevard begins its long route in the outer city amid the pastel stucco houses of the working class, then winds through the heart of the Latino barrio, and traverses a decaying industrial zone near the once-prosperous waterfront. It is this final section of Folsom Street that fascinated me the most, as it has at least three generations of queer men. As if in a dream, I would drive down those last thirty blocks in darkness. I imagined myself on a river, navigating black waters to the bay. Strong currents of lust pulled me after the red trail of light vanishing silently into night.

To undertake this journey, one had to pass between the steel pilings of San Francisco's major overhead expressway. It was a ceremonial gate, of sorts, and old frames of reference and personal limit were best deposited on the other side. Then came the stations of my need: the Stud, all redwood and redolent of the sixties; FeBe's, conjuring up multiple images of Brandos on bikes; then the Brig and the Red Star, casting their spell on full-moon rites. The Barracks. The Ramrod. South of the Slot: the archetypal cheap hotel where no questions were asked. The walls there were so caked with grease, so went the joke, the place would burn for days if it ever caught fire: a votive candle on a reliquary of released desire.

Then, past homeless men in doorways of decaying warehouses, past newer facades of prefab stone and reflecting glass, and finally to the foot of a granite cliff, where a bridge is bolted to bedrock. It was there, at water's edge, that I'd stop my solitary passage, look up, and marvel at glistening silver cables soaring out of sight into mist. There was shelter here, among the cast-out, for I knew this was where some men came to mix shit and cum and piss and tears with earthiness.

Shadow Play

By my twenty-eighth year, Folsom Street had become a substitute for the haunted house I had visited so often as a boy. The terror that unnerved me there now stalked this corridor of concrete and its dark places. Basement playrooms were negotiated as cautiously as if I were in the Minotaur's lair; I was destined to meet the beast, but my escape route was nevertheless noted. "Nice boys" weren't supposed to tread where I was traveling. More than slumming for forbidden thrills, I thought I was going to hell.

My cowardice was as shaming as my shame itself. Finally, one February night in 1980, I realized the choice I had to make. I was in a storefront loft in the Mission district with about thirty other men attending a reunion of radical fairies; those of us locally who had been at the previous summer's gathering in Arizona. Gaily costumed and sweet in our glee, we were like Bedouin lords on laughing gas. A canopy of exotic fabrics hung over the dimly lit space, sheltering the men below who were languidly piled on dunes of oversized cushions. Curling plumes of incense and dancing shadows from numerous candles lent the room a sanctity it would otherwise not have. I felt myself floating away in the scented twilight, as if on a cloud.

My detachment was partly induced by the intoxicating spell of soft light and brotherly bonhomie cast around me, but a certain perverse indifference had set in as well. A week before, an invitation to another event for the same evening had mysteriously arrived in my mailbox. A newly formed fraternity of leathermen was hosting an inaugural party and the announcement was my ticket in.

I'd carried the paper with me for days and by now this well-worn scrap had burned a hole in my pocket. I was racked with ambivalence. It would be so easy to stay put on my cushion and drift through the rest of the night. No sharp edges, anxiety soothed by gentle voices meaning well. Why upset the placid flow?

But disruption—rude and uncompromised—is what I really sought. A certain part of me had been shunned for too long not to require otherwise. Here, among the fairies, my gentlemanly persona would find all the agreement it needed. Yet beneath that mask existed a wild child—a rather nasty boy—who longed to come out and play.

Finally, something in me spoke: I had to get out of the room. The scene around me was a bewitching illusion and meant nothing more. Giving vent to that abandoned kid inside would not happen through comforting means such as this, but through risk. The banal facade of a suburban upbringing cracked right down the middle had seen to that. Of all the members of my broken family, it was I who had striven the most to uphold middle-class manners. Now it was time to let nicety go, to let the brokenness really show.

No, I didn't need more comfort. With great care and attention, I needed to be ripped apart.

An expert at self-sabotage, I couldn't resist betraying even this one honest insight. Feeling remorse over leaving, guilt for being bored, I slid off my cushion and stealthily departed the room hoping no one would notice. But once I pushed through the plate-glass door opening onto Valencia Street, the stranglehold of suffocating emotion ceased. I immediately felt liberated from all past notions of propriety. Crossing that threshold represented more than accepting an unusual invitation.

My fey outfit of drawstring pants, silk blouse, and t'ai chi slippers was the flimsiest of insulation against the frigid air outside. By the time I arrived at my battered Volkswagen Bug, parked down a narrow side street a block away, my fingers were frozen stiff. Still, I felt blasted awake, near impervious to the freezing temperature. With methodical moves, I opened the car's front hood and stripped off my clothes, exchanging them for a paper sack containing jeans, a leather jacket, and boots. Standing naked in the quiet alley, even for a minute, felt exhilarating.

I could hear the thudding beat of my heart as it worked to pump warm blood through my body. I noticed myself becoming aroused, too, a miraculous act considering the chill. My erection signaled spontaneous delight more than it did calculated eros, for I was being remade by the moment. I stood motionless for another few seconds, tuning in the hushed sounds of a city asleep. Then I pulled on the second suit of clothes, got into my car, and drove off humming; transformed and ready for whatever fortune the night might still hold.

The address on the invitation was a cavernous building on Army Street, not too far away but distant enough for me to recover some warmth and a sense of mission. I had no idea what to expect, and realized I was shivering now more from nervousness than the cold. I parked and walked toward the entrance with purposeful strides; the clumping of heavy boots on pavement was reassuring. Once inside the door, I was greeted by a man dressed in a leather vest and chaps. A piss-stained jock hung low in front, but the sight of his bare ass sticking out behind struck me as slightly ludicrous. He'd have none of my flippant attitude, though, and gruffly waved me past after checking my name off a list.

The long corridor ahead was gray with smoke and about a dozen men leaned against the walls, either conversing or cruising the passing parade. I wasn't ready to face inspection of any kind and lowered my head as I advanced down the murky hall. I was still looking downward when I turned a corner and entered a gymnasium-sized room. The sudden jolt of music at full blare wrenched my head up. I gaped at what I saw.

The space was filled with men of all descriptions, about forty in total, sharing activities beyond my wildest dreams. It was a theater of all possibility, a netherworld playground with the strangest games imaginable. There were men hanging from the rafters on the ends of chains; men bound to crosses in throes of pleasure and/or pain; men tied spread-eagle on racks against the walls; men encased in plastic, congruent mummies all; men in harnesses whipping other men, naked and in bliss. There were laughing men, crying men, men devoted to service. And best yet, everyone seemed to be having a wonderful time.

After a minute or two, I shut my mouth and swallowed hard. I could feel my wild child stir, wanting to jump into the fray. But the bashful grown-up part balked and ordered me to retreat to an inconspicuous corner. The room appeared to be harmoniously divided between dominants and submissives; well-matched pairs of opposites having fun. Yet I stood stymied while these corresponding elements within my conflicted psyche battled for supremacy, one over the other, never in tandem. My libido was gridlocked. As much as the mind said *move,* my body wouldn't.

Certain that I was invisible to everyone present, my lonely impasse lasted an hour as the party's heated crescendo continued to build without me. I was surprised when someone walked out of the crowd to ask if I'd like to join him. He must have read my shaken look as an affirmative sign and, without further discussion, commanded me to follow. Mesmerized by his boldness as much as by my fear, I silently complied and trotted across the crowded room to a device made of two crossed beams leaning against a far wall.

Then we stopped a moment and studied one another. My confident new friend was in his early forties, I surmised, and his short-cropped beard was streaked with silver. It bothered me that his blue-gray eyes were devoid of humor. But when he perfunctorily said, "Okay, now strip," I obediently did as he asked. He turned to adjust the leather restraints clipped on the X-shaped contraption as I stood facing the wall, naked and waiting. Then, with aplomb, he shackled my hands and feet to the end of each beam.

I was helpless now, a fact that slowly sunk in as I awakened from my passive state. Something told me I should have looked a little more carefully before leaping into these arms. But now it was too late. Seeing my anxiety level noticeably rise brightened my captor's mood.

"You think you're pretty smart, don't you?" he leered.

I couldn't tell if he was really serious, or if the ominous tone to his voice was part of the game. Then I heard some rummaging sounds as he dug into the long nylon bag he had carried with him. Stepping up to the rack, the top man clenched my head with one hand and twisted it sideways so he could peer directly into my eyes.

"See these?" he exclaimed, holding a tight bundle of whittled birch rods before my face. "I'm going to use every one of them on you."

Being a tyro at the sport, I didn't know what the rules were at this point. Was I supposed to be afraid, or pleading, or humble? For the life of me, I couldn't remember what *The Leatherman's Handbook* had to recommend about the etiquette of the situation. Was I to be punished for my lack of proper training, or was generic punishment justice enough? All I could think to do was to shut my eyes and become immobile again.

I heard the top heave a long, hollow sigh. Maybe this wasn't going to work out, after all. My first big scene was already a dud, and there was nothing I could say or do to prevent it from being otherwise.

Much to his credit, my partner persisted. He selected one of the switches, stepped back a few feet, and began to dutifully administer regular strokes. They were stinging, but not as painful as I had imagined. In fact, I was even enjoying the treatment. He continued to rhythmically whack away, until, finally, I couldn't resist speaking up.

"How am I doing?" I cheerily asked with a backward glance. He immediately stopped, a look half mixed of disbelief and dismay coloring his face.

"The scene is over," he flatly announced, releasing my bonds. Without uttering another word he gathered his implements and left. It was the ultimate punishment.

I spent the next several hours roaming the premises cloaked only with self-reproach. My clothes were left in the pile where they'd been dropped, and at some point I lost track of them entirely. Before leaving the site of my disgrace I'd dug half a Quaalude hoarded for such an emergency out of my pants pocket. It didn't take long after downing the crumbly tablet to lose track of myself completely.

The inner kid had grown too cocky, and now he was paying the price: from banishment to oblivion, in no time at all. More than anything, I was disappointed in myself.

By five in the morning, the party was over. Only the diehards remained, picking over the dregs and those too drugged to go home. I'd had plenty of opportunity to explore the building, which contained several other rooms (*side chapels,* I thought) besides the main play area. It was in one of these smaller spaces that I finally collapsed, fatigue and emotional exhaustion winning over at last. I was on my hands and knees, wondering if there was one ounce of energy left, when a pair of polished boots stepped into view.

"Would you like a massage?" the resonant, deeply accented voice politely asked. Coming from on high, it seemed like an odd question.

Startled awake, I stared past the boots planted before me and upward along black leather chaps, beyond a studded belt and white shirt framed by fringed vest, and then focused on a kindly but intense face inset with bemused eyes. The bearer of this tailored finery was a middle-aged Latin man of slender build, and as he spoke he extended his hand down in greeting.

"Good evening," he warmly intoned, "My name is Alexis."

A wave of enormous relief—of inexplicable trust—flushed through my body. Suddenly, I was no longer cold. I sat down on the dirty carpet, feeling never more naked but safely, gloriously recognized at last.

The hour was well beyond the time when words mattered. The dignified stranger was standing tall above. But in the leveling calm of imminent daybreak, I saw reflected before me an equal other. I knew what kind of "massage" he had in mind, the brand of touch so freely proffered this crazy night. I needed it, wanted it—we both knew that—and not many further words were necessary. We talked amiably for another minute, and then it was time to consummate the act.

I got back up on my hands and knees, only to bow down respectfully before Alexis's boots. He removed the knot of thickly braided leather strands hanging from his waist and swung them into the air. I knew instantly that I had now traveled a long distance from home; my ivory-colored tower on Buena Vista hill was a galaxy away. Once again, I lowered my head to the floor. Alexis stood strong, swinging the whip in circles until it whistled. And then he brought it down.

"Yes, yes," I cried at the sound of the first crack.

How joyous, indeed, to be freed like this: My big, round butt thrust toward heaven, getting beaten in the rosy light of a new dawn.

Gay Body

Suffering as Grace

The crunch of wet, pristine sand made a satisfying sound as we walked along the storm-cleansed beach. It seemed as if we had been talking for hours; the trail of white footsteps dotting the shoreline marked the sure progress of our conversation. With all the candor I could muster, I was coming out, once again, to my friend Cathy.

We had gone through school together at Carmel High and knew each other well; both loners, we'd taken Thoreau's advice to heart long ago: to march to a different drummer, "however measured or far away." Neither one of us was particularly surprised when we announced to the other that we were queer. It was just one more declaration in a lifetime of shared intimacies. Now it was time for yet another revelation: my growing involvement with sadomasochism and the South of Market leather scene.

Entering the leather world was like coming out a second time, I carefully explained to Cathy as we sidestepped the darting waves. Announcing my homosexuality was child's play compared to the struggle I'd had in admitting to my interest in leather sex. It was like there was another closet within the closet, and bogeymen lived inside even that guarded space. I had been so afraid to investigate that inner sanctum and confront its demon voices until now.

"I want you to do whatever is going to make you happy and whole," said Cathy, after hearing my confession. "Besides, you help to open doors for me as we go along. But what is it exactly that you are so worried about?"

"I believe I'm most afraid of what other people will think," I quietly replied.

My friend only smiled as we trudged along the coast while I continued to unload my pent-up feelings. Monterey Bay seemed to curve forever into a blue cosmos of matching sky and water. The low rumble of the incoming tide and the persistent squeal of hungry sea birds overhead filled the silence between us when we finally came to a halt.

"It's all right, Mark," she responded after a while, reaching out to offer a speckled feather found on the sand. Her brown eyes were full of understanding. "I trust your exploration and accept what you're doing without any problem at all. It's your soul medicine."

Cathy's simple observation rang so true it left me embarrassed for the rest of day. Here I was trying to hide from myself and others activities thought to be shameful. But the real shame and source of immediate discomfort was my inability to see the truth of my experience. I had been too locked up in false myths and memories from childhood, which, too, were submerged in shame. In fact, a sense of shame, systemic and overshadowing, had permeated my being so thoroughly I could hardly imagine life without it.

I had gravitated toward the heaviness of the leather scene because of its weight, its mysterious ability to pull one down into depths that might not ordinarily be ventured. It was tricky business navigating a way into the pitiless well of one's psyche, but the chains and restraints, the brunt of the whip, even the scent of the leather itself, all assisted in making this passage possible.

The blunt, heavy means of dark eros was the best transporation I had yet found to help me go into my own terror, that awesome, ever-rising fear I had known all my life. By submitting at the feet of a masterful guide, I was, in effect, signing a contract wherein my ego-driven self could be temporarily annihilated, loosed from its mooring. My surrender to the demands of the scene marked a descent into an inner domain of similar upheaval and disintegration, of other things that immobilize and sting. Being a masochist gave me the permission and the means to face my total being: the self that exists in both worlds.

Voyaging South of Market was a good thing, not bad. It represented a new kind of vision quest; a spiritual search involving reconciliation with the past, catharsis in the present moment, and, with any luck, birth of clarity for future life. To die, to be reborn, and to be made stronger: These were necessary things, and somehow I had been able to find them best on Folsom Street. Soon, I discovered I was not the only one.

"We're the new American shamans," a fellow traveler in the scene perceptively told me. Rather than playing out a pathological instinct, a small community of men were experimenting with the risky, sometimes violent, always challenging edges of leather to heal our souls. There is no denying the curative power of dark eros's rigorous intensity: It is one way to touch deeply, when adroitly applied. It telegraphs a wake-up call to the Self: that despite all the obstacles, hard places, and blows, it too is cared for—perhaps even unconditionally loved.

Still, the onus of masochism clung to my consciousness like an old skin that could not be shed. Even the word itself—*masochist*—seemed like an indecent thing, mainly because of people's reluctance to talk honestly about it. As I became more relaxed about discussing my adventures South of Market, I found that not everyone was as tolerant as my friend on the beach. *So! He's a masochist,* I could almost hear some listeners think behind their unflappable smiles. After all, the sexual revolution was still being waged and it wasn't considered chic to judge another for his erotic tastes, however *outré* they might seem.

But beneath the studied nonchalance, I could tell that people were deeply unsettled by my tales of submission and surrender, of dark eros and its liberating effect on me. More than a peccadillo or odd preference, to explore one's masochism was thought a despicable thing. For most people, *masochism* remained a dirty word; one of the most troubling if not downright taboo words in the collective lexicon.

As always when one feels the weight of oppression lifted, the urge is to share the good news. My naïveté about the pervasive nature of prejudice was short-lived, however, and I soon curbed my enthusiasm about discussing this new turn in my life. Besides, I had no real need to confess anything other than my delight in finding a means toward wholeness. If anything, being less talkative about my forays into radical sexuality made me more self-reflective about what had attracted me to this path in the first place. It was time to start owning my projections and see what the shadows in this particular closet were actually about.

I meditated atop my hill, and soon realized that the first time I got clobbered by a bully on a grammar school playground—and didn't hit back—marked the start of my shame. I delved further and remembered the time at age four when I reached out to my father and tried to lovingly show my feelings. I was rebuffed, even subtly humiliated, for so naturally expressing myself. My shame grew even more corrosive the day I heard the word *sissy* hurled my way. The word stuck. I was suspected of not being normal in other people's eyes, self-doubtful in my own.

From then on, I was forced to live in a world of private suffering. The assaults on my developing sense of self continued, in ways that were both psychologically and physically injurious. Insult followed injury, time and time again, and there seemed to be no way to escape the damaging consequences of these blows other than to stuff them down into the deepest realms of my psyche. An acid rain had fallen where I lived, seeping through my innocence. Like cracks in the pavement that erode into dangerous ruts, my soul was pocked with secret misery and shame. By the time I was sixteen years old, the pain had been transmuted into a strange kind of pleasure: masochism. I derived a sickly satisfaction in knowing that no matter how hard the beating, I would survive.

In the curious way that elements are reversed and become their opposite thing in psyche's dungeons, my humiliation became powerful food for my soul. The denial of my full humanity by others, based primarily on the observation that I was a gender-nonconforming boy, certainly had its onerous effects. My spontaneity and joy were robbed, among other things taken in the theft of my selfhood, but not my resolve. If I'm less afraid to fathom life's dark places, it's because I have been living there for a long, long time.

Yet I know this is not always the case for others who have been similarly wounded. Because being gay has been linked with painful associations for so long, it's difficult for many men to mine the riches that lie within the ore of past hurts. The inability, or willful refusal, to dredge up and claim the contents of our shadow places cripples us in innumerable ways. Denial about what haunts us creates a waste dump of noxious emotion that can rage hysterical and vindictive when finally exposed.

Jung's assertion that there can be no birth of consciousness without pain offers another way to look at masochism. Because the soul, a place of ceaseless dying as much as generation, requires suffering in order to do its work. Masochism is testament to that. But when the soul's need to suffer is denied, its shadowy contents grow morbid, a putrefaction that often spills out in lacerating attempts to contaminate the soul of others. The deadly consequence of such stagnation was demonstrated to me during a phone conversation that occurred years after my stroll on the beach.

A high-powered gay man I had once worked with called to object to some words I had written about him. He was very angry, pointedly abusive. Yet I kept on the line wanting to make sense out of his tirade. I wanted to know what had ignited his ire, but he would have none of my inquiry.

Building up to a thunderous climax, he screamed, "You, you masochist!" And then he hung up.

At first I was stung, then shattered when I realized he was right. He had detected the peculiar scent that masochism emits and showed no mercy in exposing it. But then I considered the source of this hateful attack. My offending words were not directly about the caller, but rather described a situation in which many had failed—despite his best efforts. I had obviously come too close in touching an insecure nerve within himself, a place left unexamined, or, if looked at at all, quickly pressed back into unconsciousness. I suspect what fueled his rage was that place where all the pain of his life and memory of past failure was kept hidden from scrutiny.

His dazzling, quick-witted public persona was only the flimsiest of lids on a deeply compromised, darkly churning inner life in which his own masochistic tendencies were sublimated for the sake of self-preservation. Like the schoolyard bully who has to defend his own insecurity by bringing others down to his level, my caller had to sadistically project this most despised part of himself—the shame of supposed weakness we call masochism—onto someone who had been less afraid to admit his gay wounding.

Obviously, my accuser regarded masochism as a form of moral failure. But our conversation left me wondering if masochism is less about weakness and more about the potentials of unknown strength. We need to establish a new relationship to our masochism, just as we've had to reconfigure other notions that would define us in terms of sin and sickness. To perceive pain as a gateway to liberation and know suffering as its path is one way to relate to masochism.

When we suffer, we literally embody the spirit of the word, which means "to bear below," "to submit," "to undergo," "to experience or pass through." Establishing a conscious relationship with our suffering therefore means to return, time and again, to the character forming—or *deforming*, as the case may be—landmarks of inner reality. My exploration of dark eros has meant navigating its fiery byways to those monuments of past injury and shame within myself. Revisiting those sites, even in lightning moments, has given me, if nothing else, the confidence of a traveler who finds himself in distant, but oddly familiar, territory.

"Masochism is the indispensable condition of submitting fully to an experience," observes Jungian analyst Lyn Cowan, "encompassing realms of sex, religion, relationship, and death. It . . . throws an odd twist in 'ordinary' or 'normal' experience. Masochism may become, with careful attention and radical curiosity, an encounter with the inevitability of one's essential character."[1]

By facing the essential character of one's wounding—whether it be shame, or abandonment, or the trauma of being gay in a horribly homophobic society—it is possible to transmute pain into spiritual nourishment. As I learned in Folsom basements, one way to accomplish this is to use the suffering itself as the agent of transformation. As any sage healer knows, a malaise is often cured by a tincture of what ails, not its opposite. So, too, I sought to turn lead into gold, the heaviness of my heart into a source of enlightenment, by suffering with awareness.

The point in exploring dark eros, I found, was not to formulate an identity as either a masochist or a sadist—they are, after all, opposite sides of the same construct—but rather to ask what our relationship to suffering is. To be truly masochistic, in the most pejorative sense, is to remain a secret sufferer. Spiritual teacher Ram Dass explains it this way: "Suffering stinks, and then suffering becomes grace. It still stinks, but it's grace. You'd rather not suffer, but if you do suffer, you work with it and experience what it's showing you."[2]

Queer men are no strangers to suffering and its strangulating defenses. Through the purification, or catharsis, which the exploration of masochism allows, one can shake loose the foundations of personality, its falseness and mortar of pride. A journey to Self always exacts the return to one's original humiliation: for therein lies the source of humility, without which we cannot find the key to that backroom known as shadow. It is there, in psyche's basement, at the level where masochism lives, that we suffer and die so that we may be reborn anew. Perhaps, in the final analysis, masochism is about the soul's need to properly mourn.

Critics sometimes fault the probing of masochism as an experience "complicit with a culture of death."[3] But they confuse outer mannerism with inner meaning: Submitting to a symbolic passage of death is not necessarily to agree with the demands of a culture that says one must either submit or die. For many queer men, the creative exploration of dark eros has contributed to the making of a culture uniquely their own. In their Dionysian way, gay leathermen are practioners of an age-old spiritual technology, comparable to the initiation rites of Eleusis and other ancient mystery religions.[4]

Masochism becomes a problem when it stays no more than cowardly play: a narcissistic wallowing in the crimes against Self rather than a cognizant return to and healing of them. To face one's "indispensable condition" requires a fearless treading into the inflamed location of one's suffering and shame. And this, above all else, is the work of the hero.

A soul's blackening must occur before any new light can dawn. This alchemical act of transmutation has happened in my life, as it has in others', through surrender to dark eros and the curious, healing properties of its combustible power.

Dark Eros

From the beginnings of modern gay identity, queer men have sought masculine initiation through dark eros and its clannish rites. It is an underground milieu made out of many cultural remnants, but is a world peculiar unto itself and greater than the sum of its parts. For those men outcast from the acceptable male world, and who have taken their outlaw status to heart, this subterranean place is where self-love has frequently been forged and mutual trust found.

Many gay men abstain from its practices, though, even express abhorrence, echoing mainstream society's unilateral condemnation of this least-understood part of gay male life. Nonetheless, dark eros holds a shadowy sway over the collective imagination of gay men. Its icons and argot have undeniably shaped our language of manhood. In one way or another, we have all made the trip down Folsom Street.

The fellowship of leather has been shaped through myths of its own making: life after dreams, image after art. It is a cult where the boundaries of male initiation have been expertly drawn and followed, largely inspired by the sexual fantasies of artists who began to work openly after the Second World War. For the first time in the history of art, an iconography crystallized a culture of men, giving it visible form.

In the 1950s, Helsinki-based artist Tom of Finland emerged as the creator of sleek, hypermasculine figures. These influential and much imitated gay prototypes appeared unapologetic in their lust for one another. With only superficial characteristics to distinguish them, Tom's homoerotically charged men of action were near-identical reflections of one another—the image of heroic twins.[5]

A decade later, San Francisco illustrator Chuck Arnett captured the bawdy attitude of rugged gay men living on society's edge. His widely disseminated works of the 1960s rudely deflated previous effeminate stereotypes and set the tone for an entire era to come. Arnett's men were uncompromised loners, outcasts by choice, who had loosely banded into an affectional brotherhood where rough sex and plentiful drugs were the common tie.[6]

Arnett's graphic imagery, like much of the work by numerous artists that followed, contrasted the reality of soma (body) with that of logos (mind), a crucial distinction to be made in the consciousness of the time. Taking clues from Arnett's art and life, many gay men allowed themselves to go out of mind and into body. Through intense ecstatic experience, they were able to give up the judgments of a patriarchal ghost while not in any way negating their own personal sense of masculinity.

By the 1970s, New York artist Rex was further delineating this underworld fraternity with dozens of moody, evocative scenes, often picturing older and younger men in positions of dominance and submission. These potent images, with their context of initiatory ritual, illustrate the passing on of male experience through cross-generational or brother-to-brother bonding. The incestuous undercurrent seen throughout all of these artists' works has been apparent to a generation of post-modern queer men who've been failed by a hierarchy of fathers and so kept from achieving their own masculine power.

The imagery of the leather world is compensatory in nature, just as dreams emanating from the unconscious are. Germinal in its themes and depictions, it is sacred art. Over the past fifty years, creative voyagers have plunged into the libidinous realm of lunar phallos and have brought back pictographs of a hidden side of gay male life. This forbidden imagery has communicated a way of masculine passage that has been mostly lost or sublimated in our mass culture.

The inhabiting of animal skins and the nighttime earth, tactics of containment and release, submission to a power beyond oneself, are all ways to reconnect with lunar, or chthonic, phallos. "Chthonic phallos is the means by which a man moves through ego limitation to ecstatic merger with the archetypal world in sexuality," states Eugene Monick. "It is the numinous source of his being as a male. It is the silent god within, prompting his creative action, standing behind his erectile strength, facilitating the explosion of his fertilizing seed."[7]

Practitioners of leather sex intuitively know lunar phallos, a presence that remains unbidden in most men's lives. Men who find contact with this dark masculine force undergo a form of initiation—as shamans do—that strengthens and prepares them for merger with the archetypal world. This is a rite of passage needed by all men but not always experienced. It is certainly lacking in a culture such as ours where pseudo-initiation is more often the rule. Sometimes, as in the transmutational ordeal I underwent one rainy winter evening, that passage is achieved.

This particular ritual happened between Alexis and me about a year after our first introduction. We had become good friends since that piquant meeting on the dungeon floor. Aside from our sexual compatibility, we'd quickly discovered that the same things made us laugh. Alexis exercised a wry wit that could pierce the ponderousness of just about any situation, including the archaic codes of the leather scene that made serious devotees appear literally hidebound at times, even humorless. He loved nothing more than a good laugh, even if it was at his own expense.

Alexis's sophisticated sense of amusement was naturally abetted by his status as an immigrant; he had arrived in the United States from South America in the early sixties, a young man in search of spiritual asylum. His intolerance of fascist behavior was heightened by the infractions of petty dictators observed in his native land, and thus he was always on guard for the taint of fascism inherently possible in any sadomasochistic enactment.

After we had settled in for the night, my friend told me about a big dinner party of leathermen he had recently attended, where the host, a gay Republican, had crudely tried to defend American imperial policy in Latin America. Alexis said that he had come to know a thing or two about fascism—as much in the playrooms of some at the table that evening as anywhere else—and quickly excused himself.

"You should have seen the look on their faces," he raucously laughed, puffing out his cheeks in mimicking indignation. I was lying naked on the black leather sheet he used to cover his bed, and joined in with his guffaws. Alexis's room looked like the den of some medieval alchemist. Flickering tapers in wrought-iron sconces lit pictures of bound men and other artwork covering the walls. Whips and chains hung in orderly rows, and tiny jars of human hair, neatly labeled with names and dates, were displayed trophylike.

"You and I are very much aware of the fact that we are all actors throughout our entire lives," continued Alexis. "Some people take the acting too seriously without leaving any room for comedy. We combine the dramatic with the comic. We are not only rebels, we're romantics. Only romantics understand each other, no matter their different cultural backgrounds. Romanticism is a universal bond."

Despite the thick accent which sometimes hampered his speech, Alexis was sounding particularly eloquent tonight. I nodded for him to go on. "S-and-M is a ritualistic dance where the spirit and the body are acting in unison upon a great stage," he said. "But the dance is no good, Mark, if it isn't spiritual. I always want to give you *spiritual* lashes."

Alexis chuckled, stroking his elegant goatee before reaching over to pat the skin on my ass. My friend recognized the capacity of leather sex to take its players to the edge of an existential abyss, which can be a very lonely place. Perhaps his claim on spirituality was a defense against that. Whatever the reason, it was one we both shared.

Alexis was more than just a compassionate comrade: He was a teacher, guide, and, at times, stern administrator, even though neither one of us felt that traditional S-and-M role-playing was necessary to our relationship. "Our approach to S-and-M eludes any stereotypical definition," he often told me. In his view, one could be dominant or submissive without having to become a "slave" or "master." We both interpreted our intense brand of lovemaking as sensual magic, a crimson flying carpet to some other realm, where healing takes place. Mutual respect, leavened with a healthy dose of absurdity about the human condition, made our bond strong.

And so I could kneel before him or lie prone, shackled to the four corners of his square, wooden bedframe, and receive without hesitation what he wanted to offer. We could play for hours, but this night we traveled far, as far as we had ever dared to go.

Way past midnight, I finally peer into a mirror—eyes dilated, mouth agape—and am confronted with a scary reflection. My body is covered with blood. I've been supplicant for hours, channeling beatitude during the beating. The blows had come like the driving rain; washing, watering deep, drumming out all other sensation. And now the skin is cut in many places, lacerations weeping in rivulets of brownish red. My body has been turned inside out.

I put one finger to the tip of my tongue and taste—salty, wet. Then I put palms on face and rub all over, putting down broad swipes the color of fresh-dug earth. The image in the mirror is the boyhood vision I once had of myself: alone and naked in the forest, in search of the man I would one day grow up to be. Tonight, I see myself as if for the first time: false face erased, something remarkable and real spied in the moment.

Men find their worth, define their manliness, through trials of endurance such as the one I sought out and received that night. They must expose their limits, submit to fiery tests, in order to spiritually grow. It is the hero's obligation to meet these rites of passage with faith intact, for they balance the eternal conflict between the claims of ego and the Self.

Initiation must necessarily involve ritual death—that is, transcendence of ego—before a deeper awareness of life can be reached. "Initiation is, essentially, a process that begins with a rite of submission, followed by a period of containment, and then by a further rite of liberation," explains analytic psychologist Joseph L. Henderson. "In this way every individual can reconcile the conflicting elements of his personality: He can strike a balance that makes him truly human, and truly the master of himself."[8]

The prototypical leatherman, as envisioned by Tom of Finland, Chuck Arnett, Rex, and others, is a potent image of queer manhood, yet he is more than a tribal icon. Beneath his perpetually sly grin, I perceive Tom as a knowing guide, entreating us with the seductive command to "Follow me!"

Each of us lives in two worlds. Clinging to the conscious "I," we maneuver our way through the waking world of appetites and ambition. Like a vessel adrift on an uncharted sea, ego keeps us afloat on the surface of the vast unconscious. But at night, we are pulled into turbulent depths by our dreams. The unconscious is a reality of endless strata: Beneath the water lies mud, and beneath that is fire and ice. It is the primordial inner world from which all of human consciousness has sprung. In the night, this world is revealed through the symbols that rise up to meet us in our sleep.

"I am looking for a friend in a sewer," writes one friend in his dream journal. But his search comes to a halt. The sewer is guarded by a leatherman stoically smoking a cigarette. "I feel fearful, but not devastated," the dreamer relates. He proceeds past the silent figure and after a while sees two women—a queen and a princess—driving by in a car. He follows the car, which descends into the earth until it arrives in a musty, cavelike room. Then, "the car doors open and two lovers emerge. They are bearded men dressed from head to foot in black leather, chains, and spikes. . . . I knew right away where the queen and the princess had gone!"

This is one leatherman who dares the dreamer to go deeper into his truth. Stripped of his queer trappings, this black-clad traveler of the night could be envisioned as Hermes, guider of souls. A god of audacious masculinity, Hermes is the "spirit of a completely concrete 'world-like' aspect of the world that accommodates us always again in a special realm—he is a spirit of the night."[9]

Hermes is a prankster who disregards boundaries. But unlike Trickster who abolishes limits, not least the boundaries of sex, Hermes is not a god of disorder. He is a facile messenger who crosses borders and shifts levels with ease; an archetype of connection that negotiates the distance between Apollonian rationality and Dionysian freedom. Many men go through life assuming they must forgo one for the other. But Hermes mediates this dilemma and shows the possibilities inherent in both. This mercurial communicator serves to mend our incompleteness. Even his healing caduceus, a staff intertwined with two serpents, is a symbol of regeneration and opposites balanced.

Hermes stands on the threshold of the underworld, gatekeeper to the mysteries of initiation, which marks passage from one stage of life to another. He encourages our ventures into the unknown and fortifies our will. Without his transforming touch, boys do not grow up to be men, and men lose sight of the boy within them. A precocious adventurer, Hermes is the deliverer of our phallic wonder.

Myths are the speech of psyche, and thus possess the timeless certitude of rain on rock. But they can all too easily be left to languish in the mythic realm: that is, a place of reflection. This is how myth is primarily absorbed today, through reflection in mass culture which projects only the lifeless, blood-drained husks of myth. As I've found, myths must be enacted to be made real. To really know the hero myth, for instance, one must be heroic.

In contemplating all the circles I have participated in—from groups of "soft men" exposing their vulnerability with intermittent tears to men physically testing their hardness—I see how the liberation of buried pain and rage has been made possible. It is here, in these circles, where past life stories are recovered and present life passages bodily inscribed, that I've learned the necessity of *enactment*. To find the real meaning and power of a myth—or a mythic god—requires no less than this.

Psyche desires risk, relationship, delight, and eros. This is the real promise of being a queer man in America today: We are dynamic in a deadened world. For having given birth to ourselves, in awakening to our adventure, we are giving birth to a new myth. Nothing should be more important to us now than to follow its call. That is the essence of the hero myth: the one who goes to follow a vision, who senses that there is an adventure waiting for him. And it is Hermes, ever the traveler, who encourages him—and us—onward.

The god was vividly summoned one summer day when a small band of leathermen, self-proclaimed "fairies with black leather wings," gathered in the foothills of the Sierra Mountains. They had spun off from the original fairie tribe in the late eighties to better connect flesh and spirit in ways that seemed more indigenous to them. When Hermes speaks, wise men listen—for he brings luck. Though some may think us fools playing to a distant echo, we who gathered on those granite slopes heeded his friendly urging.

The box of small rubber balls sitting by the edge of the meadow was a kind of post-modern answer to the fruit and citrus customarily used in India for our ritual dance performed on the second day. As with the ages-old Hindu practice, the balls are attached to thin wires which are then sewn lightly under the skin. Participants in the ritual wear as many balls as they want or as can be withstood. The purpose of this adornment, however, is not to exercise one's tolerance of pain. The object, rather, is to build up levels of sensation as the body naturally reacts with a flow of endorphins, pain-mitigating and euphoria-inducing chemicals released by the brain during times of stress.

One man, undressed and spotted all over with reddish-brown antiseptic liquid, observed that the piercings in his chest, back, and arms had all the bite of bee stings. While other balls were being stitched onto the dozen men partaking in the ritual, the rest of us assembled an orchestra of drums, rattles, and flutes. The red, blue, green, gold, and silver orbs gleamed brightly in the afternoon light as the men dipped and turned, testing their weight. Then a circle was formed, the first notes of music sounded. More instruments joined in, and with a cautious sway the men in the circle began to move.

With growing confidence, the dancers spread out across the field. Their graceful steps and our percussive music harmoniously merged, the rhythm of the beat matching the repetitive motion of balls bouncing against bodies. As the rite progressed, the dancers gradually slipped into an altered state of mind, a kind of heavy-lidded trance. So emboldened, they rapturously twirled. One after another, the balls began to tear loose from their bodies, spotting the grass like luscious flowers. The dancers' bliss was palpable.

The masochistic fervor of the dance was a way of piercing habitual defenses—to expose the self beneath. We, who have suffered the consequences of rejection and hate, know all too well the borders of pain. Often, we've gone to extraordinary means to numb the suffering, but no amount of alcohol, drugs, or diversion is capable of repairing a bitter heart and its betraying insecurity. We are no strangers to pain. But here, this afternoon, men flew on its wings in order to penetrate the thick skin of denial.

The dancers were intent on achieving *enthousiasmos,* or possession by the gods. As Westerners, we were inviting Dionysus, who attends to soul-making through the body, and Hermes, who communicates knowledge of the healing arts, to make their presence known. But to awaken the soul's receptivity, one must first allow for its humility.

Like the Sadhus, India's mystic holy men, the dancers were seeking liberation from earthly bonds in their pursuit of inner light. The members of that ancient sect strive to change their perception of mundane reality by reprogramming their minds and bodies in various ways, including renunciation, meditation, mortification, and other austerities. By piercing the worldly "veil of illusion" (*maya*) one may experience the greater truth behind it. Their self-chastisement is not a matter of atonement, a repentance of imagined sin, but rather a means toward releasing the spiritual energy—the "inner heat", or *tapas*—that burns within.

Our dance was a devotional act, a sacrifice to that inner fire. The dancers on the field had surrendered the last vestiges of superficiality and pride in order to dance themselves into a state that is at once holy and horrific, where the bonds of illusion and memory are shattered wide. For that to happen, radical feats are sometimes required. Even something as strange as this pagan rite on the lawn.

7

Departures, Sacred and Profane

In service to the irrational gods of chance, fate, and whimsy, as nobody else, poets walk a line in life invisible to most. This is why they are thought to be crazy, or irrelevant, at best, in a society so overly calculated that it is going mad from its own assuredness. It is a poet's job to doubt and wonder, to ask *what for* and *if*. Poets are truly the governors of that liminal space known as hope.

That is why the death of a poet, and I have seen the passing of more than I wish to count, carries me to a realm beyond sadness. The demise of a poet, especially one taken by AIDS, chokes like an ignoble defeat. For it marks the disappearance of yet another brave watch against the boorish juggernauts of certainty, which would, if they could, pave over innocence itself.

The death of my friend, the poet Paul Monette, was observed with all the literalism that the sight and sound of fresh dirt flung on coffin can provide. I had never actually stood at a gravesite, shovel in hand, returning freshly exhumed earth to the hole from which it'd been dug. It seemed like such a barbaric rite for so cultivated a man, but

Paul had a pagan heart beating loud and clear beneath his well-bred Christian manner.

Like any fine writer, he appreciated dissonance as much as well-crafted cadence in his lines. Here, on the grounds of the Hollywood Hills Forest Lawn cemetery, there was both. The surreal arbitrariness of life in late–twentieth century Los Angeles abutted the absolute rhythms of laying a loved one to rest.

A half mile to the south from where Paul's mourners stood in prayer is a replica of Boston's Old North Church, perfect in every detail as if the building had been wrested from its Revolution-era foundations and dropped among the sagebrush and newly carved suburbs of Southern California. A towering edifice made to look like Mickey Mouse's cone-shaped, star-spotted hat from *Fantasia* looms a short distance to the east, and beyond it lies sprawled the rest of the Walt Disney fantasy factory.

Rising to the west are the dry lands of vast Griffith Park; its steep slopes guard against the intrusions of the world as well as any studio gate, for in magic spots among rugged peaks and valleys another kind of escapism is pursued. Gay men have congregated there for decades, fucking among the chaparral as if their lives depended on it. All that, and just a stone's throw from the manicured green lawns of the dead.

No doubt there was a *petite mort* or two happening nearby as the last handfuls of earth were scattered over a good gay poet's grave. Ashes and orgasms, mixed together on a Saturday afternoon. How appropriate. The irony of the juxtaposition would have been richly enjoyed by my friend, who savored his own becoming as much as he longed to chronicle the laments of lost opportunity.

Everything must go full circle and, over time, become its opposite. In a microscopic world, where nanoseconds matter, queer sex is metaphor enough for that. We gay men spill our seed, shoot our wads, unleash our loads, for no other reason than the pleasure of the act itself. Each splash of semen, unfettered as it is by any responsibility to procreation, represents a little death, and we are hated for this. But in our release, we give back to the spirits of earth and air the essence of ourselves by which to feed future self-generation.

Through sex, we come back unto ourselves: When making love with one of the same, a gay man connects with the sacred wellspring of his bliss. The myth of Narcissus concludes with the story's namesake drowning in a pool of his own reflection. But that is not the end, only the start of a whole other story: a journey that begins through submersion in the image of an equal other.

By the spring of 1982, the search for my double self had led me even further into the South of Market underworld. I liked the idea of going down to a place apart, a subversive world existing almost like a phantom realm beneath the city's humdrum facade. The men who gathered there during late-night hours were doppelgangers of their daily selves, white skins made all the more pale when sheathed in gleaming black leather, parading in circuitous routes along the boulevard in search of their perfect match.

Even the street signs underscored the region's shady aura: Clementina, Minna, Zoe, Harriet, Isis, Clara, and Grace were all supposedly named after the whores who had once worked the neighborhood. They had set up shop along the narrow alleys off Folsom to satisfy the lusty needs of the single men who descended upon the city after the 1906 earthquake. San Francisco lay in ruins and hordes of workers were needed to restore its glory. Two-and three-story boarding hotels were among the first new buildings erected, made from hastily milled redwood harvested north of the bay.

South of Market was a boomtown, a thriving district which

expanded even further when rubble from the old city was pushed into the bay in order to make room for the new. Those who stayed after the reconstruction was done, married and moved outward to blue-collar enclaves like the Mission, Glen Park, or Potrero Hill to better raise their families. Now, more than half a century later, the long, high-ceilinged halls of those solid hotels were left to the very poor or to faggots in heat.

For the gay men streaming into the neighborhood from the sixties on, architecture was destiny. Without the easy availability of these neglected structures, many of which were purchased for pennies down, there would have been no place to go—no turf to stalk horny and naked and call our own. By the mid-seventies, nearly a dozen of the area's old hotels and rooming houses had been converted, with varying degrees of inventiveness and expense, into sexual playgrounds unique to their time and place. Gay men came from all over the globe to partake of the pleasures awaiting them in spartan rooms. The menu of sex offered in these establishments was more exotic than found almost anywhere else. Any act that could be done was achieved; the boundaries of imagination were the only limits.

As incongruous as it may seem, I found a deep solace and spiritual comfort padding down the grimy corridors of Folsom's sex hotels. Most of them were well-equipped with slings and crude beds constructed out of heavy timber, four-by-fours, and big slabs of plywood. Short lengths of plastic tubing for cleaning out the ass and fingernail clippers were always on stock at the front desks. The reek of marijuana smoke and stale poppers circulated constantly throughout the air.

When one checked in to such a place, one signed away any claims on normal reality. You were admitting yourself into an existential limbo where time, along with all other signatures of a regular self, was quickly abandoned. It was a scene beyond seedy, or decadent, or any of the other clichés that might come readily to mind. Stepping across those thresholds meant descending into a world truly below.

One Friday night, I found myself pretty much alone in one of the last of these places to open before the plague swept through the neighborhood like an all-consuming inferno. It was called Animals, a name that appealed to me as much for its primal simplicity as for its rather classy ring. It was a tall, narrow structure four levels high, and was located on about the worst block in town. I usually arrived early to insure close parking, which also meant forfeiting much company inside until several hours later.

The interior of the building had been painted a flat black—even the floors—and the only illumination came from small red bulbs randomly installed along the lengthy corridors. The hypnotic throb of American soul and new-wave British dance music echoed throughout the empty space. Every board of the building seemed to vibrate with the pulsating, seductive beat.

I had checked in, stripped and scrubbed, and was now touring the premises alone and nude. The sound of my bare feet slapping against the dusty floorboards was the only noise aside from the music, which ebbed as I climbed the central, looping staircase. To be so utterly free of clothes and the company of others was pleasurable by itself. If nothing else happened this night, the experience of being adrift in this warm, womblike environment would be enough.

The doors of many of the rooms were open, revealing a stark tableaux of beds in box, rendered in shades of charcoal gray, like pieces of some somber installation created by Louise Nevelson or a window dresser from hell. I continued my rounds, the solitude suiting me just fine. It wasn't until I reached the final room on the top floor that I discovered I was not alone.

At first, the sight of the hotel's only other guest startled me: All I could see was a luminous white face floating in midair. The room was pitch-black except for the narrow beam of light focused on its occupant who was comfortably suspended in the pouch of a sling. Hanging with a mischievous grin plastered on his face, the man reminded me of the Cheshire Cat at the height of lewdness. The image was mercurial and irresistible, like staring into a shiny and slightly absurd funhouse mirror.

"So . . . why don't you come in and join me?" the man in the sling coyly asked after a few seconds had passed. I could hear the chains rattle from their bolts in the ceiling as he shifted his weight.

With studied flair, he lit up a joint, took a puff, blew the match out on the exhale, and then casually offered the joint to me. Without knowing how or why, I suddenly felt we were reenacting some golden-age movie scene. Circumstance aside, his invitation was as affectingly romantic as the smoke was thick in the air. I faltered for just a moment, then took the bait.

It didn't take long before I warmed up to this curious fellow who had made an entrance from nowhere. We spent the rest of the night together, taking turns in the sling and telling our stories. His name was Barry, he said, and he worked as a clerk in a downtown insurance company. He'd been in the Bay Area just a few years, having come north from Los Angeles, where he'd lived during a good part of the seventies after escaping his hometown of Fort Scott, Kansas. It was obvious Barry intended to go no further: He had wasted little time in finding his niche on San Francisco's pleasure playground. It felt more like home than home ever had.

Barry's story was typical of so many gay men who had fled the horrific consequences of being the village sissy. The only child of loving but uncomprehending parents, Barry was taunted and teased mercilessly for his soft, gender-nonconforming appearance. He was a sweet boy, buttoned up in his mother's handknit cardigans, and he didn't stand a chance. The sexual extremities he currently sought and favored others with were in some way compensatory acts for the torture and pathos he had endured as a child. Barry excelled in sex the way others excel in the playing of a violin: He could hit all the notes and then some.

We stayed up until thin blades of sunlight began to intrude through the cracks in the blacked-out windows. Then, after a short nap, we stumbled out of the hotel and onto Sixth Street, blinking in the bright morning sun, our unwashed hair and skin slick with Crisco. Animals, indeed.

It was about nine o'clock and we were both ravenous from not eating the night before. I invited him to join me at a neighborhood hangout, an old railroad car converted to a greasy spoon. As we sat chewing our breakfast, looking much like two greasy bears who'd just crawled out of hibernation, I couldn't help but overhear the remarks of a nearby gay couple who were eyeing us disdainfully.

"Don't they know what they're doing?" said one man to the other.

"They're fools," nodded his neatly attired companion. "There's a plague going on out there."

Of course we knew. How could we not help noticing the sudden disappearance of familiar faces or fail to register the brewing controversy over plans to enforce closure of the bathhouses and other venues of unchecked sex in San Francisco. But we were denizens of our world, not theirs, and therefore understood the rules—and the risks—of the games we were playing better than they could possibly know.

Beneath this tableside dismissal lived a deeper dislike of what we were doing. Being subjected to prejudicial remarks because of one's sexuality was hardly a new experience for me, but it's always a little disconcerting when such slander is issued from fellow queers. The intimation of scorn, that caustic vote of disapproval from those who should know better, can become its own infection if not closely watched.

The form of sex Barry and I were intent on exploring is confrontational, to be sure, even to other queers. The idea of one man allowing himself to be deeply penetrated by another is so transgressive that most men—gay or straight—find it repugnant. To lie back in a sling, legs hung wide apart, your butthole presented as a receptive cavity to be plumbed, is outrageous.

Fingers, then hand, as phallos: It is the most radical act of queer love-making imaginable, one that bears the stigma of feminine submissiveness that nearly all men in our culture despise. Little do men know the asshole, that constant source of derision and shame, as a gateway into the temple of male mysteries. When properly opened, it becomes a portal through which the spirit of homo-masculinity can impregnate one's soul.

To begin, one must first imagine the entire body as an erotic instrument. Most men constrain their sexual pleasure to the tip of the penis. But, in truth, every limb, finger, and toe, each bodily surface, from the soles of our feet to the topknot on our heads, can be awakened to rapture. With deep, measured breathing and correct visualization to assist in one's relaxation, the whole body becomes orgasmic.

Esoteric sexual practices, such as the one Barry and I explored, have long been a part of ancient, non-Western cultures, which celebrated the spiritual potentials of erotic bliss. Tantric Yoga is one tradition that has harnessed the energies of the body to lift people beyond the mundane. The body's vital life force is thought to flow through a subtle network of conduits known by practitioners of acupuncture and other healing arts as meridians. Along the meridian on the spine are seven key focal points, or *chakras*.

At the bottom of the spine, near the anus, lies the first or root chakra. The other six are located around the genitals, belly, heart, throat and mouth, forehead or "third eye" area, and crown of the head. Each chakra is associated with a particular psycho-spiritual state. The energy generated by the first chakra is most concerned with base survival, for instance. The second chakra holds properties associated with sexuality. The third chakra, located as it is in the solar plexus, relates to power, control, and the ego.

According to this system of belief, most of humankind's vital energy is kept essentially locked within the first three chakras. But through spiritual meditation, and other focused practices involving the body, it is possible—indeed, evolutionarily advantageous—to free one's life energy into the higher functions of love and affection, creation and communication, wisdom and justice, and, finally, just pure knowingness. Ultimately, the point is to have the energy of all seven chakras well-balanced and working together.

This raising of consciousness is accomplished with the aid of the Kundalini, a concept key to Tantric Yoga. The Kundalini is metaphorically pictured as a serpent wound tight around the first chakra. As the serpent uncoils and travels upward along the spinal column, the other chakras are progressively opened, producing an ecstatic state which, ultimately, results in connection with the divine.[1]

On a crude level, it would be easy to see Barry's and my play as nothing more than sleazy sex, manipulative and regressive in nature. But, for us, it was a ritual of rare devotion, an erotic tango requiring mutual trust and a commitment to achieving ecstatic awareness. By opening our assholes with consummate care, we were attempting to liberate the taboo places where personal power and profound wisdom are stored. Many were the nights when I literally sang the body electric, howling with delight and astonishment for being so alive, so very awake in every nook of my being. Having another man's hand thrust deep into your ass is like being plugged into all the currents of the universe.

Muscles hold memories, the dual rings of the sphincter retaining those from early childhood. I copiously wept the first time I was so deeply touched. The tears were quickly followed by laughter, though, as much from relief for the lifting of repression as gratitude for the recovery of lost images and emotions. Then a sense of being rebirthed soon enfolded me. It's as if one were being delivered all over again: through the dawning of light and time and beyond, from the loss of innocence to some mature and tranquil place in the cosmic order where all is eternally well.

What is shocking is not the possibility of the act itself, but the actual fact of two men sexually engaged as equals, exchanging their power in loving and balanced accord. A man's mind must also be open, free from rapacious urges to dominate and control another, before the rite can work its magic. If Barry and I were fools, we were holy ones, ingenuous but not unintelligent in our play.

What concerned me most in the ensuing months after our meeting was not questions about sexual habits but our increasing dependency on drugs. We had become regular partners soon enough, renting the room where we'd met or some other similar space, usually on a Friday night. At first, the casual use of pot seemed enough. But augmenting our high with some other hallucinogenic treat meant we could extend the sensual possibilities of our play, often into the early morning hours. The introduction of one tooth-grinding powder or another had grown ever less occasional, becoming almost mandatory.

Having difficulties in establishing firm boundaries for myself meant that it was almost impossible for me to set limits with others. Without quite knowing how or why, I became a midwife to Barry's chemical habit and birthed my own co-dependency within weeks. It didn't take long for me to realize that we weren't having meaningful fun anymore.

To be sure, experimenting with drugs was hardly a novel experience for me. I had smoked my first joint during senior year in high school and had enjoyed partaking of the weed ever since. Nor had I left more potent substances untried; LSD, psilocybin mushrooms, and other psychedelics had all been ingested on special occasions, usually under the rationale of doing "spiritual research."

I had even plunged a needle full of heroin into my arm the previous autumn. I was with someone I hardly knew, which was stupid enough, but his sexy wiles, the hypnotic ritual of laying out the works, and the fact that it was Halloween night broke through my guard. It took only a minute after the syringe was emptied before I felt the drug's rapturous warmth flow into my body through the tips of my fingers and toes. I could see how people could easily get hooked and, understanding my own thirst for escapism, vowed that night never to shoot up again.

The journalist in me justified these flirtations with altered states as suitable investigations into the human mind. In fact, the prudent use of reality-bending agents has played a necessary and beneficial role in my personal evolution. Helpful allies in the pursuit of awareness, one might say. But my habit of drug-taking with Barry was hardly an act of consciousness. It soon became less about elevating to some new plateau than about avoiding old pain that neither one of us had the gumption to name.

Of course, we were not the only ones struggling with this problem.

Drugs were readily available everywhere, high octane fuel for one of the biggest parties then happening on the planet. But there were casualties, the burnouts legion. Sometimes, in the dead of night, I'd stand alone on Folsom imagining a scarlet river of drugs flushing spent young lives out to the bay in the old brick sewer that runs under the street. Why were we such willing participants in our own self-destruction?

A wounded man has difficulty taking responsibility for his life. Something in him has been abused, and the harm permeates his soul as a basic truth. Being the victim is the emotional standard against which all of life's experience is judged. He internalizes the pain and learns to assimilate its acid. Usually, his fear and shame become addictive. Rather than let go, he holds on to his abuse selfishly. Somehow, it seems safer to stay where he is. The purpose of an addiction is to erect a buffer between a man and his true feelings. This is what happened to me—as it did to others—as I became ever more desensitized under the advancing tide of amphetamine addiction.

I was a weekend abuser, which meant that I spent pretty much the rest of the week recovering only to go under the influence again. It was a vicious, exhausting cycle that, if not stopped, would spiral downward to the end not only of my relationship with Barry but also of my life as I knew it. Friends commented on my increased moodiness and shaggy looks, but I breezily deflected their concern, thinking I could hide what was occurring. In truth, I was ashamed and miserable.

My unhappiness finally erupted one Sunday afternoon during a drive in the country. I was confronting Barry with the dismal reality of our situation, but he wanted to hear none of it. With jaw clenched, he kept a steady gaze on the road ahead, impervious and remote within his cocoon of denial. Patience lost, I emphatically smacked the dashboard with the edge of my hand. To the shock of both of us, it cracked wide open.

Barry stared at the gash in the plastic and foam covering as if the San Andreas fault had just opened up to swallow him. He had never seen me this angry and it bothered him beyond words. We drove the long distance back to the city in strained silence. When I dropped him off at his apartment, I thought we would never see one another again.

But if my lover had suffered the debilitating effects of being labeled a sissy, it had not impaired his strengths as a survivor. Barry had considerable willpower when he wanted to harness it, and he curbed his appetite for drugs the very next day. As unsettling as the episode had been for me, I figured it was my strongly defended middle-class values that got compromised more than my health.

This flirtation with drugs had been relatively brief, but was long enough to tell me something about myself, where before I had been clueless. My easy tendency toward addictive and self-harmful behavior had revealed, as never before, my considerable investment in shame; of feeling bad about myself even under the guise of feeling good. I could see this same pattern at work in Barry as well, not to mention in countless other gay men I have known in the years since that tense reckoning in the car.

My friend, the poet, got it right. "I've come to learn that all our stories add up to the same imprisonment," wrote Paul, who, through the travails of becoming a healthy, whole gay man, broke free better than most. Before death claimed him, I was privileged to witness Paul's lifting of "the lead weight of my self-hatred," his liberation from the lethal bonds of internal exile which seems the peculiar fate of queers, no matter when or where we're born.

Through late-night revels, drugs, and radical sex, I, too, had sought to unburden myself of the psychic weight that kept me sluggish and, over time, would have incapacitated me completely. But opening the gateways of consciousness was not enough. Once over the threshold there were choices to be made. The seeds of queer masculinity might be planted but they had to be properly nurtured in order to grow. For all that I had said and done, the extremities ventured and toeholds gained, the real work of my soul-making was yet to come. Without facing up to my terrifying, enervating shame, my promise as a man would surely lie fallow in that pathless wasteland known as no hope.

Cleaning House

The mirrored playrooms Barry and I loved to romp in were very much like certain places of the heart: secretive. We had let ourselves into the first, but the keys to the latter had yet to be found. My wounded inner kid had the company he deserved at last, but it was fun and games without much introspection—the drugs were the hedge against that. Without going to the source of the wounding, what was the point? We were just two more feckless youths running amok without map or guidance among the city's big tribe of lost boys. Clearly, it had come time to say good-bye to the narcissistic indulgences of Pleasure Island and move on to more substantial ground.

In the language of dreams, descending into one's unconscious is often symbolized by going south—moving to the more heated land that lies below. This is what I did, quite literally. A year and a half after my relationship with Barry began, I was presented with a job opportunity that would require me to leave the city and reestablish my life in Southern California. The choice was an agonizing one to make. It would mean abandoning a lifetime of cozy associations and inhabiting the belly of the beast known as Los Angeles.

I hated the thought of it—as did my circle of family and friends—but knew I had to take the journey for reasons beyond articulating. On one cold March morning in 1984 I closed the door to my beautiful aerie for the last time. The movers had already claimed the big stuff, and my car was loaded down with the few essentials I would need while I searched for new quarters in the southland.

Barry was waiting for me on the street, visibly stressed over the fact that I was indeed departing. He had refused to believe it at first—denial was as much a part of him as the oxygen he breathed—but the irrevocable moment of our separation had plainly arrived. *Save yourself. Don't leave that work up to me!* I was shouting inside my head. But somehow, even in the final clench, I couldn't say it aloud. It was evident now that my exodus was as much about breaking away from what had become a dysfunctional, engulfing relationship as it was about seeking career advancement.

Still, I loved Barry as no other. We were truly soul brothers, born to and bred in the same dank chambers of unhappiness and shame. We were both crying as I climbed into the car and drove away from Buena Vista hill forever. The view that had once seemed so wondrous was now a blurred haze in the rearview mirror.

A decade later, I returned to climb into Barry's bed one more time. It would be our final embrace. We had maintained our friendship over the years, of course, letting time heal the hurt of our parting and bring us closer together as men less dependent on one another and more admiring of autonomous strengths. Barry had changed a lot in the intervening years and chronicled this growth in his typically eccentric fashion. He had decorated his skin with numerous tattoos—bold tribal patterns, satyrs with hard-ons, yin/yang symbols, and more—plus piercings in almost every available nub of flesh. It was his way of reclaiming the self that had been ransacked and stolen; inch by inch the battle against the insults of the past was waged until finally there was not one area of his body that had not been left victorously marked. On these terms, as excruciating as they seemed, he had won.

His compact build, once so charged with vitality, was now distressingly shrunken. He looked like an emaciated mandarin, wan and hollow cheeked, fingernails grown clawlike and hair prematurely gray. Barry was rapidly dying of AIDS, and many functions of his body as well as the brain were permanently impaired. In fact, I had been warned before my visit that my old friend might not even recognize me. It took just one glance for me to know that Barry, ever the Trickster, was his familiar self. Let others think what they may, but this one, adept as he was with smoke and mirrors, was still here.

"How are you doing in there," I bluntly asked, crouching before his chair to look deep into his eyes.

"I've been cleaning my house," he replied with an ironic but steady grin. "Each and every room of it."

I knew that Barry didn't mean the living quarters around him. Imminent death had hastened another kind of cleaning. I had never been more proud of my friend than at that moment, for I knew he was telling the truth. We exchanged a few more words, mostly banalities about treatment and care, but the important part of our conversation was done. After a while, I helped him into his bed and put a record on the stereo, Beethoven's Sonata No. 23 in F minor.

With the lush sounds filling the room, I climbed into the bed myself and gathered Barry in my arms, cradling him without words while a scented spring breeze stirred white curtains on the open window and the music played. He was asleep by the time the sonata's final measure sounded. I kissed him gently on the cheek and closed the door behind me as I left. A month later, Barry was dead.

The tragic loss of my friend led me to think about the house cleaning we all need to do—the examination and putting in proper order the contents of our soul—and how we shouldn't wait until calamity looms. It's difficult and often unpleasant, but the consequences of not doing this crucial work far outweigh the effort. Barry's last words told me he had finally found the missing keys to rooms he had avoided earlier in his life; that he had been able to examine and take inventory of his whole being. Witnessing his courage has empowered me to do the same, particularly to see those places within myself I don't want to own.

My shame, I've discovered, is heaped in a room near the bottom of my soul. It's where every deceit, secret, and denial of my life ended up and is stored. It's an ugly, embarrassed, and wounded place—the sum of the betrayal of my feelings—and I don't like to visit there very often. In fact, I don't even want to know that it really exists. But it lives each day as I do, growing like a putrid, leaden mass. Sometimes, when I least suspect it, the stench of it is overwhelming. Others notice, too, and then my shame pile grows even larger.

All gay men, whether they know it or not, are being called to examine that wounded inner place. The cost to our well-being is simply too high if we do not. As John Bradshaw points out, by refusing to look at our shame we remain caught in that "all-pervasive sense that I am flawed and defective as a human being." This denial results in "internal bleeding . . . a sickness of the soul," a self-generating feeling of being isolated and alone. An individual thus afflicted "becomes an object of its own contempt, an object that can't be trusted. . . . A shame-based person is haunted by a sense of absence and emptiness."[2]

This blight of the soul is killing our dreams, crippling our better nature as surely as any plague, a fact I saw all too well illustrated in the halls of *The Advocate.* Like most collective groups of gay people, *The Advocate* existed in the way a crazy hall of mirrors does: reflecting back and amplifying in multiple ways the noxious effects of internalized homophobia and the shame it breeds. This phenomenon went largely unacknowledged to the detriment of those employed there. To be sure, the publication was the product of many sincere and hardworking individuals, but earnestness in and of itself is no cure—or excuse—for such myopia. No people are as homophobic as gay people themselves, or as oblivious of the struggles of others, as we often are for this very reason.

One morning in 1988, during the height of the international embargo of South Africa for its history of racial discrimination, I arrived at work especially early. I had some calls to Europe to make and needed to adjust for the time difference. Thinking that I was alone, I had about made it to my office door when I was suddenly stopped by the sounds of muffled sobs coming from farther down the corridor. Deciding to investigate, I soon enough discovered the source of the noise. It was a heterosexual coworker, a beautiful black woman who worked as a part-time clerk in the distribution department when she wasn't pursuing her career as a fashion model.

"Deborah, whatever is the matter?" I exclaimed upon finding her pitifully hunched over a desk. She clasped a wadded tissue in one hand and had obviously been crying for some time.

"I've had enough," Deborah declared. "I simply can't take it anymore." In a few short sentences, she explained the situation. It seemed that Deborah's bosses had asked her to report to work early this morning, too. Sprawled across her desk were copies of the various gay male erotic magazines that the company distributed in addition to its own product. For some unimaginable reason, she had been told to hawk the titles on the phone to outlets in South Africa.

I was rendered speechless by the insensitivity of the situation, not to mention its political incorrectness. How could the managers at *The Advocate* be so lame? How could any gay person be so unaware of the fight for social justice elsewhere in the world? Having a woman of African descent do their dirty work in a land of apartheid only added insult to the injury already done.

"You've got to get out of here," I finally told my colleague. "This is no place for you."

My own struggles to counter the blind-sightedness of the place came to an end in June of 1994, just a few weeks after returning from saying farewell to Barry. The more I pushed for an expansiveness of editorial vision, not to mention insight into the personal shadows of those controlling it, the more hostile *The Advocate*'s home environment became to me. I'm sure this is partly why, when it came time at last to say good-bye, there was absolutely no ceremony made of my leave-taking.

At five o'clock, on my final day, I picked up a box filled with a few mementos gathered from over two decades of journalistic activism, and walked out the door with hardly a handshake. No going-away party. No appreciative public words spoken. Sadly, there was a conspiracy of silence about so many things there, most certainly about the horizontal homophobia that all queer people are naturally heir to. Entrusted chroniclers of the gay movement should simply know—and do—better.

Nonetheless, contributing to *The Advocate* over all those years was one of the most significant experiences of my life. I retain genuine affection for many aspects of the magazine—certainly for the talented writers, editors, photographers, and artists I was privileged to work with—and I continue to admire the ways it strives for effective change in a world so invested with homophobic and sex-negative attitudes, so intent on propagating a hurtful cycle of shame and punishment.

In cleaning their own spiritual houses, however, gay men need to understand not only the reasons for their shame but where to find it. By its very nature, shame is elusive and hard to see. For this stagnant complex of unctuous feeling thrives in the most impenetrable archetype of our soul: shadow. The notion of the *shadow* is used here in its most profound, psychological sense: to define the unconscious, split-off, and disavowed parts of a collective or individual mind.

As the poet Robert Bly reminds us, the shadow is "the long bag we drag behind us," and different cultures fill the bag with different contents.[3] Because queer people seem to emerge from—indeed inhabit—the realm of the shadow we personify for others the hidden ingredients of that bag, usually in its most threatening form: The shadow is unconsciously projected and queer folk become its screen.

We exist as an unfortunate mirror for those things left unseen, or wished not to be seen. Rather than deal with an inclusive reflection of itself, society reacts to us with hostility and rage. We live in a culture of extreme denial, and nowhere is this better evidenced than in the lives of those it has attempted to purge. The violence, the rejection, the sorrow, that pierce to the center of our hearts are the result of society grappling in fear of itself.

"In a society where the good is defined in terms of profit rather than in terms of human need, there must always be some group of people who, through systematized oppression, can be made to feel surplus, to occupy the place of the dehumanized inferior," says Audre Lorde, a black lesbian feminist poet. "We do not speak of human difference, but of human deviance."[4]

Therefore, in a patriarchal society, women and those qualities deemed feminine—like open emotionalism—are oppressed. In a racist society, people of color or of "otherness" are viewed as "lesser than." In an erotophobic society, individuals living out their spontaneous ecstatic feelings are censored. Men who are unable to integrate these alienated aspects of themselves express their repression through violent means, their bloody subjugation of women, queer people, and the disadvantaged being the signal act of our age.

That gay people display a primal link with eros threatens those who have deeply repressed their own sexuality. They project distant, twisted instincts elsewhere; the *homo* of their sexual prejudice is merely a pretext for unrecognized private distress. Every day in America, gay women and men are demeaned, abused, and even killed because they carry with them society's projection of its darkest, most despised, and least integrated aspects of Self.

I have no doubt that the archetypes which speak most directly to gay men—those we tend to gravitate around—are the very ones most deeply repressed in our larger culture. Thus we are made to appear as a people without honor, and certainly as a people without a basis for being. For the soulful ground in which we find nourishment, self-creation itself, has been devalued and buried deep in icy shadow.

When we claim the shadow, integrating what society cannot tolerate, a distanced part of our self is brought near. I understood this when I was able to shed the miserable onus of being a faggot. To be a faggot, I had learned, is to be shunned. By being removed from the trust of others, I was kept distrustful of myself.

Years of inner work were required before I could heal this wound, for I had internalized society's damning views about differentness. The reclaiming of my shame taught me that there was nothing flawed in my own being. On the contrary, the problem originated with the heterosexual majority's destructive effort to control its homosexual minority.

Jung says that archetypes are psychological mechanisms for transforming energy within us. With this insight in mind, I could now see the symbol of the faggot as an apparition of society's collective shadow. Being perceived as this shadowy figure, and having that projection reinforced in tragic ways, even by my parents, had kept me emotionally leaden. By owning the symbol of the faggot on my own terms, I could begin to release the transformative energy buried beneath.

What had been suppressed was the archetype of the Trickster, a fount of aliveness, curiosity, and risk. The Trickster became an important ally once I had rescued him from my shadow bag. Today, he enables me to find ways around obstacles—like someone's rejection or hate—that would have previously stopped me cold.

My friend, the passionate player—he got it right, too. Barry figured his salvation as a gay man lived in the dark as much as what cursed him. In our crude and fumbling way, we played in the dark together, even with darkness itself, in our search for light. Barry, the Trickster, at loose in two houses of many black rooms. Opening doors in one helped him find a way into the other. That, and a little luck, meant a damaged life was healed.

How I wish I'd known years ago, as a boy adrift in his own dark house, what Barry finally discovered: That the name of the thing rising up to haunt me was shame.

Departures, Sacred and Profane

On Wing

Like a massive curtain hanging north to south, the Cascade Mountains divide the state of Oregon neatly in two; the coastal, lesser half is all forested and green, the eastern side is exactly the opposite. One does not think of deserts in Oregon, but here I was, one summer day in 1990, traversing its dusty plains in search of my father.

I had spent the morning going over the rugged volcanic range, driving through primordial stands of mist-shrouded trees, and then descending into Klamath Falls, an old Western town like so many others: one quaintly historic main street and a plethora of newer spurs where the used-car lots, fast-food franchises, and concrete malls counter any claims to uniqueness. By now, the last signs of pop civilization had far receded and only the timeless vistas of the Oregon prairie lit golden in the late afternoon light filled my view. After decades of harrowing grief, my father had managed to find some measure of peace on these stark but beautiful lands.

Fifteen years had gone by since we'd last seen each other. Our distance was about more than a father and son merely losing track; each in his way had sought oblivion from the past. My headlong rush into the fast lane of gay life had not rested with him well, that much I knew. But I had little idea of what else he thought about me, or even if he was concerned at all.

Howard had found succor after an ugly, demeaning divorce from my mother through a loving relationship with a woman who happened to be a skilled therapist. After her untimely death from cancer, he resettled with his sister in southeastern Oregon where they operated a sprawling eight-hundred-acre cattle ranch together. This much I knew about him. . . . But no words had passed between us.

Information was exchanged by family members, including the news that he, too, now suffered with cancer. Sensing there was little time to waste, I broke our long mutual silence. Finally, the moment avoided by both of us was here: the chance to talk as grown-up men and fellow survivors.

The rattling of the car as it rolled over the cattle guards embedded in the dirt road that swept up the hill toward my father's house compounded my nervousness: Would he like me? What would we have to say after all these years? We had cautiously scheduled only two nights and a day. Would that be enough time or too little? More than anything else, I needed to hear him declare he was proud of his oldest son. And there was something I desperately needed to say in return.

I had spent nearly all my life lugging a bagful of secrets, not all of them my own, behind me. It was an odious burden, and one I wanted to drop. The biggest secret of all was the fact that I had saved my father's life, something I knew he didn't know. In most families this piece of news would most certainly be celebrated, but I had withheld the truth from anybody's knowledge for many years. After much agonizing, I committed to writing a few lines about the incident in a published essay. But I knew these words would never be read by my father. Now it was time to tell him the truth directly.

The event occurred late one night in my eighteenth year. It had been another acrimonious evening, in an interminable string of awful nights, between my parents. This one was worse than most, however. The battling match had started the moment everyone arrived home from work or school and continued until well after midnight by which time both parties were numb with exhaustion. My brothers and sister and I had long escaped into our bedrooms. Sleep was impossible, of course, but at least we were out of the line of fire. The fighting had been physically violent and especially soul-shredding; I could not imagine how our parents could possibly go on this way—indeed, how any of us could continue to live in such a bad climate of hate.

Silence finally fell on the embattled household, the muffled sounds of someone crying alone in the dark the only distraction as I drifted off into a fitful sleep. I awoke a few hours later, restless with nerves and despair, and went outside to take in the fresh, ocean-scented air. I could hear the far-distant rumble of waves in Carmel Bay and the autumn sky above was brilliantly aglow with stars. Time was at a standstill; if only it could stay this way.

I soon detected another sound, ominous static grating the sweet morning calm. An engine was running idle somewhere nearby, curious for such an early hour, and I decided to investigate. I did not have to go farther than my backyard to discover the source of the noise. There, plainly visible in the full-moon light, was my father sitting in his truck, one end of a garden hose attached to the exhaust pipe, the other end stuck through an opening in the cab's side window. He was motionless but awake, and would surely be dead in minutes if not intercepted.

It was a horrifying sight, yet I felt oddly devoid of emotion. I calmly crept around to the rear of the truck and removed the hose. And then, without a backward glance, I kept on moving through the night.

I ran across the yard and over a fence and down the long furrows of a vast field abutting our house. The spiny stems of the artichoke plants cultivated there tore my pajamas as I stumbled by, and so I shucked them and continued naked through the field. For some reason, the waist-high crop had been left unharvested, and the edible bulbs of the plants had now blossomed into fist-sized thistles. The purple-hued center of each prickly flower glowed eerily in the silver light. I was but a speck in a huge pointillist canvas of violet dots, my white body an errant splash in an otherwise seamless pattern of foliage and thorns.

I ran until I could go no farther; my feet were cut and bleeding, and for the first time since leaving the house, I noticed the cold. Yet I could not move, breathless and heart pounding, until the eastern horizon began to brighten. Then I retraced my steps back through the field of thistles, over the fence, past an empty truck, and into bed.

It was now dawn. I had saved my father from dying this passing night and, in so doing, had unwittingly birthed my own initiation into manhood. The tragedy was not so much the scene itself, but the fact that the act and its repercussion were left unspoken. Until now, over two decades and lifetimes later, when death once again imposed the only real connection available between us.

"Do you remember that night?" I asked my father the evening of my arrival. We were sitting on the sweeping front porch of his home, bourbon in hand, savoring the final minutes of the setting sun. I had built up to my question carefully, steering the conversation during the previous couple of hours to this decisive point. He reacted to my story of what had transpired with a startled sideways look, and then peered straight ahead into the fiery ball rapidly sliding from view.

"I just don't recall," he wearily exclaimed. "I was so out of it then. There was a lot I wanted to forget."

"Including me, I guess," I replied with bitterness in my voice. This time, my father looked me right in the eyes. It had been hard for him to accept the truth that I was gay, he said, although he somehow always knew. But after our separation, he had in fact followed my activities, even going out and buying copies of the gay magazine I worked for. He knew of my hard work, commitment, and activism.

"I'm proud of you, son," he gruffly concluded, his deeply tanned, still handsome face half-lit in the amber afterglow. "But let's go in now. We have a lot to do in the morning."

We spent the next day surveying the ranch, checking herds penned in various pastures. When we came to a locked gate, I'd hop out of the truck to unlatch it, waving my father through. Somehow the opening and closing of gates facilitated our conversation throughout the day as we picked through what little we shared from the past. That night, after packing for an early departure the next morning, I told my father that I loved him. They were my last words of worth to him: the following June he was dead from cancer.

I could not attend his memorial service, but was told that people from miles around crowded into the tiny country chapel where his many acts of kindness to others were observed. I did not cry when I heard my father had died, but shed angry tears upon hearing that strangers knew him better than I. Intimacy with my father had happened only once for me, years ago, at the end of a rubber hose.

A month after my father's funeral I returned to Oregon in order to perform my own rite of remembrance—and forgiveness. Sometime before his death, I had considered undertaking the Sun Dance, an ancient ritual of the Sioux Nation. Men of the Cheyenne, Dakota, Oglala, and other Plains Indian tribes would fast and purge themselves in preparation for this grueling "dance without drinking" that could take up to four days to complete. Federal authorities were imprisoning participants by 1883, however, and outright banned the dance in 1904 as "immoral and barbarian." It was rarely practiced, and then only in secret, until a revival of traditional ways in the 1970s. Yet even today, the Sun Dance is seldom performed.[5]

When the opportunity to participate in a version of the ritual was first presented to me, I read what historial accounts I could find. While it is physically torturous, the Sun Dance is a ceremony dedicated to the renewal of life. With the recent death of my father, the loss of numerous close friend to AIDS, and my own perilous HIV-positive status, attempting the dance seemed not only correct but necessary.

Still, I was concerned about plundering another culture's sacred tradition. How could a white middle-class man like myself justify playing a part in the ongoing appropriation of native peoples' culture? No matter how sincere my interest, how could I even begin to understand what this mysterious rite really meant?

But as I learned more about the Sun Dance and its cycle of mortification, sacrifice, and renewal, I grasped its significance for me. The dance takes place on two levels: the mythical and real. In simultaneous worlds, the submission can be experienced as a sacrificial act—suffering as a meaningful initiatory ordeal. But what was I wanting this initiation to stand for exactly? My earlier testings in the leather scene and elsewhere had helped me to separate from the negative consequences of my personal mother and father, kickstarting a process of healing that would lead, over time, to a more beneficial relationship with these primal archetypes.

Perhaps what this particular ritual of transformation needed to initiate was a state known as *immanence,* that final stage of individuation which, according to Joseph Henderson, "forces a man to obey the immanent law of his own nature in order to know himself as an individual."[6] In other words, the point of one's most truthful reconciliation with Self, an arrival at a unique space which requires no further rites of passage. If my life's journey had been about anything at all, it was to attain this. In my heart, I knew I was still far from inhabiting this place. Yet the Sun Dance, which seemed to me the most self-confrontational act of all, might symbolically represent my best commitment to that end.

I concluded that the Sun Dance embodies a mythological way of thinking available to all men. Its enactment belongs in the world's great storehouse of sacred rituals and myths. If correctly approached, the ritual is capable of rendering a fresh, if not shattering, new vision of life. I decided I could so honor the dance in that spirit.

I awoke nervous and empty the morning of my dance, having fasted the day before. Many weeks of focused thought had prefaced this moment, and I felt as prepared as I could be. Although the August sky was still hazy with clouds, I was confident the sun would shine. After the other dancers and ritual helpers convened, we all walked quietly through a large grassy meadow toward the ceremonial site. In the distance stood a grove of towering firs, including the one tree we had selected as the centerpoint of our dance.

We spent the next several hours readying ourselves and the grounds. Someone climbed the tree and attached five long cotton ropes near the top. The ends were taped and staked fan-shape to the ground, about twenty yards from the tree's base. Some of us meditated, others anointed themselves with oil or decorative markings. I painted rows of tightly spaced white dots—energy channels—down the back of each arm and someone else daubed my spine.

At midday, we took hands and formed a ring. Each man stated his name and the intention he had brought to the dance. There was drumming for a while. Then we sat silent, mute in anticipation. Soon the ritual's leaders came and led us one at a time to a nearby shaded spot for our piercing.

When my turn came, I removed the last of my clothing and lay down on the waiting blanket, grabbing hard onto the arm of a friend there to assist me. A small red circle was drawn on the skin above my heart. I inhaled and let out a deep breath. Then a sharp metal skewer—about the size of an ice pick—tied with an eagle feather was pushed through my flesh within the circle. The pain was brutal, shocking, almost unbearable at first, but softened with continued breaths.

After the fifth man was pierced, we each took a place at the foot of a rope, which was then lifted up and attached to our skewer. The sun was radiant, now shining high above the grove. I could feel its heat penetrate my body. Fastened halfway up each rope was a silver bell and a small medicine bundle of objects special to the dancer. In mine, I had put bits of blue turquoise, some obsidian beads, and the dried remnants of flowers collected at Delphi. The words chiseled on the oracle there—"Know thyself" reverberated in my mind.

Bright tinkling sounds filled the air as we stepped back from the tree, testing the weight and tautness of our lines. By now, the pain from the wound in my chest had become oceanic, flooding my body with tsunamis of intense sensation.

I looked at the other men around me; Josh and John to the left, and to my right Doug and Barry, who had journeyed from San Francisco. A chef, computer programmer, physicist, and office worker—each man with a different story, a reason for dancing uniquely his own. Barry had declared that his soul was in need of healing. "I want to purify past mistakes," said John. Josh stated that he was seeking an opening to his "inner world." And it was Doug who dedicated his dance to love, "so that I can better love myself and strengthen my relationship with the man I love."

In expressing our intention, unlike wants had been exposed—as nakedly bared as we here stood before the sun. But differences were of no importance now. We were five men of one mind. There was no past to cling to, only the immediacy of the present moment. In this, we were united.

Another minute or two of silent contemplation passed before Fakir, the ritual leader, stepped forward with a prayer to the spirits of sky, earth, and wind. "Father in the Sun, Mother in the Earth, accept now the offering of our bodies to you. Fulfill our prayers," he said. Smoke from an abalone shell filled with burning sage plumed upward. Then, with a resounding beat of the drum, the dance began.

I closed my eyes and let out another captive sigh, trying to surrender my resistance. Suddenly, I did not know why I was performing the dance. The pain was beyond anything I had ever experienced. I became angry, then resentful, then I felt trapped—even foolish. All this emotion, and only a few seconds had passed.

When I looked up at the sun again, I could see my rope stretched straight before me. It seemed to soar past the trees and into the sky, connecting me with the light. My reluctance ebbed, and bits and pieces of me began to let go. The bass beat of the drum infused the air. The more I leaned back from the tree, the more I let go. The sun burned deep. I was slowly disintegrating.

By now, the skewer was tugged inches from my chest, skin elastic, refusing to be cut through. I had no choice but to abandon myself to the dance. The tree became a steadying post as long minutes went by. A voice from somewhere said, "Pull, pull!" I dug my toes deeper into the ground, feeling the fertility of the field and the roots beneath. I tasted salt and sunlight itself. Despite the awful hurt, my dance was absolutely a commitment to life.

Earlier, I'd stated that I wanted to overcome fear about disease, anxiety about dying before my time, before my work was completed. But at that moment I *was* dying, relinquishing parts of myself I would be unable to covet again: my shame, my fear, my ignorance. *Take them,* I prayed to the sun. *Burn them forever in your fire.*

At that instant—and with a reverberating pop—the skewer ripped out of my chest. The rope snapped, snaking wildly through the air. Everything around me stopped, and I stood naked and alone. The other dancers had apparently disappeared, and I could no longer hear the drum. There was eerie silence, a sense of absolute calm. I looked toward the hills rising above the meadow and saw the world as never before.

I was wedded to the earth; there was no separation between me and the sky and nature's vibration. We were inseparable. The tranquillity and feeling of oneness were profound. I gazed in wonderment in every direction: All things were unique, yet wholly connected. Even the blood dripping from the open wound above my heart, staining my feet and the dirt below, was a precious reminder of this. My gay body had come home—home to itself.

The moment seemed endless, but eventually I reentered the surrounding scene. The drum was still beating. A man to my left fainted and fell to the ground, but quickly got up and continued his dance with renewed vigor. One by one, I could hear the popping sounds of the other dancers' release and their joyous shouts. I saw amazement and ecstasy etched in every man's face. Our ritual dance was done.

I had traveled far, to the sun and back. Yet as awesome as the experience was, its purpose was to remind me of the never-ending journey ahead. I'd been reborn a powerful man this day, but it was just one more turn on the ceaseless wheel of death and rebirth that any soul in the making must take.

I first knew what being a man is the night I saved my father's life. Now, through this sacrificial act, I had saved the life of the father within me. Redemption does not lie outside ourselves, but in finding our truth and strength within. If my search for the meaning of masculinity has taught me anything, it is this: We queer men must father ourselves. This way, no matter how many times we die, we live as the resurrected.

Epilogue

⊠ ⊠ ⊠

How We Die

To be wounded is not enough. We can claim our shame, count off each infraction against the Self as we would list souvenirs from a once-in-a-lifetime trip around the world. We can exalt that martyrdom, too, festooning the flesh with new wounds to better declare the one festering inside. But it is not enough only to see and then say what happened. There comes a time in every man's life when he must ask: What is to be done about it? The hurt and betrayal, the feelings which exist as facts, those time-blasted pinnacles of memory as real as any monumental rock.

Our wound is not the soul's germinal seed, but merely the gateway to that which grows beyond its other side. It is a point of entry, a way through to where that plant of eternal life we know as gay love takes root and prospers. Our gay wound is the gods' gift to us surely, but in itself is nothing to either celebrate or covet. It is the means toward the creation of a Self rather than its meaning.

Creation requires sacrifice, and what is gained stands in proportion to what of oneself is given up. Certainly, one must relinquish past insult and injury in order to spiritually grow. That is the hero's way. But we gay men have to sacrifice our attachment to the wound as well. What, at birth, seems inevitably fated, cannot alone be our destiny.

For, at some point on the journey, the hero's work is done. The heroic myth itself must be sacrificed before self-creation can continue. From Gilgamesh to the Grail knight, to the gay shaman-warrior of today, each must finally put down the sword and let that part of himself which clings to the wound die. In other words, we must die before death itself, sacrifice what is most prized in order to truly live.

The choice is ours to make, and I look in wonderment at when and how it is made by some and avoided by others. Often it is the circumstance of literal dying that determines the question of how we gay men die inside. Whatever the case may be for each individual, there is no denying the wholesale fact of our physical leave-taking. Stories about final moments abound, with dizzying proximity, in my life and the lives of those close around me. On either one level or the other, sometimes both, we gay men have become pros in the necessary act of dying.

Young men become burdened before their time, sifting through a heavy necrology of lovers and comrades. I, too, grow old just thinking about the good-byes—from hasty to prolonged—issued in such gross quantity. I am no longer sentimental about death, merely awed by its various nature. Hushed and bowed, I can't help but catalogue the ways in which some men around me have encountered death.

Carl swallowed a fistful of capsules, collected one at a time, and serenely listened to a favorite concerto until his breathing stopped. Wayne cashed in all his possessions for a cherry-red Rambler convertible, which he drove off a cliff with giddy abandon. John lay

andering stream. It was Kirk's grove, a spot of his own choosing.

We dismounted and put down our knapsacks, then gathered in a clearing in the center of the grove. Reaching out, we grasped one another's hands and bowed our heads: a new American family observing its covenant to love. One by one, we went around and spoke our minds—quiet, sad words shared in the dry midday heat. Then I opened my backpack and took out the brown plastic box that held Kirk's remains. With obstinate fingers, I slowly peeled the seal off the box and removed the lid. The ashes had the consistency of course, lumpy sand, and, after a deep breath or two, I reached in and grabbed a handful. They could be sprinkled decorously among the fronds on the forest floor, or even tenderly placed into the earth beneath. But, somehow, I knew that neither of these approaches would be correct in honoring the spirit of Kirk.

With an impetuous swing of my arm, I threw the ashes high into the air. They made a beautiful plume, glistening white in the shafts of light penetrating the thick canopy above. The solemnity of the occasion was lifted by my abrupt action. With smiles now, we passed the box and each took turns scooping out brimming handfuls of Kirk. The stately grove was decorated with dozens of talcum arcs shooting out in all directions until the box was empty. It was closure, for sure, and just as he would have wanted it. I took solace in the thought that when it rains, Kirk will not only return to the earth from which he came, he will contribute, if even infinitesimally, to the growth of this ancient wood.

My brother and I both held the same, simple view of life: that everything about it goes in circles. Not just the obvious cycle of birth, maturity, and death, and then the reincarnation of that life force into some other form, but cycles of interiority—of feeling and memory.

As much as one might try, neither of us believed that we could erase the past or even "make it better." That's the false myth of pop psychology: that if we just do the work, then somehow we'll be cured, become well, get over the inflictions from the past. What psychotherapy and the pursuit of mindfulness do offer are useful tools in understanding our fated lot, giving us a new place to stand, a fresh vantage to behold it. But it can never make what happened go away.

I feel these circles turn in me like the gears and flywheels of some fantastic timepiece. They are of various sizes, so whatever is inscribed or scarred upon their surface comes round at different times. Feelings about a mother's love and a mother's madness are calibrated in separate ways. Recollections of a father's concern or his coldness are never lost, but appear, recede, then reappear at unexpected points along each inextricable revolution. Voices and visions from the past are never quelled. I feel strong in the face of them sometimes, as susceptible as ever before at other points.[1]

One late winter morning, about a month after I had returned from helping my brother to die, I was teetering on a ladder that was precariously perched against the side of the house I share with Malcolm. As always this time of year, it was my chore to remove the leaves and debris that had accumulated on our roof during the previous months. I disliked the job, never more so than on this particular day. Balanced on one foot, with rake in hand stretched as far as it would go, I was practically steaming with discontent about the world and my own life.

I smashed the rake on the clay tiles again and again, trying to free the pine needles stuck between them, close to screaming in frustration, when suddenly I heard my name shouted out. "Mark!" the voice urgently said. It was part reprimand, part compassionate plea to cool down. My attitude was no good, of no possible benefit to me or the task at hand. I looked around in every direction but could find no one there. Stopped short, and by now a little shaken, I got off the ladder and walked down the twenty-four steps that separate our hillside yard from the front gate facing the street. There was no one there, either.

I had recognized the voice immediately, but could not possibly admit to knowing it when first heard. It was Kirk. The tone and inflection of his voice were unmistakable. But he was dead, which meant I must be going crazy. Still, I *had* heard my name spoken, as clearly registered as if a friend had called it from across a room. I do not entertain superstitions about the dead, but somehow I was being told something of importance. Like Enkidu, who reappeared to Gilgamesh in a vision from the underworld, Kirk was revisiting me after death to deliver a helpful message.

"Let go, my brother," he seemed to be saying with the utterance of a single word. "Don't hang on so tight. Trust in life. What you need and want will come in time."

Letting go of the past—not as a way to escape it, but to accept it—is why I have told my story here. I have not written about every event or person that has impacted upon my life, nor every struggle. Rather, I've related some of the things that have been worthwhile to the making of my queer soul. This is very much an account of half a life journey, which in turn can be divided into two equal parts: the first twenty-one years, during which a false self was created, and all the attempts and extreme measures in the succeeding years to achieve a more real place. This is my tale of coming out inside. It is not the end, but the beginning of a whole other story.[2]

Wake up, brother. And this I have tried to do, releasing the past as a conflagrant act. I need to burn up encumbrance—my attachment to the wound—as a way to truth. For this, I must own shadow, as must all gay men if we are to achieve any state of grace. We cannot shy away from partnering the crushed gay boy who lives inside each one of us. How else will we "fulfill our foray" in the words of Whitman, seek our queer destiny and shining promise?

These are burning times for all of us, whether we know it or not. We're at the end of humankind's bloodiest century, a new millennium near, and old myths are dying hard. This was never more clear to me than on the day of Kirk's memorial. What had begun as a remembrance of a single life, ended as a meditation on the impermanence of the many.

It was withering hot by the time we hiked out of the gorge, the air like blasts from a furnace. I had lost track of time on the arduous trail zigzagging up the steep mountain slope. It was just enough to keep one foot planted in front of the next. When the summit was finally reached, I stopped to catch my breath and take one last look behind me. The valley walls were drained of color in the white August heat, vegetation baked dry to the point of ignition. Everything around me appeared about ready to explode and burn. Suddenly, I realized that's how I felt, too.

I pulled out a bandana to wipe the sweat from my eyes, and, as I did, was jolted into another moment when the world seemed as on fire. I was standing on a similar hillside, only with a view of the sprawling urbanscape called Los Angeles before me. It was late April 1992, and the city was in flames. The four policemen who had savagely beaten Rodney King, a black man whose only crime was speeding, had just been acquitted on all but one count by a jury as white as they. The city had been torched as a result, the cinders and ash from five thousand fires set in rage falling like incendiary rain at my feet. Many people had died during the uprising, fifty-two lives, in fact, sacrificed on the bone heap of ignorance, injustice, and fear.

This vision of a burning city passed quickly enough, though, leaving me once again on the trail summit with thoughts of Kirk and all the other sacred brothers who've perished in a conflagration kindled out of similar deadly choices. A few days after my return home, a friend asked what I thought about death. She knew I'd been struggling with questions about mortality for some time, with scores dying and my own hopes for survival dimming every passing year. Each loss of a loved one or the loss of an immune cell had brought me closer to accepting my own irrefutable end.

It is difficult to comprehend that final moment. But it's as if some cosmic bully keeps holding my hand over a flame, refusing to let go. Bully as Fate. Try as I may, there is no way to squirm out of this painful embrace other than to understand its reason.

Those of us who have a hard time keeping our feet on the ground don't like to think about the finish or closure of anything. The high flyers of the world, and that includes me and most gay men I know, love to take the leaps and bounds that get things started. We put on our seven-league boots and take great strides, barely touching earth. Or we never make contact at all, keeping airborne and aloof. To stay in the clouds is to run with the spirits of imagination, wonder, and wit. Who would want such companionship to end?

Yet here was my friend's question, so bluntly put. I replied by lifting my shirt and showing her the almond-shaped scar on my chest. It is a symbolic marker of the suffering that has helped forge my journey through shadow, my hard-won resolve to name the things that confound me. The childhood shaming, the treason of Self, the bitter loss of lovers—all those salty tears—were apparently needed.[3] Reclaiming the body—through acts both sublime and shocking—

was no less necessary. To deny the reality of suffering and all the inner deaths it demands, I finally said to my friend, is to stay dead to life. And so, to live, we must burn.

Out of the fire comes, finally, another kind of knowing. The ability to connect feelings with facts, to personify the powerful emotions experienced as love and hate, desire and envy, among other distinguishable entities living in psyche's house, is one's rich reward. The ancients knew them as gods. We cannot trivialize these feelings as being anything less. The choice is ours to make.

Once I had a dream: I am lost in a murky underworld populated by aimlessly wandering men and women—the living dead. The landscape around me is gray and formless, except for a cliff on the edge of a bottomless abyss. If I stay in this twilight world, I will become like one of the soulless figures stumbling near. My only other choice is to leap from the cliff. And so I jump.

Life is a series of moments about revelation and giving witness. It is neither preordained, nor a predicament. Who knows this better than gay people who have awakened to the extraordinary promise of their lives and who daily meet that challenge? We should never doubt to venture, never be afraid of the shadows or the light.

Queer men are cupbearers of the primal and a world to come, and because of this we shall endure. By whatever means possible, the fire under the crucible of my gay body stays lit.

Notes

Introduction

1. Robert A. Johnson, *Owning Your Own Shadow: Understanding the Dark Side of the Psyche* (San Francisco: Harper San Francisco, 1991), pp. 4–5.

2. In *A Place to Start* (Dallas: Monument Press, 1989), p. 181, theologian J. Michael Clark states: "While both personally and communally gay men and lesbians do in fact need to listen more to our depths and to nurture our inner spiritual centeredness or grounding, a spiritual emphasis focused solely on the inner life may be unable or even unwilling to motivate actions. . . . Our spiritual deepening must rather occur *simultaneously* with our activism." While Clark's basic point is well taken, I maintain that we must *first* develop a psycho-spiritual cognizance, for without knowledge of self our activism will be unconsciously motivated and thus poorly rendered.

3. In *The Human Core of Spirituality: Mind as Psyche and Spirit* (Albany: State University of New York Press, 1996), theologian and psychologist Daniel A. Helminiak summarizes six different usages of the term *spirituality*. Spirituality as the human spiritual nature,

such as that which makes humans spiritual; as concern for transcendence, as in the sense that something in life goes beyond the here and now; as a lived reality, as in an individual or social sense of advancing spiritual growth through certain beliefs or practices; as an academic discipline, of the pastoral or practical kind, which studies what to do and how to do it, or the theoretical kind, which explains why spiritual practices do what they do; as spiritualism, or communication with those who have died or other nonhuman spiritual entities; and as parapsychology, involvement with extraordinary human powers that result in "psychic" phenomena like clairvoyance and precognition.

4. Anthony Stevens, *Archetypes: A Natural History of the Self* (New York: Quill, 1983), p. 52.

Chapter One: Strange Kind of Paradise

1. In *Jung, Jungians, and Homosexuality* (Boston: Shambhala Publications, 1989), pp. 141–155, psychotherapist Robert H. Hopcke suggests that gay men find the myth of Oz powerfully attractive because Dorothy Gale's passage through this imaginative realm reflects the inner journey that they, too, must take to find their way "home"; that is, to arrive at a state of psychological wholeness—a true Self. In *The Wizard of Oz* (the first title in the book series as well as the 1939 MGM film based upon it), Dorothy must come into contact with a certain aspect of archetypal masculinity, the Wizard, and defeat the negative feminine, the Wicked Witch of the West, before she can discover the true meaning of home. Along the way she finds and integrates into her being various masculine qualities represented by the figures of the Scarecrow, Tin Man, and Lion.

2. I have no reason to doubt that Dorothy's demanding but eventually fruitful journey down the Yellow Brick Road illustrates a psychological predicament common to my life and the lives of other gay men. Since so many of us appear indoctrinated with the values of the maternal world from an early age, we are seen as having lost our masculinity and thus are negatively tainted: guilt by association in a misogynistic society. Thus, sissy boys must be rescued and brought back home into the male order, often through extreme and humiliating measures. By whatever means possible, we are coerced into relinquishing the "wicked" effects of the feminine, which only furthers our sense of shame and failure.

3. Abalone, a single-shelled mollusk, is especially sought by the region's cooks. After our catch was sorted and cut out of the shell, we would tenderize the flesh by pounding it with heavy-bottomed Coke bottles on big wooden blocks. Gently sautéed and served with steamed artichokes, our hard-earned meal—"a paesano's feast," my dad would say—was a reminder of all that was good in the world.

4. For further discussion of gay archetypes, see *Queer Spirits: A Gay Men's Myth Book* by Will Roscoe (Boston: Beacon Press, 1995); *Cassell's Encyclopedia of Queer Myth, Symbol, and Spirit,* edited by Randy P. Conner, David Hatfield Sparks, and Mariya Sparks (London: Cassell, 1997); and *Gay Soul: Finding the Heart of Gay Spirit and Nature*, edited by Mark Thompson (San Francisco: Harper San Francisco, 1994).

5. While Jung's few published remarks about gay men reflect attitudes about "psychological immaturity" widely held by his contemporaries, he did not entirely endorse their damning assessment of homosexuality as an illness. Still, could Jung's reticence to speak out more extensively on the matter of homosexuality be an aspect of

his own shadow? In the thousands of pages of his published collected work, Jung mentions homosexuality no more than a dozen times. Although the emphasis of Jung's psychological perspective was on the inner forms of human experience (sexuality did not play a major part in his theories), one nevertheless wonders why he never addressed homosexual feeling in a more depthful or personal manner. See *Unresolved Questions in the Freud/Jung Debate on Psychosis, Sexual Identity, and Religion* by Patrick Vandermeersch (Leuven-Louvain, Belgium: Leuven University Press, 1991).

6. C. G. Jung, "Two Essays on Analytical Psychology," *The Collected Works of C. G. Jung* (Princeton: Princeton University Press, 1966), vol. 7, p. 240.

7. Shaped like a hook dipped into the Pacific, the Monterey Peninsula was first sighted by Portuguese explorer Juan Rodríguez Cabrillo in 1542. Actual settlement of the area did not begin until two centuries later when Spanish soldier Gaspar de Portolá and Franciscan padre Junípero Serra established a presidio and mission along the shores of the bay on June 3, 1770. By the end of the eighteenth century, Monterey had became a regional center of commerce and trade.

The peninsula is culturally rich as well, and has been rightly called "the cradle of California." The state constitution was signed in Monterey's Colton Hall in 1849, one of many history-making events to occur in a bustling port town of quaint adobes and gracious lifestyles that today reads more legendary than real. But Monterey's days as California's capital were numbered. The decline of a once-thriving whaling industry and the discovery of gold farther north depleted its economy and population. For one hundred years—from the early 1850s to the advent of mass tourism in the decades after the Second World War—the Monterey Peninsula slumbered as a romantic set from a bygone time, its charms largely ignored except by locals.

8. The immense social mobilization required by the Second World War sent out waves of change that would forever alter the status of women, gays, and other disenfranchised groups in America. Women were repositioned as a labor and intellectual force comparable to that of men. At the same time, tens of thousands of men were being amassed, closely quartered, and then deported to the front lines from major coastal cities. Not only was social disruption widely experienced, but emotional upheaval as well. For many women and men, vague stirrings of previously unrealized homoerotic urges were being felt and oftentimes acted on. But, after the war, homosexuals in the military not careful to censor their newly awakened feelings faced severe reprisal. Lesbian witchhunts were common, and innumerable men, after having valiantly served their country, were put in "gay stockades" and cruelly treated. See *Coming Out Under Fire: The History of Gay Men and Women in World War Two* by Allan Bérubé (New York: Free Press/Macmillan, 1990).

9. Despite the emotional oppression of the postwar era, some feelings held hostage by a hostile society did find means of expression. Some men and women did not return to a heartland of wives, husbands, and families as expected. Instead, they elected to stake a claim on the frontiers of the continent and its prevailing norms. Images of the outsider and rebel, central to the American experience, were up for grabs. In cities like San Francisco, Los Angeles, Boston, and New York, all the roles—tough, soft, top, bottom—were freely played out by strong-willed women acting masculine and by men giving vent to feminine expression. Their individual choices and eventual socialization created the seedbed from which post-modern gay culture grew.

As courageous as they were, however, those deviating from the rigid gender codes of the time were still acting within narrow definitions. The mendacity of artifice, while now acknowledged, was hardly absolved. Whether parodied or taken at face value, both homosexual and heterosexual alike labored under the limitations of constructed sexualities. One of the most insidious forms of that oppression for gay men was the lack of opportunity to see who they might be simply as themselves, without odious comparisions to an opposite: If gay boys do not act like their brothers, then it must mean they are more like their sisters. Thus, the context of homosexual pathology was enforced.

10. The emerging independence of women, like that of gay people, was displaced by the propaganda of "normalcy" following the Second World War. The rising expectations of a military-industrial state, with obvious hegemony over the rest of the world, fueled a consumerist society where class and gender roles once again became another form of commodity. Women's lives were cast back within the limits of child-rearing, home, and economic dependency. A new generation of children, including a significant percentage with homosexual orientation, were easy receptacles for many women's stifled ambitions. Their sublimated anger was effortlessly transferred to boys with a penchant to please and imitate; boys who would soon enter their manhood with the unprecedented mandate of gay identity.

11. In *The Psychoanalytic Theory of Male Homosexuality* (New York: Simon & Schuster, 1988), pp. 237–38, Kenneth Lewes, Ph.D., discusses how psychoanalytic theory has drawn parallels between homosexual behavior and the characteristics ascribed to neurotic women: "In certain important respects, the analytic failure in dealing with homosexuality can be viewed as at least partly the result of an initial gynecophobic stance. Homosexuals were seen as deeply

flawed and defective because they shared certain psychic characteristics with women." Furthermore, the misogynistic bias of "early psychoanalysis, having been purged from the theory of femininity, found refuge in the theory of homosexuality, which, unlike the former discourse, did not permit its objects to participate in its formation."

12. Robert H. Hopcke, *Jung, Jungians, and Homosexuality* (Boston: Shambhala, 1989), p. 63.

13. Richard A. Isay, *Being Homosexual: Gay Men and Their Development* (New York: Farrar, Straus & Giroux, 1989), pp. 29–30.

14. For more background on the book, see Anthony Curtis's Introduction in the Penguin edition of *The Razor's Edge* by W. Somerset Maugham (New York: Penguin Books, 1978).

15. *The Razor's Edge* was an enormous success when published in 1944, and it was director George Cukor who first worked to bring it to the screen. Directing chores eventually fell to Edmund Goulding, another homosexual leading a closeted life behind Hollywood's closed doors. Power, a bisexual, was cast as Larry, and Webb, a former Broadway entertainer at home in international gay circles, was assigned the role of Elliott after his acclaimed talking film debut that year in *Laura,* another 20th Century Fox production, in which he played vitriolic gossip columnist Waldo Lydecker with queer insinuation.

Chapter Two: We, Two Brothers Clinging

1. Walt Whitman, "We Two Boys Together Clinging," from the Calamus section, *Leaves of Grass* (deathbed edition).

2. C. G. Jung, "The Structure and Dynamics of the Psyche," *The Collected Works of C. G. Jung* (Princeton: Princeton University Press, 1969), vol. 8, p. 121.

3. C. G. Jung, "A Psychological Theory of Types," *The Collected Works of C. G. Jung* (Princeton: Princeton University Press, 1971), vol. 6, p. 528. About complexes, Jung goes on to say: "Complexes obviously represent a kind of inferiority in the broadest sense—a statement I must at once qualify by saying that to have complexes does not necessarily indicate inferiority. It only means that something discordant, unassimilated, and antagonistic exists, perhaps an obstacle, but also as an incentive to greater effort, and so, perhaps, to new possibilities of achievement. In this sense, therefore, complexes are focal or nodal points of psychic life which we would not wish to do without; indeed, they should not be missing, for otherwise psychic activity would come to a fatal standstill. They point to the unresolved problems in the individual, the places where he has suffered a defeat, at least for the time being, and where there is something he cannot evade or overcome—his weak spots in every sense of the word."

4. C. G. Jung, "Psychological Aspects of the Mother Complex," *The Collected Works of C. G. Jung* (Princeton: Princeton University Press, 1969), vol. 9, part 1, pp. 86–87.

5. From "Montages of a Dream Deferred," *The Collected Poems of Langston Hughes* (New York: Alfred A. Knopf, 1994):

"Harlem (2)"

What happens to a dream deferred?
Does it dry up
like a raisin in the sun?
Or fester like a sore—
And then run?
Does it stink like rotten meat?
Or crust and sugar over—

like a syrupy sweet?
Maybe it just sags
Like a heavy load.
Or does it explode?

6. Although Langston Hughes (1902–1967) did occasionally write on gay themes, his own sexuality has been the source of much speculation. Despite the denials issued by Hughes's literary guardians, many within the black queer community—such as writer Audre Lorde and filmmaker Isaac Julien (*Looking for Langston)*—claim the prolific poet, playwright, novelist, and leading figure in the Harlem Renaissance of the 1920s as a gay cultural icon.

7. Alice Miller, *The Drama of the Gifted Child* (New York: Basic Books, 1981), pp. 34, 35.

8. Mitch Walker, "The Double: An Archetypal Configuration," *Spring 1976: Journal for Jungian Studies* (London: Analytical Psychology Club, 1976), pp. 165–175.

9. Walt Whitman, from "In Paths Untrodden," *Walt Whitman: The Complete Poems,* edited by Francis Murphy (New York: Penguin Books, 1975), p. 146.

10. Christine Downing, *Myths and Mysteries of Same-Sex Love* (New York: Continuum Publishing, 1989), p. 107.

11. It took decades of persistent effort by scholars such as Samuel Noah Kramer before the odd indentations on the tablets, now known as cuneiform writing, could be understood. The markings revealed the evolution of a civilization not previously thought to exist, predating mention in the Bible or any other historical text.

The Sumerians lived and prospered five thousand years ago in a flat semi-arid region devoid of trees, an area situated between the Euphrates and Tigris rivers and now known as Iraq. They were the first people to build cities, irrigate crops, erect temples and centers of learning, and formulate writing—a people responsible, in fact, for the development of most things at the root of Western Civilization. Over time, the Sumerians were infiltrated by peoples from the north, but their technology, knowledge, and values were adapted and used by every culture that succeeded them.

Most of the tablets listed accounts of daily life in Sumer: grain harvests, laws and codes, and other civic matters. As the fragmented records were deciphered in museums around the world, something else was noticed, too: the adventures of a king named Gilgamesh. But it was a story discovered on fragile clay shards, by now strewn across continents. Many more years of painstaking work was necessary before an epic myth cycle, a millennium in the making, could be pieced together. The story of Gilgamesh has since been adapted into various works, including free-form verse, novels, an opera, and other staged presentations. See *The Sumerians: Their History, Culture, and Character* by Samuel Noah Kramer (Chicago: University of Chicago Press, 1963).

12. John Gardner and John Maier, *Gilgamesh: Translated from the Sin-leqi-unninni Version* (New York: Vintage Books, 1985), p. 73.

13. Ibid., p. 100.

14. Ibid., p. 104.

15. David Ferry, *Gilgamesh: A New Rendering in English Verse,* (New York: Farrar, Straus & Giroux, 1992), p. 38.

16. Ibid., p. 64.

17. Another recommended translation is *The Epic of Gilgamesh,* an English version with an introduction by N. K. Sandars (New York: Penguin Books, 1960).

18. James Hillman, *A Blue Fire* (New York: Harper & Row, 1989), p. 221.

19. We see the theme of Mother separation also illustrated in the Grail myth. The young knight Parsifal must go to a river (the waters of the unconscious), discard his mother's homespun garments, and bathe before suiting himself in shining armor to pursue the Holy Chalice (a symbol of Self) in new lands. See Robert A. Johnson, *He: Understanding Masculine Psychology* (New York: Harper & Row, 1974).

20. Robert H. Hopcke, *Persona: Where Sacred Meets Profane* (Boston: Shambhala, 1995), p. 23.

Chapter Three: Wounded Healer

1. Susan Stryker and Jim Van Buskirk, *Gay by the Bay: A History of Queer Culture in the San Francisco Bay Area* (San Francisco: Chronicle Books, 1996), pp. 9–26.

2. Gershen Kaufman, Ph.D., and Lev Raphael, Ph.D., *Coming Out of Shame: Transforming Gay and Lesbian Lives* (New York: Doubleday, 1996), p. 6.

3. Carlton Cornett, *Reclaiming the Authentic Self: Dynamic Psychotherapy with Gay Men* (Northvale, N.J.: Jason Aronson Inc., 1995), p. 32.

4. Lynn Witt, Sherry Thomas, and Eric Marcus, eds., *Out in All Directions: The Almanac of Gay and Lesbian America* (New York: Warner Books, 1995), p. 211.

5. Ibid., pp. 201–206.

6. In *The Stonewall Experiment: A Gay Psychohistory* (London: Cassell, 1995), p. 82, Canadian author and activist Ian Young contends that the initial urge of gay radicalism to transform and heal North American society was stifled within a few short years after the Greenwich Village riot empowered gay people across the nation:

"The Stonewall Experiment began in the untutored hands of gay people who had had enough of being second-class citizens, partial people, never fully human. It was an experiment in reclaiming full humanity from the medical/governmental establishment. With a few years, control of the experiment had fallen into other hands, and the initiators found themselves in the position of experimental animals. The new phase of the experiment involved the development of a commercial gay scene that could be test-marketed as a prototype of the urban lifestyle of the future."

7. The word *homophobia* entered the popular lexicon in 1972 when psychologist George Weinberg published *Society and the Healthy Homosexual,* a groundbreaking study of the causes and effects of society's dislike of homosexuality.

8. Joseph Campbell, with Bill Moyers, *The Power of Myth* (New York: Doubleday, 1988), p. 5.

9. Dr. Karoly Benkert, a Hungarian physician, coined the word *homosexualität* in 1869, echoing the attempts of others at the time, such as German jurist Karl Ulrichs (who used the word *urning,* implying "heavenly love"), to define for themselves an emotional and sexual state deeply felt but as yet unnamed. In time, however, the notion of *homosexual* was co-opted by the dominant society and medicalized with an almost entirely negative connotation.

10. British writer and socialist Edward Carpenter (1844–1929) professed views about "intermediate type" people (gay men and lesbians) being the shamans, healers, priests, mediators, seers, and innovators of the arts and crafts in cultures around the world. See "Edward Carpenter: Selected Insights," *Gay Spirit: Myth and Meaning* (New York: St. Martin's Press, 1987), pp. 152–164.

11. See *The Invention of Heterosexuality* by Jonathan Ned Katz (New York: Dutton, 1995) for a thorough discussion of sexual-

identity construction. As Katz well illustrates, the construct of a homosexual subclass was further hastened by the socioeconomic upheavals of the Industrial Revolution; single people were able to leave rural, close-tied family circles and move toward more independent lives in growing urban environments where privacy and the means to explore previously suppressed desire were possible.

12. Neuroscientist Simon LeVay's 1991 study, conducted at the Salk Institute for Biological Studies in La Jolla, California, found that the hypothalamus gland, which regulates sexual behavior, is smaller in gay men than in heterosexual men. A 1992 study by Roger Gorski and Laura Allen of the University of California/Los Angeles, found that the anterior commissure of the brain, which connects and relays information between its hemispheres, is larger in gay men than in heterosexual men. And a 1994 study conducted by psychiatry professor Sandra Witelson at McMaster University in Hamilton, Ontario, Canada, found differences in the corpus callosum, which allows the right and left sides of the brain to communicate with each other during tasks that require the involvement of both hemispheres. Witelson's findings showed that the corpus callosum was an average of thirteen percent thicker in the gay men studied than it was in the heterosexual men, suggesting that gay men may have different cognitive abilities associated with verbal, spatial, and motor skills than their nongay peers. See *Queer Science: The Use and Abuse of Research into Homosexuality* by Simon LeVay (Cambridge, Mass.: The MIT Press, 1996) for a discussion of these and other attempts to find a biological basis for homosexuality.

13. See *The Lesbian and Gay Studies Reader*, edited by Henry Abelove, Michele Aina Barale, and David M. Halperin (New York: Routledge, 1993).

14. For the record, my career at *The Advocate* went like this: After

working as a freelance reporter for the publication for six months, I was offered a part-time job as Assistant Art Director in January 1976. The magazine had a small staff at the time, and all available editorial slots were filled. In truth, I welcomed the opportunity to also contribute to the visual look of the magazine, having worked my way through college as a graphic artist and enjoying design as much as the written word. As *The Advocate* was a bimonthly publication, I alternated between commuting to its South Bay offices during the week it was assembled and staying home the following week where I researched and wrote feature articles. I enjoyed both the variety and the freedom this arrangement provided: I could count on a small but regular paycheck yet not feel overly bound to a claustrophobic office situation.

During the last half of the 1970s, I was able to write on a wide range of topics, nearly all of personal interest to me. Painter David Hockney, choreographer Michael Bennett, political scientist Dennis Altman, singer Bobby Short, sociobiologist James Weinrich, photographer Robert Mapplethorpe, activist Harry Hay, and novelist Christopher Isherwood were among the numerous artists, writers, and thinkers interviewed. Longer investigative articles (many featured on the cover and occasionally illustrated by my own photography) included topics such as aging, transsexualism, heterosexual S-and-M, gender politics, leather and drag, and a series of essays examining the burgeoning gay male spirituality movement. Numerous reviews, opinion pieces, and short profiles were also contributed during this time.

In June 1981 a full-time editorial position was made available to me when *The Advocate*'s Managing Editor succumbed to AIDS, one of the first such cases reported on the West Coast. I assigned myself the title of Cultural Affairs Editor and began the task of remaking the magazine's arts and entertainment section, which I considered lagging behind the rapidly evolving independent queer arts scene. Special sections on everything from performance art to poetry to pop music were produced, and in 1985 I expanded the magazine's coverage of the arts even further by inaugurating a twice-yearly book review supplement. Soon after, I developed another new section, "En Route," devoted to broader coverage of gay and lesbian cultural issues, especially in other parts of the world. In 1990, a new editor-in-chief brought further rejuvenating changes: my title was now Senior Editor and with it came even more responsibility for the magazine's pages.

Near the end of 1992, however, my recently discovered HIV-positive status necessitated a work slowdown. I spent the last eighteen months of my tenure at *The Advocate* compiling a massive book of over half a million words and hundreds of photographs culled from its pages documenting the gay and lesbian struggle for civil rights in America. I departed the publication's offices for the last time in June 1994, exactly nineteen years after receiving my first assignment there.

See *Unspeakable: The Rise of the Gay and Lesbian Press in America* (Boston: Faber & Faber, 1995) by Rodger Streitmatter for more information about *The Advocate*'s role in the gay and lesbian movement and its internal politics.

15. By the summer of 1971, the mainstream media had caught on to the phenomenon that was the Cockettes. Profiles in *Rolling Stone, Paris Match,* and other major periodicals, plus celebrity endorsements from Truman Capote, Rex Reed, and others, sent the troupe packing to New York that fall. They opened at the Anderson Theater in the East Village on November 5 amid great hoopla and failed miserably, unable to covey the blithe, enchanting spirit that

had so captivated their audiences back home. Hibiscus had split from the group by this time because of internecine conflict, however, establishing a new company. The Angels of Light gave their first performance Christmas Eve (enacting a mock nativity scene in Grace Cathedral), and continued to entertain the city throughout the rest of the decade with lavishly staged musical productions such as *Paris Sites Under the Bourgeois Sea* and the Hindu-inspired *Holy Cow!* See "Children of Paradise: A Brief History of Queens," *Gay Spirit: Myth and Meaning* (New York: St. Martin's Press, 1987), pp. 49–68.

16. Charles A. Reich, *Opposing the System* (New York: Crown Publishers, 1995), p. 12.

17. In 1888, when he was thirty-four years old, Oscar Wilde remarked, "I think a man should invent his own myth." Later, he said, "My ambitions do not stop with composing poems. I want to make of my life itself a work of art." Wilde, through his audacity and martyrdom, is a prototypal image for gay men living today. See *Oscar Wilde* by Richard Ellmann (New York: Alfred A. Knopf, 1988).

18. The tale of *Frankenstein; or, The Modern Prometheus* was adapted to the screen in 1931 by British director James Whale. A big hit for Universal Studios, much of the film's success was due to Whale's sympathetic treatment of the monster. Although a private individual, Whale did not overtly strive to disguise his homosexuality. The talented director of *The Invisible Man, The Old Dark House, The Bride of Frankenstein,* and other classic movies of the era eventually paid the price for being gay, however. Like his monster, Whale was unjustly treated: It is conjectured that Hollywood homophobia led directly to his downfall and eventual suicide in 1957. See *James Whale: A Biography* by Mark Gatiss (London: Cassell, 1995).

Notes

Chapter Four: Tricksters in a Mirror

1. Don Paulson with Roger Simpson, *An Evening at the Garden of Allah: A Gay Cabaret in Seattle* (New York: Columbia University Press, 1996), p. 29.

2. George Chauncey, *Gay New York: Gender, Urban Culture, and the Making of the Gay Male World, 1890–1940* (New York: BasicBooks/HarperCollins, 1994), p. 297.

3. Minette, *Recollections of a Part-time Lady* (New York: Flower-Beneath-the-Foot Press, 1979), p. 70.

4. Gay folklore about Stonewall includes the story of Judy Garland's tragic death on June 22, 1969, and the effect it had in instigating the riots six days later. Apocryphal or not, the uprising is popularly portrayed as having been led by drag queens, who saw in Garland an empathetic figure victimized by the same forces that oppressed them. The entertainer was cast in the galvanizing role of martyr, an emotional touchstone for frustrated feelings long on the brink of explosion.

5. Martin Duberman, *Stonewall* (New York: Dutton, 1993), p. 201.

6. Ibid., p. 198.

7. In *The Gay Militants* (New York: St. Martin's Press, revised edition, 1995), an account of the first two years of the post-Stonewall gay movement, journalist Donn Teal reprints the words of a flyer distributed by members of the Homophile Youth Movement, pp. 8–9. "Get the Mafia and the Cops Out of Gay Bars," the statement was headlined. In response to official claims that the Stonewall Inn was raided June 27, 1969, because it lacked a liquor license, the group declared, "Who's kidding whom? . . . What is illegal about New York City's Gay bars today is the Mafia (or

syndicate) stranglehold on them. Legitimate Gay businessmen are afraid to open decent Gay bars with a healthy social atmosphere (as opposed to the hell-hole atmosphere of places typified by the Stonewall) because of fear of pressure from the unholy alliance of the Mafia and the elements in the Police Dept. who accept payoffs and protect the Mafia monopoly."

8. Thirty years after its formation in San Francisco, the Royal Court had grown to include sixty-eight similiar institutions in cities throughout the United States and Canada. Once on the margins of gay life, the Court system now attracts major corporate donors to its fund-raising events.

9. As in New York and other eastern cities, the gay bars of San Francisco were plagued by widespread official corruption. The "gayola" scandal of 1961, in which police officers were caught taking bribes from bar owners in exchange for not raiding their establishments, led to the formation of the Tavern Guild the following year. The first gay business association in the United States, the Guild fought discriminatory practices (in 1962, it was illegal to maintain a place of assembly where known homosexuals gathered) and marshaled political clout by sponsoring popular community activities such as the Royal Court. By the mid-1970s, the Tavern Guild was the most powerful gay institution in town.

10. C. G. Jung, "On the Psychology of the Trickster Figure," a commentary in *The Trickster: A Study in American Indian Mythology* (New York: Schocken Books, 1972) by Paul Radin, p. 201.

11. Ibid., p. 209.

12. Carlton Cornett, *Reclaiming the Authentic Self: Dynamic Psychotherapy with Gay Men* (Northvale, N.J.: Jason Aronson, 1995), p. 60.

13. Alice Miller, *The Drama of the Gifted Child* (New York: Basic Books, 1981), p. 38.

14. Edward F. Edinger, *Anatomy of the Psyche: Alchemical Symbolism in Psychotherapy* (La Salle, Ill.: Open Court Publishing Company, 1985), p. 11.

15. See *Dionysus: Myth and Cult* by Walter F. Otto (Dallas: Spring Publications, 1981.)

16. Jean Shinoda Bolen, *Gods in Everyman: A New Psychology of Men's Lives and Loves* (San Francisco: Harper & Row, 1989), p. 277.

Chapter Five: Burning Times

1. The *San Francisco Chronicle* reported that of the 300,000 people present in the city for Gay Pride Day, June 24, 1979, 80,000 marched peacefully in the parade itself.

2. See *The Transformation of San Francisco* by Chester Hartman (Totowa, N.J.: Rowman & Allanheld, 1984). I began to understand the magnitude of the disruption in San Francisco when I interviewed city development officials in early 1981 about their master plan. A surge in white-collar employment during the previous two decades had required the construction of thirty million square feet of new office space. As a result, a Bay Area–wide mass transit system (BART) was built to transport employees into the city's core, targeting poor and working-class neighborhoods in adjacent areas for demolition and rebuilding to accommodate this more upscale work force. By the year 2000, the equivalent of a new downtown will have been built south of Market Street.

3. Randy Shilts, *The Mayor of Castro Street: The Life and Times of Harvey Milk* (New York: St. Martin's Press, 1982), pp. 194–195.

4. For further summary of the May 21 "White Night" riots, see *Long Road to Freedom: The Advocate History of the Gay and Lesbian Movement*, (New York: St. Martin's Press, 1994), p. 182.

5. A group of two dozen San Francisco police officers retaliated later that night by attacking the Elephant Walk, a gay bar in the Castro, brandishing their clubs at everyone in sight while shouting, "Sick cocksuckers."

6. Mark P. O. Morford and Robert J. Lenardon, *Classical Mythology* (New York: Longman, 1971), pp. 417–420, p. 425.

7. J. E. Cirlot, *A Dictionary of Symbols* (London: Routledge & Kegan Paul, 1971), p. 173.

8. Eugene Monick, *Phallos: Sacred Image of the Masculine* (Toronto: Inner City Books, 1987), p. 9.

9. James Broughton, "Hermes Bird," from *Special Deliveries: New and Selected Poems* (Seattle: Broken Moon Press, 1990). With his many volumes of poetry, memoir, and plays matched by an almost equal number of films (the first, *Mother's Day,* was made in 1948; the seventeenth and last, *Scattered Remains,* in 1988), Broughton is recognized as a pioneer of avant-garde cinema as well as an outstanding visionary West Coast writer. See *Packing Up for Paradise: Selected Poems, 1946–1996* by James Broughton (Santa Rose, Calif.: Black Sparrow Press, 1997).

10. Monick, *Phallos,* p. 95.

11. See *The Young and Evil* by Charles Henri Ford and Parker Tyler (New York: Sea Horse/Gay Presses of New York, 1988).

12. Harold Norse, *Memoirs of a Bastard Angel* (New York: William Morrow, 1989), p. 77.

13. For additional information about the origins of the radical fairie movement, see "This Gay Tribe: A Brief History of Fairies," *Gay Spirit: Myth and Meaning* (New York: St. Martin's Press, 1987).

this book's structure of seven chapters. According to J. E. Cirlot in *A Dictionary of Symbols* (London: Routledge & Kegan Paul, 1971), the number seven is "symbolic of perfect order, a complete period or cycle. It comprises the union of the ternary and the quaternary, and hence it is endowed with exceptional value. . . . It is the number forming the basic series of musical notes, of colours and of the planetary spheres, as well as of the gods corresponding to them . . . and, finally, it is the symbol of pain."

3. As Jung and other students of metaphysics and alchemy have implied, salt (suffering and tears) cojoined with mercury (trickery and flight) produces Luna, the developed feminine principle in a man. In the Introduction to Jung's *Aspects of the Masculine* (Princeton, N.J.: Princeton University Press, 1989), editor John Beebe explains that Luna "corresponds to an anima who is no longer naïve; who has suffered enough. . . . Luna is an initiated unconscious that is ready to interact with the initiated heroic consciousness that is Sol to produce an integration of personality."

About the Author

⊠ ⊠ ⊠

MARK THOMPSON was born and raised on the Monterey Peninsula, California, where he was exposed to a wide range of spiritual beliefs and practices. In 1973, he helped lead the Gay Students Coalition at San Francisco State University, and has worked for gay and feminist causes since that time.

He began his career in journalism with the national gay newsmagazine *The Advocate* in 1975, reporting on culture and politics in Europe. He continued to serve the publication during the next nineteen years in a number of capacities—as a feature writer, photographer, and senior editor. In 1994, he completed his tenure at the magazine by editing *Long Road to Freedom: The Advocate History of the Gay and Lesbian Movement* (St. Martin's Press), a massive volume of half a million words and over seven hundred photographs documenting the gay and lesbian struggle for civil rights. The book was nominated for two Lambda Literary Awards.

Thompson's other work includes the acclaimed 1987 anthology *Gay Spirit: Myth and Meaning* (St. Martin's Press), which examined gay spirituality from different perspectives. *Leatherfolk: Radical Sex, People, Politics, and Practice* (Alyson Publications), a 1991 collection, and *Gay Soul: Finding the Heart of Gay Spirit and Nature* (Harper San Francisco), a 1994 book consisting of in-depth interviews and photographs with sixteen writers, teachers, and visionaries, have also been nominated for Lambda Literary Awards.

Thompson has contributed to a variety of other publications, including *Hometowns: Gay Men Write About Where They Belong* (Dutton), *Positively Gay: New Approaches to Gay and Lesbian Life* (Celestial Arts), *Out in Culture* (Duke University Press), and *Gay Men at the Millennium: Sex, Spirit, Community* (Tarcher). He frequently lectures on contemporary aspects of gay male experience, and has spoken at the University of California/Los Angeles, City University of New York, and the University of Wisconsin, as well as to groups ranging from the National Organization of Changing Men to the Unitarian Church. Thompson lives in Los Angeles with his longtime life partner, Episcopal priest and author Malcolm Boyd. He is currently working toward a graduate degree in clinical psychology at Antioch University.